HOW TO SCREEN ADOPTIVE AND FOSTER PARENTS

A WORKBOOK FOR PROFESSIONALS AND STUDENTS

JAMES L. DICKERSON, MARDI ALLEN, AND DANIEL POLLACK

NASW PRESS

National Association of Social Workers
Washington, DC

James J. Kelly, PhD, ACSW, LCSW, *President*
Elizabeth J. Clark, PhD, ACSW, MPH, *Executive Director*

Cheryl Y. Bradley, *Publisher*
Lisa M. O'Hearn, *Managing Editor*
Sarah Lowman, *Project Manager*
Dac Nelson, *Copyeditor*
Wayson R. Jones, *Proofreader*
Bernice Eisen, *Indexer*

Cover by Metadog Design
Interior design by Electronic Quill Publishing Services
Printed and bound by Sheridan Books, Inc.

Library of Congress Cataloging-in-Publication Data

Dickerson, James.
   How to screen adoptive and foster parents : a workbook for professionals and students / James L. Dickerson, Mardi Allen, and Daniel Pollack.
      p. cm.
   Includes bibliographical references and index.
   ISBN 978-0-87101-415-3 (alk. paper)
   1. Adoptive parents. 2. Foster parents. I. Allen, Mardi, 1951– II. Pollack, Daniel. III. Title.
   HV875.D535 2011
   362.73'3—dc22

                                                        2010041599

Note from the Authors

To protect privacy, the names of foster and adoptive parents, foster and adopted children, and staff members at professional agencies have been changed; in some instances, composite stories have been used for case histories in an effort to maintain the strictest standards of confidentiality. This book is intended to enhance the effectiveness of care that is delivered to children by diminishing inappropriate selection of adoptive and foster parents.

We are aware that administrators, social workers, and adoptive or foster parents are operating in a litigious climate. As meticulous as we have tried to be in our choice of words, we recognize that, by their nature, words are capable of being interpreted in a variety of ways, or even misunderstood completely. We acknowledge that there is also, of course, room for healthy disagreement with and application of our guidelines. These guidelines are offered primarily with a view toward moving the fields of adoption and foster care to a higher level of practice. They are not necessarily offered as legal benchmarks.

Dedication

Daniel Pollack dedicates this book to his wife,
Rivka Rachel Pollack.

James L. Dickerson dedicates this book to the memory
of F. David Rice, a social worker's social worker.

Mardi Allen dedicates this book to Sydney, Austin, Max,
Logan, Sam, Brayden, and Karlie. Always know there is hope.

Contents

About the Authors

James L. Dickerson is director of "You've Got a Friend," a social work program funded by a federal grant awarded by the Mississippi Council on Developmental Disabilities. He has nearly 10 years' experience as a screener for adoptive and foster parent applicants, and he is coauthor of two books on adoption.

Mardi Allen, PhD, is a psychologist who counsels families in private practice, clinical liaison for the Mississippi Department of Mental Health, president of Mental Health America of Central Mississippi, and a former president of the Association of State and Provincial Psychology Boards.

Daniel Pollack, MSSA (MSW), JD, is professor at Yeshiva University, School of Social Work, New York City, and a frequent expert witness in foster care and child welfare cases. He is author of several books of interest to social workers.

Acknowledgments

The authors would like to thank R. S. Fenemore, retired director of Family and Children's Services in Brockville and the United Counties of Leeds and Grenville; Edwin C. LeGrand, executive director of Mississippi Department of Mental Health; John Lipscomb, director of Hudspeth Regional Center; the late Jean Gardner; Alex A. Alston; the late Florene Brownell; the late Reg Barrett; Sharon Gary, whose friendship and counsel is always greatly valued; the production team at NASW Press; and Lisa O'Hearn, managing editor at NASW Press.

PART ONE

Interviewing

What You Need to Know Before You Begin Interviews

We advocate a team approach to adoption and foster care placement in which private and public social agencies designate specific social workers, known as screeners, to be responsible for screening adoptive and foster applicants; a second category of social workers, known as child care specialists, to be responsible for supervising children once they have been placed in adoptive or foster homes; and a placement team composed of the screener, the child care specialist, the protection worker who worked with the family before the child came into care, and an adoption or foster home supervisor, to be responsible for matching the child with the caregiver. All have important roles to play in the process, but the screener establishes the pace for everyone else and determines the ultimate disposition of the child.

Our purpose in writing this book is to help facilitate best practice guidelines for adoptive and foster care selection. Our evidence-informed recommendations for raised standards may initially reduce the number of approved adoptive and foster home applicants available for use by public and private agencies, but we are convinced that whatever shrinkage occurs as a result of raised standards will be compensated for by more stable placements with fewer disruptions. When it comes to adoptive and foster care placements, *less is more* if it results in greater stability among caregivers and a better quality of life for children. Far too many adoptive and foster homes fail, resulting in new placements for the child, a cycle that, once begun, sometimes stretches to six, eight, 10, even 20 placements, each taking a destructive emotional toll on the child.

Adoption disruption seems an overly sterile term with which to describe the enormous emotional pain that accompanies adoptive breakdowns. For children who have endured multiple foster home placements prior to adoption, a breakdown of their "forever" family cannot help but be devastating. The percentage of adoption placements that fail is smaller than it is for foster home placements, and the reason for that can be found in the different motivations that define adoptive and foster parents. Those differences will be explained in later chapters.

National statistics on adoption failures owing to inadequate screening are hard to come by, but one in 10 is a reasonable estimate (estimates in Michigan run from 3 percent to 15 percent). Accurate statistics on foster home breakdowns are easier to access. Recent data shows that 34 percent of the children in foster care in Oklahoma have been moved four or more times, with 17 percent subjected to six or more placements (see http://www.childrensnsrights.org).

Basic math reveals that half of all foster children in that state experience more than four placements. Statistics gathered by the Pennsylvania Department of Public Welfare show that 41 percent of the children in foster care in that state experience two or more foster home placements (Rubin, Alessandrini, Feudtner, & Mandell, 2004). In Illinois, about 40 percent of children in foster care experience three or more relocations (see www.cfrc.illinois.edu/LRpdfs/PlacementStability.LR.pdf[1]) In the lawsuit, *Braam v. State of Washington,* which sought to improve the quality of foster care in that state, it was disclosed that Jessica Braam, for whom the case was named, experienced more than 34 placements after being removed from her parents and placed in foster care at age two (see Roberts, 2005).

The fallout from failed placements extends to every facet of society: Adults who were placed into foster care as children in Oregon and Washington suffer posttraumatic stress disorders twice as often as U.S. war veterans; one-third of former foster children in Oregon and Washington live at or below the poverty line, three times the national poverty rate (see Roberts, 2005).

Although placement failure rates vary from state to state, the emotional damage that results from those failures is consistent across the nation, regardless of geographical location. In 2010, a Tennessee woman made international headlines when she asked her mother to put her seven-year-old adopted son on a plane to his homeland of Russia. With the child was a note that stated that she no longer wanted him because he had emotional problems. It was an uncaring thing to do to a child and will likely have lifelong effects on his ability to form relationships. It was just the latest in a string of adoptions involving Russian children that went horribly wrong. In 2008, a Utah woman was sentenced to 15 years in prison after pleading guilty to killing a Russian infant in her care (Associated Press, April 9, 2010). Two years earlier, a Virginia woman was sentenced to 25 years in prison after being convicted of beating to death her adopted two-year-old Russian daughter. The child was kicked and punched between her eyes, and across her back and stomach. The woman testified that she killed the child because they never bonded (Vargas, 2006). Typically, severe abuse against adopted children is attributed by the adopted parent to behavioral problems exhibited by the child. Sadly, such stories are not all that unusual, because behavioral problems among both foster and adopted children are the rule and not the exception.

---

1. See Children and Family Research Center, School of Social Work, University of Illinois at Urbana-Champaign at www.cfrc.illinois.edu/LRpdfs/PlacementStability.LR.pdf. Also see Hartnett, M. A. et al., 1999 and D. Webster et al., 2000.

Studies have found:

- More than 80 percent of foster care children have developmental, emotional, or behavioral problems (Kaplan & Sadock, 1995). Forty-four percent of young adults who have been in foster care reported being involved in delinquent activities (Rosenfeld et al., 1997).
- Two to four years after leaving foster care, fewer than half of the foster care alumni had jobs, according to one study, and among women, 60 percent had given birth, with fewer than one in five described as self-supporting. Overall, for both genders, nearly half had been arrested and a quarter had been homeless (see http://www.aecf.org).
- Children in foster care who have experienced multiple placements are more likely to incur mental health costs than children in more stable placements, and they are more likely to experience higher medical costs in general (Rubin, Alessandrini, Feudtner, & Mandell, 2004).

There are those who attribute these problems to factors other than inadequate foster home care. They point to dysfunctional birth parents and attribute foster home breakdowns to genetic considerations or improper nurturing by birth parents. They say that some children are simply born "bad" and cannot be rehabilitated. If they are moved from foster home to foster home, so the argument goes, it is their own fault because they are disruptive.

Beyond a doubt, children who are abused or neglected by their birth parents enter the foster care system at a parenting disadvantage, for they often present destructive behaviors and unacceptable modes of thinking that must be corrected if they are to have a chance of ever living a so-called normal life. Our position is that there are no "hopelessly lost" foster children, only children in need of guidance and inadequately screened adoptive and foster parents, many selected by ill-prepared screeners, few of whom have ever had college-level courses on the subject or adequate in-service training by experts in the field. That should not come as a surprise because there are only a handful of schools of social work in the United States and Canada that offer courses on adoptive and foster parent screening.

Reform of the system frequently has come from the legal profession. Today, when change occurs at the state level in departments of human services, it is often the result of a lawsuit that has forced agencies to confront their failures. It is an issue that the social work profession should seize as a natural outgrowth of its historical mandate for social justice. The first step in doing so is for social work professionals to demand that every social worker who works as a screener be properly trained. There is a direct relationship between the skill of the screener and the number of breakdowns that occur at the caregiver level. The more skilled the screener, the fewer the breakdowns in adoptive and foster homes—and the fewer children who are emotionally scarred by multiple placements.

We all want the best for our nation's foster and adoptive children. The foundational building blocks are excellent caregivers. That is why departments of human services are always seeking dedicated, professional caregivers. The purpose of foster care and adoption is to improve the quality of care of children and to reduce unacceptable and illegal behaviors of caregivers. Clearly this means that the selection of a caregiver should be done with the needs of the child in mind. To be good adoptive or foster parents, individuals should be caring, empathetic, compassionate, and able to communicate well with any child who is placed in their home. They should also be responsible and organized. Emotional stability is also very important because they may often be faced with emergencies and other difficult situations. Does this sound demanding? Some of the characteristics necessary to be a good adoptive or foster parent are inborn; others can be developed. As is often the case in life, the difference between desire and reality can be stark, and not every person who wants to be a caregiver is qualified. For most prospective caregivers, if the applicants are motivated, stable, caring people and genuinely interested in helping children in need, they are on their way to becoming good adoptive or foster parents.

As a social worker, you need peers with whom you can share concerns. For this reason it is important to take time to build a solid professional network, such as people from your agency, a group of peers from other agencies, older colleagues, or other professionals. Take the time to identify those colleagues in your state or county foster care or adoption world. Ideally, you can turn to your predecessor for some general guidance, and for specific guidance regarding the caseload you have. Your coworkers and supervisor are also there to give you helpful tips. An experienced office secretary or administrative assistant can be invaluable as well. Take the time to talk with all of these people to find out how you can work together. You also need to make and maintain external contacts. Again, take the time to find out who can be most helpful in assisting you with selecting the right caregiver for the right child. Remember, the caregiver is the linchpin for a successful placement.

Caregiver Selection Can Be a Critical Legal Decision

Foremost in the selection of a foster or adoptive home is that the placement will be effective, safe, and child friendly. This means that everyone involved will be focusing on the particular needs of the child and that the parents caring for the child will have the appropriate training and skills to provide high-quality care that meets all legal requirements of the state. All parties involved in the care of the child should be treated with respect and given the support and information they need to understand and cope with each child's unique circumstances.

If you are a social worker, selecting a caregiver can seem daunting, largely because you are not sure what to expect. It is easy to feel overwhelmed. Elsewhere in this book are suggestions that may help you gain a sense of control over the tasks that you face. To be emphasized at this point is that *the selection of a caregiver is a critical legal decision.*

If you are sued, you may be required to appear at a deposition or go to court. In court, if it is determined that you did not follow the standard of care, you and the agency may be held liable for monetary damages. This is not said to frighten you, but to alert you to the realities of working in this profession.

The better informed you are, the better able you are to do your job within the legal boundaries that are expected of you. Even if you think you have done everything correctly, somebody else may believe otherwise when something bad happens to a child while in placement. As society becomes increasingly litigious and increasing demands are imposed on child welfare workers, you become a growing target for a lawsuit.

Building a Safe Home Study

By "safe," we mean a home study that will protect the child, the foster or adoptive parents, the birth parents, the social worker, and the agency. A home study, when properly done, is an in-depth psychosocial analysis of a foster or adoptive applicant's potential as a parent, complete with a detailed look at a series of interrelated social and emotional variables that have shaped the individual from childhood to the present. The challenge is to look at the past with enough clarity and insight to be able to make informed inferences about the future.

For the screener the first goal of a home study is to evaluate the applicant's potential for sexual, emotional, or physical abuse toward a child. Until that can be determined, everything else involved in the home study process is secondary. Once the screener is satisfied that the applicant is not a risk to a child, the other areas of concern are the individual's emotional stability, the nature of the individual's relationship with his or her spouse and family members, and the individual's attitudes about major parenting issues. Another area of concern is the individual's relationship with society as a whole (as documented by arrests or treatment for alcohol or drug abuse).

The screener should approach foster or adoptive applicants as if they are a mystery to be solved. Is the applicant the person she or he seems to be? Or is the applicant someone who has been coached about "right" and "wrong" answers?

The home study that we advocate in this book is the optimum level of assessment we consider appropriate for screening foster and adoptive applicants. Admittedly, some agencies hold their screeners to a lower standard, especially when it comes to details of the applicant's personal relationships. We do not approve of shortcuts in the home study process because we think it puts children at risk. Our hope is that increased scrutiny of the process will elevate professional standards to a level commensurate with the responsibility of the task.

Doing a first-rate home study requires a lot of thought. Unfortunately, issues arise from time to time that make the work more difficult than it should be. Because there is no regulation of adoption or foster homes at the national level, there are no uniform standards for home studies and the requirements vary widely from agency to agency, even within the same state. Screeners who do home studies for public or private agencies that allow applicants to read their home study must constantly second-guess themselves about the information they include in the report for fear of violating privacy rights, or for fear of being sued by an applicant who disagrees with the assessment. This second-guessing can have a chilling effect on the truthfulness of the report by intimidating a screener into withholding critical information from the home study. Failure presents serious legal consequences, not only for the child and adoptive or foster parents, but also for the social worker.

Being named as a defendant in a lawsuit is not something child welfare workers want to think about. They enter the profession with a sincere desire to help children. Yet there is some risk that comes with being in the profession. This risk should not be minimized. No matter how competent you are, you can still be sued if someone thinks you made a mistake that resulted in harm. Foster parents and the state department of human services explicitly agree that they will uphold certain standards in caring for a child. In legal terminology, these are called "standards of care." In comparing your behavior against the appropriate standard of care, lawyers and courts view the child welfare standards that were in effect at the time of the alleged incident. Any changes to the standards subsequent to the incident are excluded.

Standard of Care for Foster Parents

Foster parents and the state department of human services explicitly agree that they will uphold certain "standards of care." For instance, the *South Carolina Handbook for Foster Parents* (2008), notes that the "failure to comply with one or more of these standards of care may result in removal of foster children from the home and revocation of the foster home license." Should something adverse happen to the child, the failure to follow the standards of care may also lead to a lawsuit. What are some of these standards of care? From the South Carolina handbook, the following are included (see https://dss.sc.gov/content/library/manuals/foster_care_licensing.pdf):

- Each child shall be provided with adequate health and hygiene aids. Space for a child's possessions shall be provided.
- No child may routinely share a bed or a bedroom with an adult, except for a child under one year of age.
- Children of opposite sex sleeping in the same bed must be limited to siblings under the age of four years. Children of opposite sex sleeping in the same room must be limited to children under the age of four years.
- Children shall sleep within calling distance of an adult member of the family, with no child sleeping in a detached building, unfinished attic or basement, stairway, hall, or room commonly used for other than bedroom purposes.
- Foster parents shall follow instructions and suggestions of providers of medical and health-related services. If receiving medication, a child's prescription shall be filled on a timely basis and medications will be administered as prescribed, and otherwise be kept secured.
- Foster parents shall obtain emergency medical treatment immediately as need arises, and shall notify South Carolina Department of Social Services (SCDSS) and child placing agency staff, no later than 24 hours after receiving such care.

- Foster parents should contact SCDSS for coordination of any elective or non-emergency surgical procedures as far in advance of the procedures as possible.
- Any injuries sustained by a foster child must be reported as they occur and no later than 24 hours after an incident.
- Foster parents are responsible for notifying SCDSS and child-placing agency staff as soon as possible when a critical incident has occurred such as: (a) death of any child in the home; (b) attempted suicide by the child; (c) child is caught with a weapon or illegal substance; (d) child is charged with a juvenile or adult offense; (e) child is placed on homebound schooling or is suspended or expelled from school; (f) child has left the home without permission and has not returned.
- Religious education shall be in accordance with the expressed wishes of the natural parents, if such wishes are expressed.
- The use of corporal punishment as a form of discipline is prohibited.
- Infants and children shall not be left without competent supervision.
- Foster parents, in conjunction with SCDSS, shall keep a life book/scrapbook on each foster child placed in their home. Children's records and reports shall be kept confidential and shall be returned to SCDSS when a foster child leaves the foster home.
- Firearms and any ammunition shall be kept in a locked storage container except when being legally carried upon the foster parent's person.
- Foster parents must be able to secure/supervise access to swimming pools and maintain adequate supervision during periods of swimming.
- No unrelated lodger or boarder shall be allowed to move into a foster home without the agency's concurrence.

Home Study Interview Model

The interview model required of the home study process is different from those used for family therapy, individual counseling, or crisis intervention interviews. The purpose of a screening interview is to gather information that can be used to determine eligibility, define personality, evaluate parenting potential, and provide insight into an individual's opinions on a variety of issues. That purpose differs significantly from a traditional social work interview, in which the ultimate goal of information gathering is to provide therapeutic services.

Basically, there are four interview models used by social workers and psychologists, all based on the following theories:

- *Cognitive–behavioral.* This interview model is a hybrid, drawing on the common elements of cognitive psychology and behavioral psychology. It focuses on the present to change future behavior, while establishing the interviewer as the "teacher" and the client as the "student."
- *Psychodynamic.* These interview models have their roots in the works of Sigmund Freud and are based on the belief that today's problems can be traced back to childhood experiences, with a focus on personality change.

- *Humanistic.* This interview model is based on the belief that each individual has within himself or herself the resources to solve problems. The role of the interviewer is to form a positive relationship with the client that will allow the client to focus on the present and not the past.
- *Postmodern.* This interview model takes the position that success is dependent on a negotiated interaction between interviewer and respondent. It is largely based on the writings of Michael White and David Epston (1990), coauthors of *Narrative Means to Therapeutic Ends.* The basis of this model is a belief that reality is a social construction that can be affected by stories that highlight the relationship between therapist and respondent. Puppet therapy for children is a familiar example.

All of the above interview models have a place in social work, but none are entirely appropriate for social workers engaged in screening adoptive and foster parents. As Alfred Kadushin and Goldie Kadushin (1997) point out in their book, *The Social Work Interview,* "Social workers try to maximize clients' participation, to encourage the development of the interview so that it follows the clients' preferences, to minimize standardization and maximize individuality of content. Social workers have no set interview agenda and attempt to keep their control of the interview to a minimum" (p. 13). The screener's goals are just the opposite: to control the interview so that the quantity and quality of information obtained from clients can be maximized.

The interview model presented in this book has been developed by the authors specifically for use in screening adoptive and foster home applicants. It borrows from some of the above-mentioned interview models, but it is more similar to the forensic models used by psychologists involved in custody evaluations and the investigative models used by journalists than it is to the type of therapeutic models taught in schools of social work. We have named this style the Dickerson–Allen–Pollack Model (DAP, for short).

DAP Goals:

- To determine applicant motivation
- To evaluate family and significant-other relationships
- To catalogue positive and negative parenting abilities
- To screen for mental health disorders
- To screen for financial stability
- To screen for health issues
- To screen for home safety
- To screen for child abuse potential

Child custody evaluations are forensic instruments that seek to evaluate a parent's suitability for guardianship of a child or children, usually in the wake of divorce or death. According to the American Psychological Association (APA), the child's needs and well-being are paramount in the evaluation. "Parents competing for custody, as well as others, may have legitimate concerns, but the child's best interests must prevail . . . during the course of a child custody evaluation, a psychologist does not accept any of the involved participants in the evaluation as a therapy client. Therapeutic contact with the child or involved participants following a child custody evaluation is undertaken with caution" (APA, 1994, pp. 677–680).

Investigative interviews conducted by journalists are structured in such a way as to maximize both the interviewer's control of the interview and the quantity and quality of the information obtained in the interview. The interviewer arrives at the interview with a list of preformulated questions that have been determined to be critical to the purpose of the interview. The interviewer is not interested in helping the subject solve a particular problem. The entire focus is on obtaining information deemed to be important to the interviewer.

A social worker engaged in a therapeutic interview does not gather health or financial information from a client to determine eligibility for services (the screener does). The social worker conducting a therapeutic interview will not deny services based on the client's motive for seeking services (the screener will). The social worker conducting a therapeutic interview will not deny services if the individuals seeking services have serious marital difficulties; indeed, the social worker will seek to assist with resolution of the difficulties (conversely, the screener's job is not to help applicants with marital problems, but rather to determine whether those problems are too severe to allow them to take children into their home). Unlike a social worker involved in a therapeutic interview, a screener identifies antisocial tendencies in a client, not to counsel, but to evaluate for unacceptable behavior.

These differences exist because it is the role of the social worker conducting a therapeutic interview to assist the client. There is no confusion about the identity of the client; he or she is the person who has approached the social agency for help in solving a problem. The opposite is the case for the screener. Applicants who approach a social agency to request children for adoption or foster care are seeking approval to augment their family. Strictly speaking, they are not the screener's clients. The screener's client, the individual to whom the screener is responsible, is the child who is in need of a family. All decisions made by the screener are defined in terms of his or her advocacy for the child. This is sometimes difficult for social workers to accept. The natural inclination is to want to help the applicants make their dreams come true. Screeners must remember at all times that their job is to find a home for the child, not to find a child for the applicants. Of course, when things work out well the screener looks out for the interests of both the child and the applicants.

Basics of Interview Assessment

Once an adoption or foster home application is received by an agency, it is important that it be delivered to the appropriate screener without delay. A telephone call to the applicants on the day of receipt to set up an appointment is appropriate, even if the screener is unable to arrange time for the interview right away. If the screener waits

FIGURE 1.1

HOME STUDY FORMAT (SHOULD BE 15–25 PAGES IN LENGTH)

INTRODUCTION
An explanation for the applicant's contact with the agency.

INTERVIEWS
Dates and structures of the interviews with the applicants.

FAMILY HISTORY
A detailed history of each applicant's family background and social history, beginning at birth.

EDUCATION
Schools attended, graduation dates, majors or field of study.

EMPLOYMENT HISTORY
Complete work history, with dates and summaries of responsibilities.

MARITAL (OR SIGNIFICANT OTHER) RELATIONSHIPS
A detailed analysis of the applicant's relationships.

EXPERIENCE WITH CHILDREN
An analysis of the applicant's experience with children.

ATTITUDES ABOUT ADOPTION (OR FOSTER PARENTING)
Discussion of applicant's views on adoption and foster parenting.

HEALTH
Discussion of any health problems that could affect ability to care for children.

REFERENCES
Names, address, telephone numbers of the references, along with quotes from each person.

RECOMMENDATIONS
Post-placement recommendations
Statement of acceptability as adoptive or foster parents.

Source: See Dickerson and Allen, 2007, p. 78 (Reprinted with permission of publisher).

until a few days before the available day to call the applicants, it will get the interview process off to a bad start because it will feed perceptions held by many that social service agencies are more concerned about bureaucratic process than they are in meeting human needs. Successful screeners are acutely aware of the impact that their actions have on applicants, and they use that awareness to enhance the odds for a successful placement for the children in their care.

That same line of thought should be followed when the applicants arrive for their first interview. As Kadushin and Kadushin (1997) point out, for the interviewee the interview begins when he or she first arrives at the agency, not when the interview actually starts: "If clients have waited a long time, interviewers may find it helpful to recognize explicitly at the beginning of the interview clients' annoyance at having been kept waiting, to openly acknowledge that clients might have some strong feelings about this, and invite them to discuss their reactions" (p. 75).

If the screener realizes shortly before a scheduled interview is to begin that he or she will be late because of an emergency (long-running staff meetings are not emergencies), an effort should be made to speak to the applicants so that an explanation can be personally delivered (do not ask the receptionist to notify applicants that you are running late; do it yourself).

Once the interview begins the screener should pay close attention to how the applicants are dressed. Are they in sync with each other? Is one person dressed in a revealing low-cut dress, transparent blouse, or radical T-shirts with a message such as "s**t happens" and the other dressed conservatively? Is one person dressed casually and the other person dressed in business attire? Are they wearing the same colors? Are they wearing opposite colors (as in black and white)?

Interviews should take place in an office with a door that can be closed to ensure privacy. Interviews should not be done behind partitions in a room in which there are other people. If the screener does not have a private office, interviews should be done in a conference room or other private area. If the screener has a comfortable sitting area in his or her office, it should be used instead of a behind-the-desk arrangement. This will make the applicants feel more relaxed and enable the screener to manage the conversation more easily. If your agency allows it, use a tape recorder for the interview, after asking the applicants (on tape) for permission to record the conversation, and keep a notepad nearby so that you can make notes about follow-up questions. If you take notes on paper, do not become so absorbed in your note taking that you are unable to observe body language when questions are asked.

Importance of Eye Contact

Eye contact is critical for social interaction. Inappropriate eye contact, whether it is avoidance or glaring, speaks volumes about an individual's mental state. It demonstrates, for a variety of reasons, a reluctance to establish a temporary rapport with another individual. The reasons for that reluctance may be based on deception, anger, shyness, disapproval, disinterest, or a host of other nonemotion-related factors such as autism.

Appropriate eye contact is one of the key components in a successful social transaction. If you are the speaker, you know that the person that you are engaging in conversation is interested in what you are saying if they return your eye contact without glaring and demonstrate accompanying facial characteristics devoid of anger, frustration, or impatience.

Is lack of eye contact a sign of deception? Not necessarily. Children who are being deceptive are apt to avert their gaze in an effort to avoid eye contact with a parent or teacher. However, as individuals mature they learn how to maintain eye contact while being deceptive. That deception is not revealed by strong eye contact, but by the mock sincerity that usually accompanies it, or by the sudden displays of anger, contempt, or disapproval that flash momentarily about the eyes and the mouth.

The key to using eye contact as an interview tool is to understand its relative importance. Eye avoidance, followed by critical or argumentative words spoken by the interviewee, angry expressions, unexplained sweating, or sudden panic attacks may be indicative of deception.

Dr. Stephen Porter, a psychology professor at Dalhousie University, conducted research that concluded that smirking or eye blinking accompanied by a sad face often were reflective of deception (see ScienceDaily.com, 2008).

He also determined that some emotions were more difficult to fake than others. For example, happiness was found to be easier to fake than disgust or fear.

Listening to Body Language

Body language and clothing choices are important vehicles for nonverbal behavior. Clothing is one way for people to use body language to express their innermost feelings, and you should never be dismissive about the clothing that applicants wear to an interview, because it often says something important about the individual. Always ask yourself what image or message you think they are trying to get across to you.

If you are interviewing a couple, are both partners able to maintain strong eye contact with you? Do they communicate with each other in approving or disapproving ways while the other person is speaking? Do they sit with their arms folded, showing resistance to your questions? Do their eyelids flutter, indicating possible deceit when you ask them direct questions? Does either partner seem defensive or reluctant to be there? Does either partner interrupt you when you are speaking (an attempt at dominance), or do they interrupt each other when they think their partner is faltering (see ScienceDaily.com, 2008)?

If interviewees seem anxious during the first interview, that would not be unusual. They know they are being tested, but they don't know exactly how. Their voices may be pitched slightly higher than normal. Their words may sound breathy at times. Put yourself in their position and try to be understanding. Be supportive and maintain a friendly, matter-of-fact demeanor, but at the same time be alert to anxious mannerisms that are paired with negative body language such as shrugs or eye avoidance, any signals that could indicate negative or deceptive thinking. Look for signs of dominance—head inclined forward, with chin dropped, tightened eyelids, and raised outer brow—and signs of contempt directed toward the partner: rolled eyes, dimpled cheek with crooked smile, along with sarcasm and insults, even if delivered behind a mask of forced laughter (see ScienceDaily.com, 2008).

Take note of the frequency with which applicants nod and shake their heads so that you will be aware of whether they are in agreement with you on important issues, especially as they relate to policy. Richard Petty, an Ohio State University psychology professor, conducted research in which he found that head nodding and shaking not only influences other people, but it self-validates the person displaying the head movements (Petty, 2003). Sometimes interviewers nod their head out of habit when they are listening to something that doesn't particularly interest them and they don't want to spend time discussing it; in those instances, nods are seen as a way to move on to something more interesting. If you have that habit, break it; your nods are communicating unspoken approval to the applicant on subjects about which you may not wish to be offering approval.

Be aware of the influence that emotions can have on physical characteristics. Anger experienced over a long period of time can sculpt the face with telltale signs about the eyes and lower forehead that give the individual a "hard," combative look even if the individual is smiling at the time. It is very difficult for a person to control facial expressions because human anatomy has been wired in such a way that facial muscles react to a stimulus twice as fast as the brain can process it. In other words, humans react faster than they can think about reacting to a particular stimulus. As a screener, that gives you the advantage, but only if you are clever enough to understand the signals (Petty, 2003).

While doing research on how emotions affect the face, Paul Ekman and Wallace Friesen (1975), both psychology professors at the University of California, determined that facial muscles are capable of producing 43 movements that can create 10,000 different facial expressions. Some expressions, they concluded, can be seen as "microexpressions" that are displayed in less than a fifth of a second. Ekman and Friesen discovered the existence of microexpressions while studying films of a depressed woman seeking a weekend pass from a mental hospital. The first time they viewed the film, the woman appeared stable. It was not until they switched to slow motion and studied her face that they caught flashes of the despair she attempted to conceal: The corners of her mouth were pulled down and the insides of her eyebrows arched up, fleeting expressions that were camouflaged by a broad smile. Fortunately, the doctors at the mental hospital turned down her request for a pass—a good thing because it later turned out that she planned to leave the hospital so that she could commit suicide. Ekman and Friesen characterize facial expressions that are revealed in quick bursts as emotional leakage that betray a person's true feelings.

The coauthor of this book, James L. Dickerson, became aware quite some time ago of the type of emotional "leakage" described by Ekman and Friesen (1975) when he observed it among female children and adults who have been sexually abused. He first

FIGURE 1.2

Alice and Josh were a study in contrasts. Alice wore a pastel pantsuit with frilly cuffs and a white blouse that was set off with an antique necklace; Josh wore jeans and a black T-shirt that broadcast the message "Life Sucks!" The screener let the T-shirt message slide until the individual interviews, at which point he made inquiries about it.

Alice apologized and made it clear that she did not approve of Josh's attire. "I don't know why he does things like that," she said. "He knew better than that." Although he did not apologize, Josh readily admitted that he did know better. He explained that a friend had asked him to help move his mother into a nursing home that day and it took longer than he expected and it left him no time to go home and change clothes.

Josh grinned and said, "I guess you see all kinds, don't you?"

The screener acknowledged the truth of that and had decided to overlook the fashion error when the second shoe dropped with a thud.

"To tell you the truth," Josh added, "I'm not sure I would have changed, even if I had time. Alice gets too uptight about how I dress sometimes." Josh winked at the screener. "I think the T-shirt taught her a valuable lesson, don't you?"

DISCUSSION

(1)   What was Josh's real message?

(2)   What does Alice's apology tell you about their marriage?

(3)   How do you interpret Josh's statement, "I guess you see all kinds, don't you?"

(4)   Why do you think that Josh's comment about the "valuable lesson" learned by Alice should raise questions about their suitability as adoptive or foster parents?

Source: Dickerson and Allen, 2007, p. 80 (reprinted with permission of publisher).

noticed it in women who had confided in him about their abuse as children. The leakage manifests itself in the form of a distinct smile, fragile in appearance and marked by minute tugs at each corner of the mouth, not unlike the smile of movie icon Marilyn Monroe, and intense, searching eye contact that falls just short of a stare. Once, while the author was working as a consultant for a group of psychologists, he passed through the waiting room while it was filled with young girls that ranged in age from five to eight. As he walked past, one girl in particular caught his attention with the telltale smile and stare. After he entered the inner office he asked the receptionist why the girls were there.

"They're being tested," the receptionist answered.

"For possible abuse?"

"No."

"One of those girls has been abused."

"Why do you say that?"

"I just know."

"What girl?"

"The one in the blue sweater."

The receptionist pulled the girl's file and quickly read through it. Suddenly, she gasped. "You're right," she said. "She was sexually abused."[2]

Emotional leakage is always at work on the human face, affecting the way individuals look, if only for a fraction of a second. There is no scientific basis for the author's observations about the relationship between sexual abuse and facial expressions, but there is an intuitive basis for that conclusion that has been influenced by many years of observation.

A screener should react to intuitive insights during an interview with follow-up questions, even if he or she does not exactly understand why the questions are necessary. Future research may well prove intuition to be a reaction to the microexpressions discovered by Ekman and Friesen (1975), intellectual calculations that occur too rapidly for the human brain to register as anything other than a vague feeling. Sometimes intuition is a screener's best friend. A screener should never base a decision about application approval based solely on intuition, but it can be a useful tool when used as a "tie-breaker" in cases in which the positives and negatives seem evenly balanced.

Understanding the Ethics of Screening Interviews

The interview process is fraught with ethical minefields. That's because nothing is ever simple—or safe—when it comes to dealing with powerful human emotions. A good way to walk through that minefield is with the knowledge and expectation that anything that is observed, spoken, or written is subject to potential review by a judge in a court of law. Psychologists who conduct child custody evaluations do so with the understanding that they are subject to questioning under oath by a judge or by attorneys hired by the participants in the evaluation.

---

2. See Dickerson and Allen 2007, p. 82 (Reprinted with permission of publisher).

So it is with an investigative journalist. Everything gathered in an interview and written in a published story is subject to legal scrutiny for possible libel, defamation, or invasion of privacy. Journalists must always be prepared to testify in court about what they have written, although they have constitutional protections that are not extended to social workers.

Social workers should never write anything in a report that they cannot prove. If you write something that is your opinion, clearly label it as opinion, and never express any opinions that could damage the reputations or careers of individuals who have come to you for children.

Privacy and Confidentiality

In the course of adoptive and foster parent interviews, information invariably will come to light that must be protected by the screener. Examples, include details of sexual experiences, marital infidelities, family secrets of various kinds, confidences revealed by an applicant that have not been disclosed to the applicant's partner, and myriad other confessions that sometimes defy comprehension.

Your agency should have a confidentiality policy in effect to address such concerns. If there is no policy in effect, it is helpful to remember that your first concern is for the welfare of any child placed with the applicants. Your second concern should be for the individual that provided information of a confidential nature to you. Screeners have confidential sources just as investigative journalists have confidential sources. You have an obligation to protect those sources. There are exceptions, of course. In its *Code of Ethics,* the National Association of Social Workers (NASW, 2008) recommends that social workers protect the confidentiality of all information obtained during the home study process: "The general expectation that social workers will keep information confidential does not apply when disclosure is necessary to prevent serious, foreseeable, and imminent harm to a client or other identifiable person. In all instances, social workers should disclose the least amount of confidential information necessary to achieve the desired purpose; only information that is directly relevant to the purpose for which the disclosure is made should be revealed" (p. 10).

At the start of the interview it is important that you explain to the applicants that although you will maintain confidentiality regarding their comments, you will put those comments into a home study that will be read by your supervisor and others at the agency, and possibly opened by court order. This process is known as *informed consent,* a legal term that means that the applicants understand that the information that they provide to you will be shared with other professionals at the agency. Incorporating informed consent wording into the application itself is recommended to avoid any misunderstandings at a later date.

Many states grant some segments of the population *privileged communication.* Included are lawyers, physicians, journalists, and clergy. Privileged communication means that protected groups cannot be compelled by the courts to share information obtained during confidential interviews with clients, except under unusual circumstances that recognize that "protective privilege ends where public peril begins."[3] In practical terms, this means that any promises made by a social worker to observe strict confidentiality may be subject to revision if it becomes clear that failure to disclose the information could result in harm to a child or some other person.

One area where confidentiality often is breached is with home studies. When an agency makes home studies available to applicants, it addresses the right of individuals to have access to records compiled about them by a social agency, but it also raises serious questions about confidentiality. For example, if one partner discloses during an individual interview that she is unhappy with her husband's sexual performance but has learned to live with it—and that information is dutifully reported in the home study by the screener—its disclosure to the husband could damage the couple's relationship. The wife's expectation that her comments will be kept in confidence is in conflict with her husband's expectation that anything written about him in the home study will be made available to him as part of the agency's responsibility for full disclosure. The same dilemma often is faced with references. It is customary for an agency to state in its letter to a reference that the information provided will be kept in strict confidence. However, it is essential that the information be included in the home study. Does an applicant have the right to override the agency's pledge to a reference? Does a spouse have the right to override confidentiality granted by a screener to the other spouse? Obviously, that is not the case, but it occurs with alarming frequency because screeners are not always consulted when information is released. If confidential information is not redacted from home studies before they are released, it puts the screener and the agency at legal risk. Breach of confidentiality is a violation of the social worker's code of ethics: "When providing clients with access to their records, social workers should take steps to protect the confidentiality of other individuals identified or discussed in such records" (NASW, 2008, p. 10).

This puts the screener in an awkward position. Sometimes, information of the sort that would be given only with an understanding of confidentiality plays a crucial role in the acceptance or rejection of an applicants' application. Other times it does not affect the final decision but offers insight into the type of child that would be appropriate for the applicants. If the screener does not include the information in the home study, for fear of breaching confidentiality, is he or she living up to obligations to protect any child placed in the home?

Perhaps the best way to navigate through potential problems would be for the screener to discuss controversial information with his or her supervisor prior to including it in the home study. That way the matter can be fully discussed before it becomes a potential problem, thus providing the agency with a proactive strategy for including or rejecting the information in the actual home study. Under no circumstance should a social worker be asked to complete a home study if the social

---

3. See National Association of Social Workers, 2008. See also *Tarasoff v. Board of Regents of the University of California* (529 P. 2d 553, 1974).

worker does not have a clear understanding of how to handle controversial information obtained from the applicants.

Sexual Relationships with Clients

Under no circumstances should a social worker have a sexual relationship with a client or member of a client's family. Legal considerations aside, such activity may be harmful to the client and may make it difficult for the social worker and client to maintain a professional relationship. Suffice it to say that such activity is a violation of the social worker's *Code of Ethics* and could result in a malpractice lawsuit against the social worker and the agency.

Likewise, it is a violation of the social worker's *Code of Ethics* to have a sexual relationship with a former client or to take on a client with whom the social worker had a prior sexual relationship (NASW, 2008) If a former spouse or sexual partner of the screener applies for adoptive or foster children at the agency where a screener works, the screener should notify the supervisor that he or she cannot take the case because of a conflict of interest.

Client Touching

Studies have reported that social workers engage in client touching more often than psychologists (Willison & Masson, 1986). Because physical contact with clients—hugging, caressing, and so forth—is so open to misinterpretation, it should be avoided in most instances. Just because a social worker's intentions in making such gestures are completely harmless does not mean that the gestures will be perceived by the client in such a manner.

Unexpected and unwanted physical gestures sometimes can be perceived by the recipient as sexual harassment. It matters little how you meant your gestures to be perceived if the recipient has a different perception. It is their perception that matters most. It may be useful to remember that some individuals grow into adulthood without a history of experiencing affection expressed through physical gestures. Such an individual could find an unsolicited hug an invasion of their privacy, at the very least, and quite possibly a distressing emotional experience.

Even so, Kadushin and Kadushin (1997) advocated that social workers not rule out touching in situations in which the client might perceive it to be expected, especially when a failure to touch might be regarded as "unnatural." If touching is done by social workers during interview situations, they recommend the following guidelines:

> The interviewer has to be clear that the situation warrants touching, that the nature of the touch is appropriate, that its intent is nonerotic, and that it doesn't impose a greater degree in intimacy on the interviewee than the interviewee wants and can cope with. The gesture must be a response to genuine feeling and serve the needs of the interviewee. The interviewer has to decide whether a touch that is theoretically correct in terms of the needs of the interview is also ethically incorrect.

CHAPTER TWO

First Contact:
The Do's and Don'ts

First impressions matter. It is during the first encounter with the agency that applicants provide some of the most useful information needed to evaluate them as adoptive or foster parents, and it is during the first encounter that the agency provides the most useful information needed by the applicants to evaluate the agency's ability to address their needs.

Unfortunately, many social agencies relegate intake interviews to staff members with the least amount of training and experience. As a result, many inquiries have a tentative or unsatisfactory conclusion. A 2005 study conducted by the Evan B. Donaldson Adoption Institute, which surveyed more than 40 states, found that 78 percent of the adults who call an agency for information about adoption or foster care will not fill out an application or attend an orientation meeting, and just 6 percent of those who call for information will actually complete a home study (Evan B. Donaldson Adoption Institute, 2005). Of the estimated 240,000 inquiries received each year by state agencies, only a small percentage of callers complete the process to adopt a child who is in foster care. Those are dismal statistics that illuminate a major problem in the adoption and foster home–finding process.

Inquiries about adoption or foster care begin in one of four ways: by telephone, by letter or e-mail, or in person by individuals who simply walk unannounced into the office. In all four instances, if the inquiries are not fielded by an experienced adoption or foster home worker who can answer questions with authority, it is important that the intake worker handling the inquiry respond to the applicants in a friendly, positive manner and not try to answer questions that exceed the intake worker's experience. If the intake worker does not know the answer to a particular question, he or she should admit that in a friendly manner and offer to obtain the information for the applicants.

What Information Should Be Provided over the Telephone?

Every agency, public and private, has nonnegotiable requirements that cannot be waived during the interview process. This is the information that can be provided by telephone by intake workers or inexperienced adoption or foster home workers. Among them are minimum age requirements (usually 21 years of age or older), marriage requirements (length of time that individuals have been married), and residency or citizenship requirements. Those types of nonnegotiable requirements can be discussed during the intake process without risk because there is little room for misunderstanding. Other more subjective requirements related to income, emotional stability, lack of a criminal record, to name a few, are best dealt with by experienced social workers during the in-person interview process.

Intake workers are more likely to give out incorrect information when they venture beyond their levels of expertise.

Sample Intake Interview

Goals: To provide callers enough information on nonnegotiable issues for the caller to self-screen himself or herself and thus save the agency time and resources.

Client: I would like information on adoption/foster parenting.

Intake Worker: What would you like to know?

Client: Basically, I want to know how to go about it.

Intake Worker: I'll be happy to answer any questions you have today, and I will send you a brochure and an application that you can fill out and return to us.

Client: Oh, good.

Intake Worker: First, let me ask you a few questions.

Client: Sure. No problem. What would you like to know?

Intake Worker: Are you married?

Client: Yes

Intake worker: How old are you?

Client: I'm 22 and my husband is 28. Do you have a minimum age requirement?

Intake Worker: Yes. All applicants must be 21 or older. How long have you been married?

Client: Four years. We got married when I was 18. Is there a certain length of time you have to be married?

Intake Worker: Two years.[1] One last question. Of what county are you a resident?

Client: Jackson County. Can I ask you a question?

Intake Worker: Certainly.

Client: How much money do you have to make?

Intake Worker: There is an income requirement, but it is not a set amount.

---

1. Unlike most foreign countries that require couples to be married for a specified period of time (in China, it is two years, unless a spouse has three or more divorces, in which case they would be ineligible for adoption; Vietnam requires two years; India requires five years, and Korea requires three years), length-of-marriage requirements in the United States vary considerably from state to state. In Mississippi, couples are required to be married for at least two years, but in New York there is no length of marriage requirement. In New York, according to the New York Bar Association's pamphlet *Adoption in New York,* an adult married person who is legally separated may alone adopt another person.

Client: I don't understand.

Intake Worker: It depends on your overall situation. Your social worker will discuss that with you during your interview. Any other questions?

Client: I don't think so.

Intake Worker: We look forward to receiving your application.

What to Look for During an Intake Call From a Male–Female Couple

Typically, the caller will be female. That is because, historically speaking, adoptive and foster families have tended to be matriarchal. Notes Dorothy Hutchinson in *In Quest of Foster Parents*, "The would-be foster parent requesting a child to board or to adopt is almost always a woman. Whether the foster father is interested or not, the idea is proverbially born in the foster mother."[2] With that in mind, if the caller is male, it raises the statistical possibility that his partner is not entirely sold on adoption or foster care or that he has a controlling personality and does not allow his partner to make inquiries about serious issues. The gender of the caller should be notated in the intake worker's report. If the caller is male and he inquires about adopting or fostering children of a particular gender it should be viewed as a potential concern that requires further inquiry. That information also should be notated in the intake worker's report.[3]

If the caller is female and asks if it is necessary for her husband to be interviewed, that should be viewed as a potential concern because it may indicate that the husband may not be 100 percent convinced that adoption or foster care is right for him. The information should be notated in the intake worker's report.

Establishing the Ground Rules for the First Interview

Before the screener begins the first interview, he or she should explain how the agency processes applications for adoptive or foster children. It should be made clear to the applicants that questions will be asked about their personal life and that their answers will be evaluated by social work professionals to determine their suitability as adoptive

---

2. Dorothy Hutchinson's (1943, p. 8.) observations were made quite some time ago, but they are consistent with the experience of the coauthor of this book, James L. Dickerson, who has placed literally hundreds of children into adoptive and foster homes.

3. Coauthor Dickerson's experience as a screener is that few male-generated inquiries about adoption or foster care resulted in approved homes. In most instances, the female spouses admitted during separate interviews that they were not enthusiastic about adoption or foster care. Typical was one woman's admission that she wanted to pursue a career and her husband wanted her to stay at home with a child. One husband admitted to the author that he wanted a child in the home so that his wife would not make so many sexual demands on him. That experience has been supported by various studies, including David Fanshel's (1966) study of foster parents, in which he found that a majority of the men questioned were more passive than their partners, reluctant to embrace views that could be labeled authoritarian or that reflected a hostile attitude toward women. Seventy-eight percent of the men questioned disagreed that going off together hunting or fishing without women was their idea of an ideal vacation. As a rule, foster fathers don't like to rock the boat.

or foster parenthood. It should also be made clear to the applicants that they have certain legal responsibilities as adoptive or foster parents.

Key Legal Advice for Foster and Adoptive Parents

Caregivers and DHS workers must rely on each other for information regarding the child they are mutually serving. Nonetheless, there are limits on the extent to which the caregivers and DHS workers can convey responsibility to each other. Each member of the team has unique legal responsibilities that can be neither delegated nor shared. These will vary from to state to state. Those responsibilities should be clearly explained to prospective adoptive and foster parents. It should be explained to each applicant that conscientious performance is expected, not just by the agency but by the legal system.

Caregivers must make every effort to operate within the legal framework of the state in which they live. The best protection against a lawsuit is to operate in such a way that prevents lawsuits from being filed in the first place. However, it should be made clear to applicants that no caregiver can be totally free from risk. There is no absolute protection against someone bringing a lawsuit against a caregiver.

Every state offers courses to meet the diverse continuing educational needs of foster and adoptive parents. These continuing education credits must be kept up to date.

Applicants should read all agency communications and make sure they accurately reflect their conversation and understanding. Agency employees and caregivers should ideally keep track of all contacts they have with each other. Neither caregivers nor agency workers should assume that what they are saying is going to be documented by the other person.

Once a child has been placed with an adoptive or foster parent, parents should be encouraged to record, preferably in writing, all objections they have with the agency. Controversial and difficult issues constantly arise. Parents should make sure their position is recorded. They should note the name of the workers they talked with and the date and time of the contact. If possible, notes should be written on the same day as the conversation takes place.

Parents should be required to review all agency plans and policies and how they are carried out. They should be advised that they should not feel a need to accommodate agency staff just because they have a working relationship with them.

Parents should know that if they feel that the agency's actions are not in accordance with its own policy, they should speak up!

Last, foster parents should be encouraged to purchase foster parent liability insurance, which will protect them if a child in their care is injured and they are sued by a birth parent or legal guardian. Policies usually offer protection from lawsuits related to libel, slander, and claims of alienation of affection by the birth parents.

Sample Questions for the First Interview with a Social Worker

The goal of these questions is to screen for early warning signals of potential problems with the application, to make initial assessments of motivation, to educate the applicants about the agency's needs, and to identify both positive and negative parenting attitudes.

Question 1:
How Long Have You Been Considering Adoption/Foster Parenting?[4]

Possible answers:

1. "Oh, gosh, I don't have any idea."
2. "For several years, I think."
3. "We've talked about it for a long time, but not until recently did we decide to pursue it."

Answer 1 is evasive. It could indicate a long-term disagreement over adoption or foster care. On hearing this response, the worker should ask which partner first raised the issue.

Answer 2 indicates possible ambivalence or even hostility from one partner toward adoption or foster care. The follow-up question should be, "Why do you think it has taken so long to make a decision?" It is important, at this point, to identify each partner's opinion of adoption or foster care so that you can track their decision-making process.

Answer 3 is an acceptable response if subsequent questioning indicates that the couple had understandable reasons for delaying a final decision, for example, if there were financial, health, or other issues that had to be resolved. Perhaps the wife wanted to spend several years on her career before committing to adoption or foster care. Perhaps the couple wanted to build an addition to their home before taking in adoptive or foster children.

Question 2:
Why Do You Think the Time Is Right for Adoption/Foster Parenting?

Possible answers:

1. "Our life is at a place where we think we have something to offer children."
2. "We just feel that children will make our marriage stronger."
3. "We have given up on having children of our own."

Of the three above answers, it is the first that offers the most potential because it is one of the answers that most often has been associated with good adoptive and foster parenting. Answer 2 is a concern and must be explored. Answer 3 is satisfactory as far

---

4. Many of the basic questions in this section are reprinted with permission from Dickerson and Allen (2007, pp. 97–99). However, all the answers to those questions and the discussion material and recommendations are original to this book.

as it goes, but it offers a potential red flag if one partner is bitter about not being able to have birth children (perhaps one partner has not "given up," thus planting a seed for discontent within the relationship, not a positive attitude with which to build an adoptive family). Answer 3 is a potential concern for a foster parent applicant if it motivates the applicant to "try out" foster children for adoption.

If they have been discussing it for a long time, what have been their respective positions? It is important to determine who was reluctant to pursue adoption or foster parenting, and for what reasons. Among the possibilities you will want to explore in subsequent interviews are the following:

- Whether one partner is disillusioned with the relationship and is reluctant to add a new commitment
- Whether one partner is fearful the relationship is in trouble and wants a child in the home to bolster the relationship
- Whether one partner is prejudiced about adoption or foster care for racial or religious reasons

Question 3:
Are You Able to Have Birth Children?

Why would this question be important? There was a time in adoption history (as recently as 30 years ago), when applicants who could have birth children were routinely rejected for adoptive and foster care. That is rarely the case now because of a nationwide shortage of foster homes and a need for adoptive homes for older children. However, the question still has relevance, even if for an entirely different reason.

Today the question is most frequently asked to help gauge relationship stability.

If the answer is "no, we can't have children," the agency may require the applicants to provide verification of infertility from a physician. A deceptive client who is able to have birth children may feel that a "no" answer will make them more attractive as applicants. Deception does not bode well for subsequent questions about intimate aspects of family and personal relationships. If the physician says they are able to have children, then you must confront them with that information (a medical report provided at the applicants' request is an exception to the confidentiality rule) at a subsequent follow-up interview.

For applicants who state that they can have birth children, you must determine why the applicants want to adopt or foster children. The first interview is not the point at which you seek to establish actual motivation, but rather the point at which you begin to establish their *stated* motivation. Why would an applicant who can have birth children prefer to adopt? One possibility is that one or both partners have an aversion to sex. If so, that would complicate their application.

Follow-up questions:

If you can have birth children, why have you decided not to?

Possible answers:

1. Because the world has too many children in need of homes.
2. Because I (or my partner) have a history of genetic diseases of a troubling nature (cancer, retardation, and so forth) and we are afraid to have birth children.
3. Because I have a fear of childbirth.

Of the above answers, answer 1 would be considered the most appropriate. Known as an altruistic response, it typically scores high on rating scales measuring satisfaction among foster parents (Fanshel, 1966). Answer 2 is a satisfactory response that has not been linked to negative child-rearing attitudes. Answer 3 is significant only if the male partner has negative attitudes toward the female partner as a result of her fear of childbirth ("She's such a wimp." "I don't know why I have to pay the price for her fears." "She's afraid of childbirth but not afraid of what those cigarettes are doing to her.")

Question 4:
How Does It Make You Feel That You Can't Have Birth Children?

Possible answers:

1. "It makes me angry."
2. "It makes me sad."
3. "It makes me happy."
4. "It's just one of those things you have to accept."

Of the above responses, it is answer 4 that indicates the most mature attitude. Resignation can be a firm foundation upon which to build a future after experiencing a disappointment. Answer 1 is the least acceptable because anger is not a good emotion with which to begin adoption or foster home proceedings, no matter how painful the antecedent disappointment. Answer 2 is certainly understandable, but if you hear that response you must be vigilant in future interviews to screen the applicants for possible depression that may have causes other than the disappointment of not being able to have birth children. Answer 3 is inappropriate because it could indicate an individual who is not in touch with reality or who has an oppositional personality. You should immediately challenge such a response by asking why not being able to have birth children would make them happy. If you receive this response, you will want to look for similar oppositional responses in subsequent interviews.

Question 5:
Have You Ever Applied Elsewhere to Adopt Children?

If the answer is yes, you must determine the status of the previous application. Was the applicant rejected? If so, you will need to ask the applicant to sign a release so that you can contact the agency. Did the applicant withdraw the application? If so, why? Again, you will need a signed release to contact the agency. If the applicants applied but then withdrew their application during the interview process you will want to discuss it with them in detail to determine their reasons. Typically, if the applicants withdrew their application before the interviews were completed, the previous agency will tell you that they don't know the reasons. However, on occasion, you will be told that the interviews were broken off because the applicants were in disagreement over one issue or another. If that is the situation, you will need to ask the applicants to explain the nature of the disagreement. If they deny there was a disagreement, you will want to interview the previous social worker so that you can determine whether there was a misunderstanding.

Question 6:
What Age Child Would You Like to Adopt?

Possible answers.

1. "An infant . . . a preschooler . . . school age."
2. "What age would you recommend?"
3. "We don't really care."
4. "I don't know—I've never really thought about it."

Good adoptive and foster home prospects typically have a specific age in mind. Beware of the applicant who says, "I don't care." Or "I don't know—I've never really thought about that." Such answers may indicate an emotional detachment from the process and raise questions about whether there may be a disagreement between the applicants over whether children are in the best interests of the family.

Answer 2 could indicate a person who has done his or her research and does not wish to limit available options (a positive indicator) or an indecisive individual who has a difficult time making up his or her mind (a negative indicator).

Answer 1 is the preferable answer. Every couple or individual who applies for adoptive or foster parent consideration should have a clear preference for the age of the child they are seeking. If the applicants are a couple, each individual may have a preferred age, which could result in the couple being open to different age groups, such as "infant or preschooler."

Question 7:
Describe the Child Who You Think Would Fit Best Into Your Home?

Possible answers:

1. "Someone with no health or mental problems."
2. "A child that looks like me or my partner."
3. "A child that needs love and guidance."
4. "A child that no longer has contact with his mother or father."

This is an important question that provides you with your first glimpse of the applicants' perception of how an adoptive or foster child will impact their family. If an applicant responds with answer 1, you will know that you will have a difficult time finding a child for them and it would be appropriate for you to suggest deviations from that limited description. For example, you might ask the applicants to clarify that position by inquiring if they mean that they could not accept children with minor or moderate health or mental problems. Ask them to be specific.

Answers 2 and 4 will be addressed with direct questions as you proceed through the interview. Of the above answers, answer 3 is the one that you would most like to hear because it depicts the child as someone who is in need of them.

Question 8:
Would You Be Able to Accept a Child Who Has Special Needs?

Few applicants will understand the phrase "special needs," so you will have to explain it to them before they answer—that is, children with physical, intellectual, or emotional disabilities. You also will explain that siblings fit the definition of special needs. Subsequent questions will allow you to discuss their reactions to specific conditions or situations.

Question 9:
How Do You Think That Adoption Will Change Your Life?

Possible answers:

1. "I don't know."
2. "I think it will make us feel more like a family."
3. "I don't think it will change our life."
4. "In ways we can only dream about."

Good adoption or foster home prospects will have an answer to this question. If the applicant responds, "I don't know" or "I don't think it will change our life," you may want to give the applicant a reading assignment that must be completed before the next interview. If they respond with answer 2, ask for more information because it could indicate problems in the relationship. What is happening in their relationship that makes them not feel like a family? Answer 4 indicates a level of optimism and openness that may bode well for a placement.

Question 10:
What Do You Think Is the Most Difficult Thing about Raising an Adopted or Foster Child?

Possible answers:

1. "Replacing the love and affection that they have lost."
2. "Helping them overcome their past."

3. "Planning for the extra expense."
4. "Sharing them with their birth family."

This is a subject that will be discussed in great detail later in the interview process, but, for now, the question provides the screener a window into the applicants' viewpoint of their role in adoption or foster care. Obviously, answers 1 and 2 are the most appropriate answers because it shows recognition by the applicants that the child or children that they receive will not be perfect and will have fears and anxieties that will have to be overcome.

Answer 3 is a response that will require more elaboration in subsequent interviews.

Answer 4 is an answer that suggests that the applicants will have a difficult time with foster care or open adoption in which the birth parents are involved in the child's care. You will need to follow up on this in subsequent interviews.

Question 11:
How Does Your Extended Family Feel about You Adopting/Fostering a Child?

Possible answers:

1. "They think we're crazy."
2. "We haven't told them since they are very much against adoption/foster care."
3. "They love the idea."
4. "They said they will support our decision."

If the applicants are evasive in their responses to this question, then you must press for details. Answer 3 is the response that you hope to hear. Answer 4 is second choice because it suggests acceptance in the face of some resistance. With this answer it is very important for you to ascertain any negative attitudes that family members may have toward adoption or foster care. Answers 1 and 2 are potential concerns that will require in-depth questioning in subsequent interviews. For now, simply ask "why" in response to either of those answers. For answer 2, you want to ask why they are against adoption or foster care. Perhaps a parent was adopted or placed in foster care as a young child and did not find it to be a good experience. Perhaps they know a disagreeable person who was adopted or placed in foster care and they blame that individual's personality on his or her childhood experiences. Perhaps there is a racial angle to their opposition.

Question 12:
How Would You Feel about Adopting/Fostering a Child with Developmental Disabilities?

Possible answers:

1. "I think it would depend on the severity of the disability."
2. "We don't think we could handle that at all."

3. "We don't know that much about it."

4. "I don't know why not. I have a cousin who is retarded."

The responses to this question could be positive, negative or something in between. If the response is that the applicant could not be accepting of a developmentally challenged child, don't try to persuade—just move on. If the response is answer 1 or 2, describe the different levels and types of disabilities they could encounter and discuss with them their ability to adopt or foster a child with mild, moderate, or severe retardation. If the response is still positive, you will still have a lot of educational work to do with the applicants at subsequent interviews. If the response is "no," reassure the applicants that they will not be penalized in any way for not agreeing to accept a child who is developmentally challenged. The optimum answer here is 4. The applicant has had experience with an individual with a disability and an open mind on the subject.

Question 13:
How Would You Feel about Adopting/Fostering a Physically Challenged Child?

Possible answers:

1. "I guess it would depend on the severity of the disability."
2. "I don't think I'm strong enough, if you think it would involve lifting."
3. "We don't think that someone with a physical disability would be a good fit for our family."
4. "We talked about that and it is a possibility, depending on the child's age."

You want to make certain that the applicants understand all the implications, both short and long range, of caring for a physically challenged child. Be specific in discussing the types of handicaps that are at issue. Answer 4 is an ideal response. The applicants anticipated the question and expressed openness to discussing it further. Any applicant who responded "yes," without elaboration should raise a concern. Answer 1 is also an acceptable response. Answers 2 or 3 are honest and should not disqualify the applicants from receiving consideration for other classifications of children.

Question 14:
How Do You Feel about Adopting/Fostering a Child with Emotional Problems?

Possible answers:

1. "I guess that all depends. Could you explain the different levels of problems in more detail?"
2. "My sister was diagnosed with emotional problems and I was sort of raised in that environment. I think we could handle it, but it would depend on the age of the child and how engrained the emotional problems are."
3. "Absolutely not! Something like that would drive me crazy."
4. "We are open to discussing it further on an individual child basis."

Before asking the questions, provide the applicants with examples of children with emotional problems and listen carefully for any reservations on their part. Also be alert to any unrealistic expectations from either partner. The optimum answers are 1, 2, and 4. It is unrealistic to expect an applicant to say "yes" without explanation or additional questions because that would suggest unrealistic expectations. Answer 3 is clear enough. It would be counterproductive to press them for more details. Accept the answer for the time being and move on to other questions. One of your goals will be to find out exactly what drives the applicant "crazy."

Question 15:
How Would You Feel about Adopting/Fostering a Child Who Had Been Sexually, Emotionally, or Physically Abused by His or Her Parents or Caregivers?

Possible answers:

1. "I don't think I could handle the stress."
2. "I was abused as a child, so I think I would have a good understanding of the problems involved."
3. "That wouldn't be our first choice, but I think we could be supportive of the child."
4. "I don't know why not—we'd treat her like we would any other child."

Before asking the question, provide the applicants with examples of the different types of abuse. Of the above responses, answer 3 is the best response because it offers hope that the applicants would be able to work with social workers in providing appropriate care to the child. Answer 1 is honest and the applicant should be given the opportunity to be considered for other categories of children. However, the screener should be alert to the frequent conversational use of the word "stress"; if the word is recurring it could be an indication of maladaptive behavior in the individual's life. You would want to be direct with this applicant: "Please give me examples of things that cause you stress."

Answer 4 is unrealistic. There is little to be gained by pursuing that line of thinking at this point, but it should raise concerns about unrealistic attitudes in other areas, such as in child-rearing attitudes in general.

Answer 2 is problematic. An applicant who was abused as a child (sexually, emotionally, or physically) does indeed possess an understanding of the problems involved, but only if they have come to terms with their abuse. Complicating the issue are various studies that indicate that there is a high probability that child sex abusers were themselves sexually abused as children.[5] To date, no one has discovered

---

5. Jespersen, Lalumiere, and Seto (2009) concluded that "there is support for the sexually abused–sexual abuser hypothesis, in that sex offenders are more likely to have been sexually abused than non–sex offenders" (179–192).

a correlation between emotional and physical abusers and childhood sexual abuse. Applicants who admit to childhood abuse should be questioned in great detail about the nature of the abuse and the manner in which it has affected their life.

Question 16:
How Would You Feel about Adopting/Fostering a Child of a Different Race?

Possible answers:

1. "We would be open to adopting/fostering a child of a different race."
2. "We could not be accepting of a child of a different race."
3. "Depends on the race. Hispanics are almost white. We could accept them, probably."

As in all other areas, you should let the applicants know that they will not be penalized for sharing their opinions about race. There is no penalty for wanting to adopt a child of the same race. However, one thing you want to be alert to in their response is a negative attitude toward a particular race. If they explain their rejection of a different-race child in terms of comments such as, "We wouldn't want a black child because they have criminal tendencies," or "We wouldn't want an Asian child since they can't be trusted," or "We wouldn't want a Hispanic child because they are trying to take over this country," then you will have to follow up on those comments during the individual interviews to determine whether the applicants' attitudes are pervasive enough to cause problems for any child placed in their care, all the more so if they live in a multicultural community. Of the above-mentioned responses, answer 1 is the most promising and requires no follow-up at this point. Answers 2 and 3 are satisfactory enough to prevent the applicants from receiving a different-race child, even if that is the most pressing need at the moment. One thing a screener doesn't want to do is try to talk an applicant into bending their bias to accommodate the screener's needs.

Follow-up questions. Follow-up questions should focus on the extent of the interviewees' prejudice, that is, whether they internalize their beliefs or externalize them. You cannot reject an applicant simply because they want a child of the same race. However, you can reject an applicant if their beliefs are extreme enough to affect the growth and development of an adoptive or foster child.

Possible follow-up questions:

1. Would you allow your child to play with children of a different race?
2. What would you do if your child had a teacher of a different race?
3. Would you allow your child to participate in a school event in which there are children of different races?

Question 17:
How Would You Feel about Adopting/Fostering a Child of a Different Religion?

Possible answers:

1. "Depends on what the religion is. I'm a Baptist. I wouldn't mind a Methodist, but I wouldn't be interested in a Jew or a Muslim."
2. "We are agnostic and we wouldn't feel comfortable carting a child off to church every Sunday."
3. "We would be fine with a child of any religion and we would do our best to see that they maintain a relationship with the religion with which they have been raised."
4. "We are spiritual but do not attend church every Sunday. Is that a requirement?

You don't give negative points to an applicant who is reluctant to adopt a child of a different religion, but you do want to be alert to negative or hostile comments about other religions because it may be indicative of a life view that would be incompatible with good parenting. Religion is a passionate issue for many individuals and could have a very strong impact on how children are raised in an adoptive or foster home. Unfortunately, religion's relationship to adoption has not been the subject of any in-depth research, and many screeners are uncomfortable with the issue. That should not be the case. Religion should be explored by the screener with the same thoroughness he or she devotes to other issues that have a bearing on an adopted or foster child's growth and development within a family.

Answer 3 is the most appropriate response. Answers 1 and 2, in and of themselves, are not enough to disqualify an applicant, but such responses are limiting in that they would severely restrict placement opportunities. If adoptive or fosters parents are approved only from children that come from agnostic or religion-specific backgrounds, they could have a very long wait for a child and they should be so advised.

Answer 4 is an honest response that would perhaps be considered appropriate for a public agency and inappropriate for a religion-based nonprofit agency. The public agency will be more interested in whether the applicant will be supportive of a child's wish to maintain a relationship with the religion in which he or she was raised. Many religion-based nonprofits give preference to applicants of the same faith, primarily because birth parents frequently attach that stipulation as a condition of surrendering parenting rights.

Question 18:
How Would You Feel about Adopting/Fostering a Child Whose
Birth Parents Are Under Court Order Not to Try to Contact the Child?

Possible answers:

1. "Parenting a child is hard enough as it is. I don't think we could cope with a crazy parent banging on our door all the time."

2. "I suppose it would depend on the reasons why they are under court order."
3. "I think we could handle that with your help."

Applicants who are apprehensive about committing to a child under those conditions should not be penalized, because caution is a fairly normal reaction to this question. As in other situations, you want to be alert to what else the applicants say while responding to your question. If the applicants say "yes" but then add, "We have enough guns to stop a small army, so we wouldn't be concerned about any trouble," you would want to pursue that line of thinking during the individual interviews because their response moves them from a "normal" category to one that requires further scrutiny. Answer 3 is the most appropriate and opens the door on later negotiations regarding what specifically can be "handled." Answers 1 and 2 could indicate a low threshold for stress and should alert the screener to limitations in the applicants' ability to handle stress.

Question 19:
How Would You Feel about Adopting/Fostering a Child Whose Parent Is in Prison?

Possible answers:

1. "Regardless of what their mom or dad has done, they still need love."
2. "I would be afraid that the child might have criminal tendencies."
3. "I would be concerned about whether the parent was convicted of a violent crime, and whether they would be getting out of prison anytime soon."

Answer 1 is the most appropriate, but you would still want to question them in more detail, in subsequent interviews, about their attitudes toward people who go to prison. Answer 3 does not close the door on a "yes" answer, but it should prompt additional questioning at a later date. Regarding answers 1 and 3, you should be alert to attitudes that later would result in the child being told disparaging things about their birth parent. For example, a situation in which a parent would discipline a misbehaving child by saying, "You are going to end up in prison just like your mother."

Answer 2 is indicative of ingrained attitudes that will not easily be changed by discussions with a social worker. The screener's job is to identify negative attitudes, not to change negative attitudes with a reasoned and informed argument.

Question 20:
How Would You Feel about Adopting/Fostering a Juvenile Offender?

Possible answers:

1. "You mean someone who has been to jail? I don't think so."
2. "I guess that would depend on the nature of the offense."
3. "Juvenile offenders need homes, too. We'll give it a try."

Answer 3 offers the most potential, but you would have to be certain that the applicants have a good understanding of the challenges they would face. Answer 2 opens the door to serious consideration. Answer 1 closes the door on this particular type of placement.

Question 21:
How Would You Feel about Adopting/Fostering Siblings?

Possible answers:

1. "I don't think we have room for more than one child."
2. "We would be fine with taking in a small family."
3. "That would depend on their ages."

This is an important question because many adoptable "special needs" children have siblings and should be placed as a family. It is important for prospective adoptive and foster parents to understand that although many children in this category do not necessarily have problems or disabilities of any kind, many may have disabilities and health issues of various kinds.

Answers 2 and 3 both offer the opportunity for successful placements. The screener should follow up with questions about what limitations they would put on such a placement. For example, could they be accepting if one of the children had physical, emotional, or developmental issues? If the applicants say they could accept siblings that have no serious problems, ask them to define what they consider to be "serious," because their definition and yours may differ.

If the applicants give answer 1, it should not be interpreted as an invitation for negotiation on the number of children that can be placed in the home, even if you think they do have room for more than one child. Most applicants feel vulnerable during the interview process. Sometimes applicants will agree to something that they think you want because they want to make a good impression. For that reason, you should never view a "soft" answer as one that can be molded to fit your needs. Sometimes screeners have to take no for an answer.

Question 22:
How Would You Feel about Caring for a Child Who Has Been Diagnosed with HIV?

Possible answers:

1. "I think we could do that. We have a family member who was diagnosed with HIV. Of course, we would need a lot of support from you."
2. "Oh, no. I was afraid you would ask that. I'm sorry to say I don't think we could cope with that."
3. "That is simply too scary for us to handle."

Answer 1 is what every screener hopes to hear. Of course, anyone who answers yes to this question must be thoroughly questioned to make certain that they understand what would be involved with caring for a child with HIV.

Unfortunately, answers 2 and 3 are the ones you will hear the most often. Fear of HIV is not a cause for rejection, but it points out the need to question the applicants more closely before placing a child with them who has serious health issues. You will want to make certain that they understand what will be required of them in caring for a child with a specific disease or ailment.

Question 23:
Once a Child Has Been Placed with You, Whether for Foster Parenting or Adoption, It Is Our Agency's Policy to Make Unannounced Visits. For Adoption, the Visits Would Continue During the Probationary Period. For Foster Parenting, the Visits Would Continue for as Long as the Child Is in Your Home? How Do You Feel about That?

Possible answers:

1. "That's fine. I understand that you have a duty to protect the children in your care."
2. "Oh, I think that would make me too nervous."
3. "Wouldn't that be an invasion of my privacy?"

Answer 1 is the obvious best response. Openness is an important characteristic of successful adoptive and foster parents.

Answer 2 is a nonstarter for either adoptive or foster parenthood. If someone is too "nervous" for an unannounced visitor from a social agency, he or she is probably a poor risk. You will need to question them in more detail to determine whether other family members feel the same way.

Answer 3 offers a ray of hope. Explain why the agency makes unannounced visits and go over what happens during the visit (make it clear that you will not walk through the house to look in closets and drawers). Often the individual will withdraw the objection and announce their willingness to work with the agency.

Using the Internet and Social Media

Babies by e-mail! That's not as ridiculous as it sounds.

The newest trend in adoption is for adoptive applicants to advertise themselves on social media such as YouTube or Facebook or Twitter, hoping that a pregnant teen will be impressed by their pitch and offer to give her unborn child to them. CNN broadcast a revealing news story on the phenomenon in 2009 and interviewed an adoptive couple and the birth mother who placed her child with them.[6] Adam Pertman, executive director of the Evan B. Donaldson Adoption Institute, told the CNN reporter that he had knowledge of other adoptions that had been arranged on the Web: "The more people who know you are looking, the better your prospects. It's a crapshoot, and you are trying to improve your odds."[7]

---

6. See "Their paths crossed on YouTube on an August night last year." CNN (March 10, 2009).

7. Ibid.

Unfortunately, navigating the Web sites is also a "crapshoot." Some are operated by established agencies with experienced adoption personnel. One of the most successful websites is AdoptUsKids.org, a clearinghouse for children in foster homes in need of adoptive homes. It is operated under a cooperative agreement between the United States Department of Health and Human Services, the Adoption Exchange Association, Children's Bureau, and Administration for Children and Families, and it is used by state social service agencies to promote individual children for adoption. It has an excellent track record of making successful placements and offers a high degree of professionalism.

Some Web sites offer little or no experience in adoption, in effect prompting individuals desperate for children to "roll the dice." They encourage adoption applicants, women with children who they would like to place for adoption, and adopted adults who simply want to get in touch with birth parents or siblings, the opportunity to communicate directly with each other. One successful page on Facebook is linked to a Web site that is operated by a law firm that specializes in adoption. Sample postings on the Facebook page, which has more than 14,000 "fans," include:

> "We are a loving, caring compassionate Christian couple that is seeking an open adoption."
>
> "I am searching for a half sibling."
>
> One woman pleads that she is looking for her son who was "adopted against my will."

This Facebook-connected Web site is staffed by attorneys, not adoption specialists. The Web site shows a photograph of a law office, but it does not offer information about where the offices are located. The site provides a good example of where adoption is headed. Children are matched with adoptive parents, and private and public agencies are asked to complete home studies either before a placement is made or after a placement is made, when the potential for conducting a proper screening is severely handicapped.

Private adoption agencies also have recognized the extraordinary coverage offered by social media. Some agencies regularly used the Web to match adoptive parents with children. Of course, it is one thing for an adoption agency to use the Web to advertise children who are available for adoption (that has been done in newspapers and on television for years), but it is another matter for couples to bypass adoption agencies to arrange private adoptions, selling themselves on slickly produced videos. That is a risky procedure that places an enormous burden on screeners to evaluate couples who have no motivation to be straightforward in their answers because in some instances they already have the child in their possession by the time the home study procedure begins.

It goes without saying that the screener should have the same access to information about an applicant that is available to the general public. For that reason we suggest that screeners conduct an Internet search for information about applicants. You should begin by using a search engine for any information on the Internet pertaining to their name and city of residence.

For example, try "John Doe New York."
Follow that up with various creative pairings such as:

"John Doe New York adoption"
"John Doe New York foster parent"
"John Doe New York foster child abuse."
"John Doe New York child predator."

Other possibilities include researching applicants on social media such as Facebook, Twitter, MySpace, Internet forums, and blogs. We do not recommend using your personal Facebook or Twitter accounts to establish contact because your name would be recognizable to the applicants. Instead, ask that your agency establish special accounts that would not be recognizable to applicants.

People often express themselves on social media with an honesty that is sometimes lacking in their day-to-day personal communications. Once your interviews begin the applicants may go online and comment on the interview process by offering opinions on a wide range of issues, such as their assessment of the agency or their satisfaction at outsmarting the screener on a certain issue. Check out their sites and you may discover inappropriate photographs related to children, opinions on social issues such as racial discrimination, hate crimes, violent militia movements, illegal drug use, child pornography, and so forth. You may also discover positive attributes that enhance their potential as adoptive or foster parents—mentions of community service, for example.

With adoption by Internet certain to increase, it is essential that social agencies develop online expertise so that they can become competitive with private online entrepreneurs to find adoptive and foster parents for children in need of homes, while at the same time developing investigative skills to use the new technology as a screening tool.

Every social agency involved with adoption or foster care should have at least one individual on staff who can counsel adoptive and foster parents, along with the children for whom they provide care, about the dangers of the Internet. In 2010, the adoption world was rocked by the case of a 36-year-old Michigan woman who used Facebook to track down the biological son that she had given up for adoption when he was only a few days old. Once she located him, they arranged to meet, at which point she sexually molested the 14-year-old, a criminal act that later garnered her 9 to 30 years in prison. Asked by reporters for an explanation for her behavior, her attorney said, "When she saw this boy, something just touched off in her—and it wasn't a mother–son relationship, it was a boyfriend–girlfriend relationship."[8]

Social media are nothing more than a vehicle. The advice you would give to a child about hitchhiking is the same advice you should give to a child about the Internet: Although it may be all right on occasion to wave to strangers in passing, it is not all right to get into the vehicle with them, which is what happens when a child establishes an online relationship with a stranger.

---

8. Associated Press. "Mom jailed over sex with 14-year-old son." Retrieved from www.msnbc.msn.com

FIGURE 2.1

FIRST INTERVIEW CHECKLIST

At this point in the process, you should be confident that you have the following information:

Names, addresses, contact information, directions to home _____
_____

Stated motivation for adopting/fostering _____
_____

Birth children status _____
_____

Application history (have they applied elsewhere?) _____
_____

Age of child desired _____
_____

Any restrictions on type of child desired for placement? _____
_____

❏ Normal only   ❏ Physical disability   ❏ Intellectual disability

❏ Emotional problems   ❏ Health problems

❏ Child who has been sexually abused   ❏ Child with HIV

❏ Child who has been physically abused

❏ Special needs

Comments: _____
_____
_____

Will the applicants be able to accept agency supervision?   ❏ yes   ❏ no

Explain: _____
_____
_____

Do you feel that the applicants will be able to share information with the staff regarding the child's behavior?   ❏ yes   ❏ no.

CHAPTER THREE

What You Need to Know about Follow-up Questions

Follow-up questions are those that occur in response to previous answers that seem incomplete or in need of clarification. They may occur during the individual interviews or home visit, or they may be scheduled after the completion of the first round of interviews. If follow-up questions occur during the individual interviews, they may fall within the natural rhythms of the interview process and the applicants will not likely become concerned. However, if follow-up interviews are scheduled after the individual interviews have been completed, the applicants may become overly anxious and fearful that something may be remiss (as indeed might be the case), even if they have been advised in advance by the agency that follow-up interviews are a possibility.

Preparation is the key to a successful follow-up interview. Not only must the questions be carefully prepared, but also the possible answers must be anticipated by the screener, and a second round of follow-up questions must be considered well in advance of the interview. Lawyers are taught never to ask questions in court if they do not already know the answer. Unlike lawyers, social workers cannot know the answers to their follow-up questions in advance, but they can educate themselves on the range of possible answers.

For this round of interviews, the screener will be at a disadvantage since the applicants, sensing that something is wrong, may be defensive and more likely to reply to the interviewer's questions with questions of their own. If the screener is not properly prepared for follow-up questions, he or she may lose control of the interviews.

If follow-up questions come after regularly scheduled interviews have taken place, the screener should request that they take place in his or her office so that he or she will have more control over external events. It is possible that someone will knock on the office door during the interview and disrupt the flow of the conversation, but not so likely as it would be if the interview took place at the applicants' home, where friends and neighbors are apt to drop by unannounced.

Three Steps to a Successful Follow-up Interview

One

Are the follow-up questions the result of your analysis of previous comments made by the applicants, or are they the result of questions raised by your supervisor? If it is the latter, it is important for you to question your supervisor about the reasons for the questions so that you thoroughly understand them. Never go into a follow-up interview with a list of questions that you will be unable to explain to the applicants. If you disagree with one or more of the questions suggested by your supervisor, do not acknowledge that disagreement to the applicants by qualifying the question with, "My supervisor wants to know . . ."

Two

Look in the mirror. Are the applicants different from you in any noticeable way—skin color, ethnic origin, sexual orientation, political beliefs, and so forth? If so, research those differences by reading what those of different backgrounds have written on the subject. Are your follow-up questions related in any way to those differences? Examine your questions for any hint of cultural prejudice.

Three

Do you know the range of possible answers to your questions? You should prepare for your follow-up interviews by writing out the possible answers to your questions. Once you have done that, analyze each answer for substance and then prepare subsequent follow-up questions for each potential answer. Just be prepared!

Interview Techniques

To be an effective interviewer, the screener must have a clear understanding of what he is expected to do, and he must transfer that understanding to the applicants in such a way that they will understand his role in the proceeding. His responsibility is to the child and not to the applicants, at least not until they have been approved as foster or adoptive parents. His job is to obtain information, not to provide therapy (Dickerson and Allen, 2007, pp. 104–105; reprinted with permission).

As a result, his interview style will be noticeably different from the other social workers at a typical social services agency, almost all of whom will be doing interviews in therapeutic situations involving emotional dysfunction of one kind or another. Unlike the professionals engaged in therapeutic interviewing, the screener can afford to be less reserved in his interactions with the applicants. Friendliness is an asset, especially when it projects an image of warmth and understanding. It is important that the applicants feel comfortable throughout the interviews. A screener who fails to create such an environment will have a more difficult time obtaining the information that he needs.

Screeners should be cautious about appearing overly stern when asking questions. Most people confronted with sternness have a tendency to shut down emotionally out of a sense of self-preservation. The best interview environment is one in which the applicants can answer each question without giving thought to the screener's motivation for asking it.

For the routine questions, it is best to establish a rhythm in which the screener asks them in quick succession, without emphasis on any one particular question. The screener should understand that if he or she asks a question and looks up at the applicants with full eye contact they will interpret that question to be more important than the others, and that will usually work to the interviewer's disadvantage. Save the full eye contact until such time as you really need it.

It would probably prevent misunderstandings if the screener explained to each applicant that he or she has no constitutional right in either the United States or Canada to be a foster or adoptive parent. It is a privilege that is granted by the state when certain conditions are met. However, because screeners cannot explain that concept without seeming overly aggressive and putting the applicants on the defensive, it usually remains unspoken unless the applicants are rejected and the issue comes up before a review panel or a judge. If an agency wants to stress that point with applicants, the place to do it is in the agency's booklets or perhaps on the application itself, where the information could be presented in a less threatening manner.

There will be times during the interviews when it will be necessary for the screener to be aggressive in his questioning, especially if he feels the applicant is being dishonest or evasive. It is all right to challenge an applicant's response, particularly if it contradicts a previous statement made by the applicant.

When the screener gets to the point where he is keying in on the essence of the applicant's family or marital relationship, or other sensitive areas, one technique that always works well is what James L. Dickerson calls the *white space effect* (others sometimes refer to it as productive use of silence). What that means is that a good interviewer will use long silent pauses to encourage the applicant to fill in the gaps in the conversation. Think of the interview as a blank canvas. You want the applicant to look at the blank canvas and feel greater pressure to fill in the spaces than you do. Most people are made so uncomfortable by a long pause that they will start talking and say things that they perhaps had decided not to say. The white space effect is a power tool. Use it sparingly when the occasion calls for it.

Role of Race in Follow-up Interviews

Racial differences exist in communication. Different life experiences, different political affiliations, different socioeconomic backgrounds, different culturally based child-rearing philosophies—all put different spins on both the language and the content in follow-up questions and answers. These differences are amplified during follow-up interviews, for the simple reason that the interviews are a challenge to the status quo of the discussion that already has taken place. Follow-up interviews are an implicit admission that previous information supplied by the applicants is incomplete at best or of questionable value at worst. Those individuals for whom race is a sensitive issue will often fear, rightly or wrongly, that the problem is race-based and their responses may reflect that fear.

> Interview participants of different races are keenly aware of the racial differences between them; nevertheless the racial factor is rarely discussed openly. It may be that race is not discussed because the participants regard it as truly irrelevant to the work at hand or that both participants conspire to ignore race because it is such a sensitive issue in American society . . . To proclaim colorblindness is to deny the real differences that exist and need to be accepted (Kadushin & Kadushin, 1997, p. 323).

The best way to clear the air if the interviewer and the interviewees are of different races is for the screener to ask whether anyone feels that race is an issue:

Possible answers:

1. "Yes, we talked about this after our last interview. We think some of your questions ignore the reality of black family life."
2. "No. The subject makes us uncomfortable."
3. "Yes. You and my husband are of the same race and sometimes I feel that influences your opinions. A few times I feel like the two of you have sided against me."

Answer 1 clearly indicates that the screener must deal with the interviewees' feelings of being treated differently because of their race. It is important for the screener to listen to their concerns and adapt, if possible, the questions he has planned for the follow-up.

Answer 2 indicates that problems already have occurred in the interview process. The interviewees may not want to go into detail about their feelings, but the screener should encourage them to do so. He should reassure them that their feelings are of legitimate concern to him. If the screener feels uncomfortable talking about race, he should inform the interviewees of his feelings and let them know that he is willing talk about it if they are willing.

Answer 3 opens the door on several conversations. First, is the statement true, or does the interviewee have a point? If yes, then the screener should address the issue. If the statement is false, the screener should explore the interviewees' racial differences. Is this a subject that comes up regularly, or only in special circumstances? Are racial differences a threat to the relationship? The screener should ask that question outright. Is there a possibility that the couple has a difference of opinion about the race of a child to adopt or foster?

White Interviewer and African American Interviewee

There are several areas of sensitivity for white interviewers when they interview African American applicants for adoptive or foster children. Focus groups composed of African Americans were interviewed by the authors to identify sensitive areas of the interview process, especially for follow-up interviews that may suggest to the applicants that they have been found wanting in some critical area.

Those areas of concern voiced by the focus groups are:

- Finances—if their income is not high, will a white interviewer factor in the historic disparities between white and black incomes, or will the interviewer discount them as adoptive or foster parents because their income falls below the average incomes of white applicants?
- Education—if one or both applicants have only a high school education, will a white interviewer be judgmental and discount them as potential parents? Will that judgment extent to their parents, who may have less than a high school education?
- Discipline—will white interviewers hold it against them if they admit that they were spanked as children and they plan to discipline their own children in the same manner?
- Social interaction—will a white interviewer keep an open mind and understand that African Americans do not always feel comfortable socializing outside their secular communities?
- Religion—will a white interviewer understand that religion often plays a more prominent role in the lives of African American families than it does in many white families?

African American applicants worry that white interviewers will be judgmental, talk down to them, treat them as if we are children, discriminate against them, and discount their cultural values. They fear that they will be interviewed by someone of a different religious faith who will not understand their religious beliefs. They wonder if it would be all right to ask the interviewer if he or she has any black friends. Burdened by a history of hurtful racial discrimination in America, they will reserve judgment on a white interviewer until they see evidence that race is not a factor in the evaluation of their family life.

Regarding finances, the screener should simply ask direct questions that are devoid of qualifying adjectives or insinuations. For example, when you ask, "What is the combined annual income for your family?—and receive an answer—don't follow up with questions such as:

- Does that include any second jobs for either of you?
- Does that qualify you for food stamps?
- Is that enough to pay all your bills?

If you feel the income is inadequate to care for an adoptive or foster child, ask the applicants if they would mind preparing a budget for you so that you can get a better idea of their finances. Don't debate the specifics of their income. Instead, have that debate with your supervisor. Just remember that the dividing line between honest criticism and discrimination is very thin when viewed by individuals who have been subjected to unfair treatment because of their race.

Regarding education, ask direct questions that will provide the information that you need, being careful not to inject value judgments into the conversation. Examples of questions *not* to ask include:

- Have you ever considered going back to school?
- Do you think you have enough education to properly raise a child?
- Would you mind reading to me so that I can judge your reading level?

Regarding discipline, keep in mind that research indicates that African Americans are more likely than other racial groups to use corporal punishment to teach children not to misbehave. A 2010 study by C. S. Mott Children's Hospital, the University of Michigan Department of Pediatrics and Communicable Diseases, and the University of Michigan Child Health Evaluation and Research Unit found that more parents used nonphysical disciple than spanking as a means of controlling behavior in children. However, larger percentages of parents who live in the West (31 percent) and the South (20 percent) were found to prefer spanking over parents who live in the Midwest (13 percent) and Northeast (6 percent).[1] A second study (Child Trends Analysis of the General Social Survey of 2008)[2] found that African American women were the leading proponents of spanking in the United States—and by a significant margin: 80 percent of African American women spank their children, compared with 63 percent of white women.

These findings are important for screeners to understand because they indicate potential areas of conflict between social agencies that are opposed to corporal punishment and African American families who advocate corporal punishment. For agencies in the South, which typically have a shortage of foster homes for African American children, it raises important questions. How do you reject African American applicants because they advocate spanking when you have a critical shortage of African American foster and adoptive homes? The situation becomes even more complex when you consider that most of the African American children who come into care have been raised by birth parents who spanked them for misbehavior.

Social agencies must decide on a case-by-case basis whether it is better to place certain African American children—for example, those who display average or below average levels of aggressiveness—into homes that advocate spanking, or better to keep them in group homes or place them in nonspanking white, Hispanic, or Asian homes.

---

1. National Poll on Children's Health, April 16, 2010. C.S. Mott Children's Hospital. Retrieved from http://www.med.umich.edu/mott/npch/pdf/041510report.pdf

2. Child Trends Data Bank's analysis of General Social Survey of 2008. Accessed on Oct. 4, 2010 at http://www.childtrendsdatabank.org/?q=node/187

According to our focus group, discipline is a sensitive subject. If social workers explain that spanking is not acceptable, they should be prepared for some resistance. One group member who professed a belief in spanking, when asked what she would say if a white social worker asked her if she planned to spank any children placed in her care, answered, "I would say no, but then do what I wanted to do."

When asking questions about discipline, do not ask loaded questions such as:

- You don't believe in spanking, do you?
- Do you feel you would be able to refrain from spanking?
- Why do you think African Americans spank more than whites?

Regarding the topics of religion and social interaction within the community, it is important for white interviewers to understand that for African American families the two topics are interrelated. African Americans, as a group, do not have the extensive social network enjoyed by whites, primarily because of decades of discrimination, which means that they do not participate in civic events to the extent that whites do. Instead, African Americans channel their civic activities into their churches. Studies have consistently shown that African Americans attend religious services more regularly than white Americans (Hart, 2001)

A white interviewer who asks African American interviewees questions about social and civic activities will likely find the applicants deficient if he does not ask similar questions about church involvement. Because of this country's long tradition of separation of church and state, white screeners may feel that they are being invasive if they inquire about an African American's religious activities. If they back away from the issue, they will not make a proper assessment of the family's social and civic interaction within the community. White screeners definitely should ask African American applicants about their religious activities, for therein lies the social framework of the family that the screener is attempting to assess.

Questions to Ask

- Is your church accepting of adoptive and foster children?
- Would you be disappointed if an older adoptive or foster child did not want to attend your church?
- How would you feel if an adoptive or foster child joined social networks outside your church and immediate community?

Questions To Avoid

- What social activities, beside church, do you enjoy?
- Do you ever allow church responsibilities to affect your social responsibilities?

African American Interviewer and White Interviewee

In many respects, African American interviewers have an advantage when interviewing white interviewees, as we have learned from African American writers, since white culture has been celebrated in books and movies to a greater extent than African American culture, thus providing African Americans with access to more information about white culture. Nonetheless, African American screeners may feel uncomfortable delving into the private lives of white applicants for adoptive and foster children. As a result of that discomfort they may come across as being tense and resistant, perhaps even distant, qualities that may be interpreted by white applicants as indicating prejudice against them.

If an African American interviewer is too deferential, white interviewees may interpret that behavior as incompetence. If an African American interviewer is too confident or too aggressive in his approach, white interviewees may wrongly feel that he is cocky and therefore prejudiced against whites. It is a very fine line indeed that African American interviewers must walk when first establishing a relationship with white applicants. That is grossly unfair, of course, but it is the reality of the situation. What is an African American screener to do?

First, it is essential that the screener be himself. Establish solid eye contact, smile frequently, and engage the applicants in conversation unrelated to the reason for the interview. Talk about the weather. Talk about a locally popular sports team. Comment on the applicants' home or neighborhood. If the interview is taking place in the South, it is essential that the screener understand the discomfort that the applicants may feel with such an important role reversal. Reserve judgment. The screener may feel that the applicants' tenseness is because of racism, when just the opposite may be the case—the interviewees may be social liberals who are concerned that the sins of their racist white neighbors may affect their ability to obtain a child.

Questions to Avoid

- Do you have any black friends?
- Do blacks attend your church?
- Could you accept a black child?

Better ways to ask the same questions:

- How would you describe your friends?
- What sets your church apart from others?
- Would you be interested in a child of a different race or ethnic background?

Racism is a difficult subject for many Americans. One problem is that people sometimes have a difficult time agreeing on the definition of a racist. Racism is best measured not by personal testimony, but by past behavior. With that in mind, we offer the following history-based test:

Racism Quiz

You May Be Racist if You Have Never . . .
. . . taken a public stand in favor of equal rights.
. . . written letters-to-the-editor or published articles in support of equal rights.

. . . attended a racially integrated house of worship.
. . . cultivated friendships with individuals of a different race.
. . . eaten with individuals of a different race in a restaurant.
. . . voted for a candidate of a different race.

Dealing with Difficult Subject Matter

When screeners first begin work, they quickly learn that there are many fun questions to ask the applicants, questions that lift the spirit, offer hope, and paint rosy pictures of a new day filled with love, adventure, and optimism. Everyone wants to be loved. There are few things in life more satisfying than physically handing over an infant or older child to loving parents.

Of course, there also is a flip side to this process.

Sometimes screeners have to ask embarrassing, painful, sometimes intrusive, questions that leave everyone, including the screener, feeling uncomfortable. You must ask questions that you would never ask friends or family members. You must be intrusive when the occasion requires it and you must be willing to look into dark corners of the applicant's life.

Sometimes your questions will make interviewees cry.

Sometimes your questions will make interviewees angry.

Always, you must remember why you are doing it: to provide a child with a better life.

Talking about Sex

As a nation we are fond of anonymous, vicarious sex with strangers, as evidenced by the multibillion-dollar popularity of Internet porn, R-rated movies, romance novels, and magazines such as *Playboy*. However, when it comes to face-to-face conversations about sex with strangers, we often are reluctant, whether because of personal shyness, strongly held beliefs about privacy rights, or religious beliefs. As a screener you must overcome any reluctance you have to initiate a dialog about an applicant's sexual history. Of all the variables that determine the long-term viability of a significant-other relationship, none is more important than the individual's feelings about his or her sexual relationship.

One of the most consistent research findings is that there is a positive relationship between sexual satisfaction and overall relationship satisfaction, commitment, and stability in heterosexual, gay, and lesbian relationships. Longitudinal studies of marriage have shown that spouses who are sexually content are more likely to be happy with their marriages and have reduced marital instability. Overall, sexual satisfaction seems to be related more strongly to relationship quality for men than women. Women are more likely than men to feel that a poor sex life is an unfortunate, but separate part of the couple's relationship (Schwartz & Young, 2009).

It is one thing to ask an applicant if they are satisfied with their sexual relationship with their significant other and quite another thing to ask the follow-up questions necessary for a proper evaluation. Among the questions that need to be asked, regardless of whether the applicants say that they are satisfied or not with their sex life, are the following three:

(1) How often do you have sex?
    Individuals aged 18 to 29 average intercourse 84 times a year. Individuals in their forties average intercourse 64 times a year (Smith, 1998).

(2) Who usually initiates sex in your relationship?
    Studies consistently report that men usually initiate sex, but wish that women would initiate sex more often than they do. Who actually initiates sex the most in the relationship is of lesser importance than whether both partners agree that they are happy with the balance they have struck.

(3) How do you rate this sexual relationship compared with previous relationships?
    Because the applicants understand that they are being evaluated, it would be unusual if one of the partners gave a higher rating to a previous relationship. However, it does happen on occasion, and a negative rating of the current relationship would be of great concern to the screener.

A major change in recent years in screening for adoptive and foster applicants is the acceptance by most states of homosexual applicants. Gays are not the largest minority in America, but they are a minority of emerging influence. That complicates sexual history screening because of the discomfort level it creates for social workers who are not gay. Until the mid-1970s, social workers and psychologists were taught that homosexuality was a mental disorder. When the American Psychiatric Association and the American Psychological Association voted to drop that classification, it created confusion among many mental health professionals. In some respects, that confusion continues to the present day.

This affects the screening process because many social workers are not educated on gay sexual practices. It may be helpful for screeners to understand that some gay couples consider hostility toward them to be in the same moral league with racism and sexism. It is important to remember that research suggests that differences in sexual orientation are not directly associated with pathology (Bell & Weinberg, 1978). Gays are no less well-adjusted than heterosexuals (Gonsiorek, 1982).

The question arises, once you have asked a gay couple if they are satisfied with their sexual relationship, where do you go from there? The answer is that you ask the same follow-up questions (see above) that you would ask a heterosexual couple.

Talking About Issues Raised by References

References are an excellent source of information for screeners. However, they can become a very stressful aspect of the screener's job if they provide negative information about the applicants. Negative references are a major cause of follow-up interviews. When that happens the screener's first task is to verify the negative information, if possible. That can be done by collateral interviews with individuals deemed by the screener to be helpful. For example, if a relative refers to something that happened at school, the screener will want to schedule an interview with the proper school official. If the negative reference refers to something illegal that happened in another jurisdiction, the screener will want to contact authorities in that jurisdiction.

Once the groundwork has been laid by collateral interviews, the screener must analyze the information and then schedule follow-up interviews with the applicants. Under no circumstance should the screener announce to the applicants that questions have arisen because of a negative reference. It is the screener's duty to protect the identity of the person who provided the negative reference.

Explanations include:

1. Information has come to our attention that makes it necessary for me to ask you some additional questions.
2. I need to ask you some additional questions because some parts of my notes are incomplete.
3. When I got started on the home study I realized that I had forgotten something.

Typical responses from interviewees include:

(1) Why do you need to ask us more questions? Is anything wrong?
    Your response should be reassuring, regardless of the allegations.

(2) Did my mother say anything to you?
    Your response should be, I can't respond to that.

(3) There is probably something I need to tell you about a previous marriage.
    In this case, your response should be to encourage the interviewee to talk to you.

If your collateral interviews and research confirm the reference's negative information, you should address the issue in a straightforward manner only if the negative information is public record (an arrest, lawsuit, newspaper article, and so forth) or is known to persons other than the reference (teachers, employers, neighbors, and so forth). In the final analysis, it is the information that is important, not the person who provided the information. You have no moral or ethical obligation to provide the specifics of your information to the interviewees, but you do have a moral and ethical obligation to protect the individuals who provided the information to you.

You may feel that this flies in the face of the American legal system's guarantee that the accused has the right to confront his or her accuser, but home studies are not a legal proceeding, and obtaining adoptive or foster children is a privilege and not a right. For that reason, the potential child's safety and well-being and the reference's expectation of confidentiality take precedence over the applicant's right to confront an accuser.

FIGURE 3.1

FOLLOW-UP INTERVIEW CHECKLIST

Identify the areas that need follow-up _____

_____

_____

_____

_____

_____

List your questions in advance of the interview _____

_____

_____

_____

_____

_____

Is race a potential problem for you? If yes, how can you address the problem? _____

_____

_____

_____

_____

_____

Is a frank discussion about the applicants' sex life a problem for you? If yes, how can
you address the problem? _____

_____

_____

_____

_____

_____

_____

_____

CHAPTER FOUR

The Individual Interview

Once you have seen the applicants interact in a joint interview, you will want to conduct individual interviews with each partner. The three reasons for proceeding in this manner are as follows: (1) to allow you to better understand each person as an individual, (2) to enable you to compare their responses to questions that are vital to evaluating their strengths and weaknesses as potential parents, (3) and to help you gauge the emotional and social parameters of their relationship. This process is applicable to heterosexual married couples, homosexual couples, and single applicants of either gender who are in relationship with a "live-in" partner.

The first individual interview (typically the second interview) should be done in the home with the partner who is responsible for most of the homemaking duties. That could be the male or the female partner, but we will use the pronoun she for convenience.

Before leaving for a home interview, the screener should take certain precautions:

- If possible, don't schedule the interview until you have read the results of the police check.
- Research the neighborhood to determine whether it is a high-crime area. If the answer is yes, notify the police precinct that you will be in the neighborhood at a certain time.
- Make certain your agency knows exactly where you are going.
- Do not wear expensive jewelry, shoes, or jackets.
- Make certain that you have enough gas in your car to get there and back.
- Drive by before you stop and park. Make certain that no one is loitering nearby.

Weeks before going into an area for a home interview, the screener should have established a relationship with local law enforcement officials. The best way to do that is to make an appointment with the sheriff or police chief and explain that you will be in and out of their jurisdiction on a regular basis to conduct home interviews with adoptive and foster home applicants. Ask them for their cooperation in providing information when it is needed about applicants and let them know that you will appreciate it if they will keep an eye out for you while you are traveling through the various neighborhoods. If you have to call for help, you want them to already be familiar with your face.

In addition to interviewing the applicant, the screener should tour the home and make general observations about living conditions. Have the applicants prepared a room for the child? If so, make notations regarding its comfort, safety, and location in relationship to the applicants' bedroom. Also, take note of the cleanliness level of the home as well as its potential for harm to the child. For example, are firearms openly displayed in the home? Are there posters or insignias that represented viewpoints espoused by organizations that advocate violence? Are there visible containers inside or outside the house that contain poison or caustic materials? In general, how aware are the applicants of the need to take special precautions to promote child safety?

If you show up for a home visit and encounter rooms filled with pets (or newspapers, car tires, unopened junk mail, ceramic figurines, and so forth), don't ask the obvious question—"why do you have so many animals (or newspapers, car tires, ceramic figurines, and so forth)?"—ask if the individual has always kept so many animals or objects in the home.

Possible answers:

1. "Pretty much since I was a teenager, I guess."
2. "Not long, actually. The neighborhood pound closed and all of us in the neighborhood took pets home to keep until we can find homes for them."
3. "Let me think . . . Probably since my first husband died. He loved dogs and I wouldn't let him have one (laughs). Now I've got eight. Go figure."

Individuals who collect large numbers of pets, shoes, newspapers, unopened junk mail, car tires, and so forth, are compulsive hoarders. It is a type of obsessive-compulsive disorder (OCD), but its exact classification is still under debate (the *DSM-V* diagnostic work group on OCD has recommended that hoarding be included in *DSM-V*). The International OCD Foundation draws a distinction between hoarding and OCD

> Hoarding symptoms are more likely to be 'ego syntonic,' meaning that the person considers hoarding to be normal behavior, whereas OCD symptoms are commonly considered 'ego dystonic' or inconsistent with one's normal behavior and sense of self. Finally, hoarding is often associated with positive and even euphoric experiences, feelings that are almost unknown in response to OCD symptoms (see www.ocfoundation.org. "Diagnosing Hoarding").

Hoarding characteristics include:

1. Onset at around age 12
2. Family members who also hoard
3. Death of a loved one
4. Social isolation

Answers 1 and 3 fit the profile of a hoarder. Although hoarders may not be dangerous to themselves or to others, their inability to control their obsession does not bode well for adoptive or foster children. Such applicants may feel that children will address their loneliness or their imagined imperfections, but that is almost never the case, and there is potential for abuse if the hoarder becomes disappointed in the child for not addressing his or her needs.

Answer 2 is unusual and may be of questionable merit, but it does not indicate an OCD and it should not rule out an applicant for adoptive or foster children. Such applicants could be approved with the understanding that a specified number of the pets would have to be removed from the home, for sanitary reasons, before a child could be placed with them.

After a tour of the home, you will want to sit down with the applicant, perhaps in the living room or den, or at the kitchen table, to conduct the second interview. This time the applicant's comfort level will be noticeably higher than it was in the office; by contrast, your comfort level may not be as high as it was in the familiar surroundings of your office. In addition to discussing the home, you will want to gather information about the applicant's childhood, family life, relationship history, and employment and health history.

The Family History Interview

Sample Questions for Second Interview with Social Worker[1]

If you want to know where a family is headed, take a close look at where it has been. Families seldom change course without a good reason. Information you need to evaluate an applicant's suitability to adopt or foster a child may be embedded in his or her family history. To obtain that information you first must construct a framework built on the basics.

When gathering this information, make your questions as routine as possible, maintain an even tone or voice, and make notes to follow up later on items about which you have serious questions. As far as interview technique is concerned, when you are asking family history questions, it is sometimes helpful *not* to make strong eye contract, so as not to suggest that a particular question has value beyond the obvious. Whether you record the interview on a tape recorder or not, you should take notes, keeping your head lowered in an effort to appear less invasive. Keep in mind that you are examining the interviewee's past, not counseling her about her future; if you are animated or overly friendly in your approach you may subconsciously encourage her to conceal information that she feels might make you less animated or friendly. Without meaning to be manipulative, the applicant will use behavioral reinforcement to influence your behavior.

---

1. Some of the questions in this chapter were previously published in *Adoptive and Foster Parent Screening* by James L. Dickerson and Mardi Allen (2007, pp. 106–108, 131–133, reprinted with permission), but the answers and interpretations are all original to this book.

FIGURE 4.1

THE HOME INSPECTION CHECKLIST

Is the exterior of the house well maintained? ❏ yes ❏ no
If no, please explain: _____

Are the grounds cluttered? ❏ yes ❏ no
If yes, please describe: _____

Do the grounds show potential for danger to children? ❏ yes ❏ no
If yes, please describe: _____

Are dogs running loose on the premises? ❏ yes ❏ no
If yes, please explain: _____

Is the interior of the house well maintained? ❏ yes ❏ no
If no, please explain: _____

Are there enough bedrooms to accommodate the applicants' request for
children? ❏ yes ❏ no

Where is the child's bedroom located in relation to the parents? _____

Are the stove and refrigerator in working order? ❏ yes ❏ no

Are the smoke alarms in working order? ❏ yes ❏ no

Are the carbon monoxide monitors in working order? ❏ yes ❏ no

Is there unfinished construction inside or outside the house? ❏ yes ❏ no
If yes, please describe: _____

Are there any wall decorations suggestive of violence or sexuality? ❏ yes ❏ no
If yes, please describe: _____

Are firearms visible in the house? ❏ yes ❏ no
If yes, please describe: _____

Do the applicants have pets? ❏ yes ❏ no

Do the applicants have any pets that could be dangerous to
children? ❏ yes ❏ no
If yes, please explain: _____

Do all pets have the proper vaccinations? ❏ yes ❏ no

Do the applicants display evidence of hoarding? ❏ yes ❏ no
If yes, please explain: _____

Do the applicants have home owners or renters insurance?
(must be verified) ❏ yes ❏ no

Do the applicants have auto insurance? (must be verified) ❏ yes ❏ no

Question 1:
Could I Please Have the Names and Ages of Your Parents (Note: This Information May Already Be Provided on the Application Form)?

Possible answers:

1. "The applicant will quickly provide names and ages, and let you know if one or more parents are no longer living."
2. "The applicant will let you know if one or more parents are no longer living and provide you with names, but falter before establishing their ages."
3. "The applicant will be unable to recall names or ages."

Answer 1 is the typical answer and it is indicative of neither deceit nor concealment.

Answer 2 is not unusual and may be indicative of faulty memory or a faulty parental relationship.

Answer 3 may be indicative of concealment or faulty memory, the result of a strained parental relationship, or it could signal deceit if the applicant has provided an incorrect age for himself or herself on the application.

Follow-up questions. Difficulty establishing names and ages of parents could be indicative of deceit for one reason or another. One reason could be because the applicant has given an incorrect age for herself on the application and is withholding her parents' ages because she knows it could raise questions. Another reason could be because of a faulty child–parent relationship or abuse.

Possible follow-up questions. (1) Would you mind calling your parents (if living) and obtain the information? (2) (If deceased) What year did your parents pass away?

Question 2:
Could I Please Have the Names, Ages, and Addresses of Your Siblings (Note: This Information May Already Be Requested and Provided on the Application)?

Possible answers:

1. "The applicants will have an address book with them and quickly provide the information without hesitation."
2. "The applicants will not have an address book with them, but they will provide the names, stumble over the ages, and ask if they can phone in the addresses."
3. "The applicant will be unable to provide a complete list of names or ages, and profess not to know where any of his/her siblings live."

Answer 1 is the best possible answer.

Answer 2 may be consistent with faulty memory or faulty sibling relationships and will require follow up questions. See follow-up questions.

Answer 3 is the worst possible answer because it may signal faulty sibling relationships at best and, at worst, concealment of serious family dysfunction such as abuse (see subsequent chapter for more details). See follow-up questions.

Follow-up questions. This is a very important question because the inability to recall or provide sibling information can sometimes be linked to sibling or parental sexual abuse.

Possible follow-up questions:

1. "I will need a complete list of your siblings and their cities of residence. What member of your family will have that information?"
2. "What are their last known cities of residence?"
3. "Where did you attend grammar and high school?"

You can use this formation to contact the school and request information about siblings.

Question 3:
Have Your Parents or Siblings Ever Been Arrested or Convicted of a Crime?

Possible answers:

1. "No—definitely not."
2. "Yes, my brother/sister/parent was arrested for shoplifting/theft/fraud."
3. "Yes, my brother/father was arrested/convicted of sex abuse/DWI/assault."

Answer 1 is what you hope to hear from an applicant.

Answer 2 is not disqualifying, but it may indicate a dysfunctional family, and you should be alert to that possibility as you proceed with the interview.

Answer 3 is the least desirable response. Most likely your agency will undertake a police check on all adoptive and foster parent applicants. If the applicants report parental or sibling arrests, you may want to request records of those arrests from the appropriate law enforcement agency, depending on the nature of the charges. Arrest records are an important part of a foster and adoptive applicant's family history. Allegations involving abuse, either sexual or physical, will be of interest, as well as charges related to drug use or trafficking.

How deeply you probe a history of arrests depends on the nature of the crimes. Obviously, if the applicant's father, mother or siblings were arrested for sexually or physically abusing children, using or selling drugs, public drunkenness, and so forth, it will be of greater concern than if the charges related to property theft or traffic offenses. The reason for that is because crimes of child and substance abuse radiate throughout the family and affect relationships in varied and substantial ways. So called ex-pedophiles, ex-drug users, ex-alcoholics, or ex-drug traffickers always remain a threat because those classes of behavior are subject to such high recidivism. It is the reason that Alcoholics Anonymous insists that members speak of alcoholism in the present tense, as in "I *am* an alcoholic." (Dickerson & Allen, 2007).

American and Canadian jurisprudence maintains that a person is innocent until proved guilty. That is an admirable principle on which to base a legal system, but as a screener whose main responsibility is to protect children you will be just as concerned with charges and allegations as you will with convictions because they may be indicative of destructive patterns of behavior. A person's right to a fair trial does not translate to a right to have a foster or adopted child.

Question 4:
How Would You Describe Your Childhood?
Was It Different in Any Important Ways From Your Friends' Childhoods?

Possible answers:

1. "The applicants may say they had happy childhoods that did not differ significantly from that of their friends."
2. "The applicants may 'split the difference' by saying that they had happy childhoods that were different from their friends' childhoods, or by saying they had a 'so-so' childhood that was no different from that of their friends."
3. "The applicants may admit to an unhappy childhood and express resentment that their friends all had 'everything they needed or wanted.'"

Answer 1 is the preferred answer, but you should be alert to changes in that assessment in answers to future questions.

Answer 2 may indicate issues with some aspects of childhood (for example, the applicant may have enjoyed home life but may have had unhappy school experiences, or vice versa), or it may indicate a tendency toward jealousy if the applicant says that their friends had better childhoods.

Answer 3 is the least desirable answer because it may indicate serious childhood difficulties. See follow-up questions.

Follow-up questions. The admission of an unhappy childhood, along with an expressed resentment of the advantages possessed by friends, is an unintended invitation for additional questions. It is essential that the screener have a full understanding of an applicant's unhappy childhood.

Possible follow-up questions:

1. "What was the nature of your childhood problems?"
2. "Your problems were whose fault?"
3. "How do you think those problems have affected you?"

Question 5:
How Would You Describe Your Partner's Childhood?

Possible answers:

1. "I think it was absolutely perfect. I'm jealous."
2. "It wasn't perfect, but I don't think he/she had had major problems."
3. "Not good at all. It brings me to tears to think about it."

There is no wrong answer here. What you are looking for is consistency. If the partner answering the question, proves to be inconsistent with his or her partner it raises questions about deliberate concealment from the screener or dishonesty between the partners, or the partner may have told you more than they told their spouse. Document the response and compare it to the partner's response. Respondent 3's response should be followed up with additional questions. See follow-up questions.

Follow-up questions. This answer is of interest if it conflicts with statements made by the spouse. Follow-up questions should be directed to the spouse, not the person who provided the information. Deceit is a caution light that has implications far beyond the seriousness of the actual deceit.

Possible follow-up questions:

1. "Your partner's description of your childhood is different from your description. Why do you think that is the case?"
2. "Is there any aspect of your childhood that I failed to question you about?"

Question 6:
How Would You Describe Your Relationship With Your Parents?

Possible answers:

1. "Ideal—it could not possibly have been better."
2. "Do I have to talk about that?"
3. "To be honest, we had problems from time to time, but we always seemed to work them out. The older I get, the more I appreciate my parents."

Answer 1 is too good to be true and will require closer examination. People who idealize their family life sometimes do so to compensate for a disappointing family life.

Answer 2 should immediately generate concern and more thorough questioning. Such statements are consistent with betrayals within the family unit. Unresolved betrayals early in life sometimes simmer during later relationships for long periods before erupting with negative consequences. See follow-up questions.

Answer 3 is the most encouraging response because it suggests that the applicant has a healthy understanding of conflict resolution.

Follow-up questions:

1. "Ideal—it could not possibly have been better."
2. "Do I have to talk about that?"

Neither of these responses can be overlooked. Any family relationships described as ideal is suspect and must be explored. An applicant that does not want to discuss his or her childhood is broadcasting the presence of possible trauma.

Possible follow-up questions:

1. Please give me some examples of why your childhood was ideal.
2. This subject may be difficult for you, but I'd like to know something about the situation you faced. What happened in your childhood that you do not want to discuss?
3. What would you like to change about your childhood (good follow-up question if the interviewee balks at providing details to question 2)?

Question 7:
In What Ways Are Your Mother and Father Different?

Possible answers:

1. "They are complete opposites. He goes one direction, she goes the other."
2. "They aren't different. That's just it. They're like two peas in a pod. They are very happy, but I don't think that I could live like that."
3. "They like the same things, mostly. They both like to read and travel. Growing up, I sometimes thought I was in the way."

There is no wrong answer to this question. It is important if it helps you understand the applicant's relationship with his or her significant other. Has that relationship mirrored any one of the family relationships defined in the answers above? Or is the relationship the opposite of the one described by the applicant?

For example, if the applicant gives answer 1 and approves of that type of relationship, is the applicant's relationship like or unlike that type of relationship? If the applicant's relationship is unlike that of the parents, is the applicant disappointed and constantly attempting to redefine his or her relationship?

If the applicant gives answer 2, does he or she have a current relationship that is similar? If so, is he or she having a difficult time "living like that?"

If the applicant gives answer 3, does the applicant have a similar relationship with his or her significant other? If so, that may speak well of the current relationship.

Question 8:
Who Is Dominant in Your Family, Your Father or Your Mother?

Possible answers:

1. "Father, without a doubt. He balances the checkbook and makes all the major decisions."

2. "Mother, without a doubt. She balances the checkbook and makes all the major decisions."
3. "Neither is dominant, I would say. They share responsibility equally."

Answer 3 is the one that is most consistent with modern American relationship models

> In a large number of families, power over decision making seems to be either exercised jointly or divided according to the individual competencies of the members, and husband and wife influence one another in a variety of direct and indirect ways, with no person being consistently 'in charge.' (Maccoby & Jacklin, 1974, p. 262).

However, research on the power-sharing characteristics of foster families depicts relationships that are under female dominance, especially on issues related to child rearing (Wolins, 1963, p. 50).

In view of research on female-dominated relationships, as applied to foster parenting, and relationships in which decision making is shared, answer 1 should be viewed as the least desirable of the three above-listed responses.

The challenge for the screener in analyzing responses to the above question is to determine the relationship between the applicant's characterization of his or her parents' relationship and the applicant's relationship. For example, if a female applicant responded to the question with answer 3 (shared power) and describes her significant-other relationship as one that is male dominated, it will be necessary for the screener to determine with more precision the applicant's happiness level in her relationship. If she grew up with a shared-power model, but now finds herself living in a male-dominated role, she may harbor deep-seated resentment, an emotion not conducive to effective child rearing. See follow-up questions.

Follow-up questions. The importance of these questions is as a measurement of current happiness. If the female applicant grew up in a family in which the man made all the decisions, she may or may not be comfortable with that power structure in her current relationship. If her mother made all the decisions when she was growing up, and her husband now makes those decisions, she may feel that she is being held back in the relationship, and she may harbor resentment toward her partner.

Possible follow-up questions:

1. "Do you feel that you have a voice in the major decisions made in your marriage?"
2. "What would you change about decision-making in your marriage?"
3. "(If the woman is dominant) Do you feel that your partner ever resents your leadership in the family?"

Question 9:
Were You Ever Emotionally, Sexually, or Physically Abused as a Child?

Possible answers:

1. "No. Nothing like that ever happened to me."
2. "I don't think so. If it did, I don't remember it."
3. "Yes."

Answer 1 is the preferred response, but as the interviews progress the screener should remain alert to the possibility of concealment. Denial is not unusual among adults who have been abused as children. Sometimes they will deny abuse, even in the face of overwhelming evidence that abuse occurred.

Answer 2 is a cause for concern because it leaves open the possibility of abuse. The applicant may have been abused but repressed the actual memory of it while retaining a lingering suspicion that something might have occurred.

Answer 3 is the response that experienced screeners dread to hear because it opens the door to an assortment of concerns, ranging from the applicant's capacity to parent without inflicting abuse on children placed in his or her care, to the applicant's ability to sustain a workable marital relationship with a significant other. See follow-up questions.

Follow-up questions. An admission of abuse, or a claim by the applicant that she does not remember whether she experienced childhood abuse, are both invitations for follow-up questions.

Possible follow-up questions:

1. "If you don't remember childhood abuse, why do you think you did not answer no to the question? Do you have a suspicion that you might have been abused?"
2. "Please tell me about your abuse. Was it done by a family member or a stranger or a family friend?"
3. "How has the abuse affected you as an adult? Have you ever talked to a mental health professional about the abuse?"

Question 10:
Which of Your Parents Was the Most Loving?

Possible answers:

1. "My mother, definitely."
2. "My father."
3. "Neither. They were both too absorbed in each other."

Love is almost never dispensed in equal measure in a family. It is difficult to grow up in a two-parent family without feeling that one parent is more attentive than the other. The significance of this question is in the belief that applicants who have had bad relationships with opposite-sex parents tend to struggle in their relationships with the opposite sex, whether with adults or children, whereas applicants who have had good relationships with opposite-sex parents tend to excel in their relationships with the opposite sex, whether adults or children.

Psychiatrist William Appleton conducted research that indicated that father–daughter relationships may have a continuing impact on the development of adult women. He concluded that the father's attentiveness and support during childhood are crucial for the adult daughter's ability to develop positive relationships with men. More than 60 percent of the women he interviewed who had a positive relationship with their father reported satisfying marriages or relationships with men later in life (Appleton, 1981; Biller, 1993).

Similarly, psychologist Carol Franz conducted research that prompted her to conclude that there is a linkage between paternal warmth, both male and female, and midlife success for both men and women (Franz, McClelland, & Weinberger, 1991).

Let's examine each response. Answer 1: If the respondent is male, that is a positive indicator for the adoption or fostering of either a male or a female child, whereas if the respondent is female, it suggests that she probably will be a better parent to a female child than to a male child.

Answer 2: If the respondent is female, it is a positive indicator for the adoption or fostering of either a male or a female child, whereas if the respondent is male, it suggests that he probably will be a better parent to a male child than to a female child.

Answer 3: At first glance the significance of this response is that the respondent grew up unloved by both parents—and that, indeed, may be the case. With no role models, parenthood may be a challenge. However, the upside is that the applicant may be able to compensate for that upbringing by providing equal opportunity love to a child of either gender.

Question 11:
Did Your Parents Ever Have Arguments about Your Behavior? If so, Describe the Behavior That Provoked the Arguments.

Possible answers:

1. "My folks said I was cruel to animals, but I didn't do anything bad. I was just conducting experiments that I read about in books."
2. "Nothing serious. Sometimes they had arguments when I asked questions while they were watching television, but that was about as bad as it got. Mother said I was just expressing myself. Dad said I never asked questions unless something important was being said on television."
3. "My parents always argued over whether I set fire to the house on purpose. All I was doing was roasting marshmallows. Accidents happen."

These are questions that tell us more about the applicant than the applicant's parents. As an interviewer, you are fishing for examples of antisocial behavior by the applicant during childhood. If an applicant set fires as a child, was cruel to animals, or instigated conversations while the parents were absorbed with television that is an area of concern, but not so much so that you would use it as a reason to reject their application. Instead, you would view it as a cautionary signal that gives you a "heads-up" to the potential for additional antisocial behavior as an adult. In the event you approved the applicant for a child and the child subsequently suffered mysterious burns, bruises, other injuries, the answer to the above question could prove to be helpful in solving the mystery of the burns or bruises. If the screener has any questions in his mind about the applicant's childhood antisocial behaviors, he or she should consider referring the applicant to a psychologist for further evaluation.

Question 12:
Did You Ever Feel You Had to "Walk on Eggshells" around Your Parents or Siblings?

Possible answers:

1. "Yes, that is exactly how I felt."
2. "No. They were both pretty relaxed about things."
3. "Sometimes. My mother was like that. You had to be careful not to set her off."

Answer 2 is the preferred response, but if the applicant responds with either answer 1 or 3 you will want to question him or her in more detail to elicit information that may suggest symptoms of borderline personality disorder (BPD). BPDs are rare in males, so the emphasis here will be on mothers.

BPD is a serious mental illness characterized by instability in moods, behavior, self-image, and interpersonal relationships. Women with BPD often need extensive mental health services and account for 20 percent of psychiatric hospitalizations (Zanarini & Frankenburg, n.d.).

Children who grow up in a household with a parent with BPD seldom have their emotional or physical needs met by the parent and often must fend for themselves, effectively becoming the parent.

An adoptive or foster parent applicant who has been diagnosed with BPD is not a good candidate for approval. Children of BPD should not be rejected by virtue of their parents' illness, but the screener should be sensitive to the symptoms of the illness—short-term bouts of anger, depression, or anxiety; sudden shifts of mood; suicide threats and attempts—in the event they appear in an applicant's behavior history. Also of interest when interviewing children of BPD patients is how well they adjusted to their parent's behavior—did they withdraw from the conflict or meet it head-on? Applicants who display symptoms of BPD should be referred to a psychologist for further evaluation.

Borderline Personality

Many individuals with BPD are dually diagnosed with depression, substance abuse, and eating disorders. Therapists often record BPD as a secondary diagnosis, influenced by the fact that some insurance companies refuse to pay for treatment of BPD because they consider it incurable no matter what treatment is offered. Also, the diagnosis itself carries a stigma and a reputation for a poor prognosis; it actually frightens many therapists away from trying to treat such patients.

The term "borderline personality" is often misleading and confusing for patients and their family. Coined during the mid-20th century, the term refers to individuals who exhibited behaviors on the edge of both neurosis and psychosis and thus were considered "borderline."

The diagnosis of BPD is difficult to make because of its complexity. Often a spouse or other loved ones are relieved when a diagnosis is made because it actually explains the patient's extremely erratic, irrational, and harmful behaviors. Frequently, the patients, themselves are not so receptive, and pushing the matter may only exacerbate their self-destructive nature. Victims of BPD can drag other victims (children, spouse, and friends) down that path of chaos with them. Intervention can be helpful for family, even if the identified patient denies a problem.

The characteristics of BPD are numerous and no one individual exhibits them all. However, the hallmark of BPD seems to be rooted in the frantic effort to avoid abandonment, either real or imagined. This ever-present impinging panic drives many of the thoughts, feelings, and behaviors of people with BPD. As patients deal with conflicting emotions, their fear of abandonment can be disguised as rage and anger. Relationships are usually difficult, vacillating between extreme idealizations to devaluation, resulting in a pattern of unstable and intense experiences. Their sense of self does not reach stability by their 20s like most of us. They continue to report feelings of emptiness, which propels an endless search for approval and nurturing by others. They can't seem to fill the black hole of despair they feel inside.

Individuals with BPD have self-damaging impulse control problems such as reckless sex, spending, eating, driving, and substance use that lead to even more personal emptiness. About 10 percent of all people with BPD eventually commit suicide, with a very large percentage of them engaging in multiple attempts, threats and suicidal gesturing. Self-mutilation can be an indicator of BPD.

This affective instability, with tremendous mood swings, can create havoc in families. Children of individuals with BPD suffer as their parent can't differentiate the importance of the child's needs over their own. They tend to be stuck at an early developmental stage, with a preoccupation concerning their emotional feelings, while ridiculing the child for being selfish by expressing feelings.

Often individuals with BPD have suffered multiple childhood traumas and/or have been raised by a parent with BPD who was not able to provide the validation and structure children need. Treatments have been gaining success within the last decade. Medications alone are not considered adequate, but are often part of the treatment. Key in the patient's progress is recognizing the disorder and wanting to minimize its effects.

Question 13:
What Are the Highlights of Your Childhood?

Possible answers:

1. "The time Mom and Dad took us on a trip out West."
2. "When I was chosen Miss/Mr. High School. It's been downhill ever since."
3. "The time I escaped after this guy broke into the house and tied me up."

There is no wrong answer to this question. You will ask it to get a sense of the applicant's life view. Is the applicant self-centered or family oriented? Are the "best" things that happened to them positive or negative? As answers go, 1 is preferable because it indicates a sense of family unity. Answer 2 is indicative of a self-centered person who is probably frequently at odds with the family's agenda.

Answer 3 is in a category all unto itself that requires further questioning. Why was the house broken into? Why was she tied up? Was the intruder someone she knew or a total stranger? Did this sort of thing happen frequently to her as she was growing up?

Question 14:
Did You Undergo Any Traumatic Events as a Child?

Possible answers:

1. "No."
2. "Just my Mom and Dad's divorce."
3. "Some things I'm not comfortable talking about."

Answer 1: "No" is the preferred answer here, but when you ask this question you never know what answer you will receive. It is fairly common and understandable for children to label their parents' divorce as traumatic (answer 2), but to be prudent follow up with questions about why the divorce was traumatic. See follow-up questions.

Answer 3 is a cause of great concern because it signals abuse. Explain to the applicant that you are required to ask follow-up questions and apologize for any discomfort that your questions might cause.

Follow-up questions. Some childhood traumas are more of interest than others when it comes to understanding human behavior. On the one hand, breaking an arm or leg and missing school for an extended time would be traumatic, but it is unlikely to have lifelong effects. On the other hand, experiencing a heart or kidney transplant at a young age could generate fears that last a lifetime.

Divorce is almost always traumatic for children. The variables are the ways in which it affected the family. If both parents work together during the divorce and afterward, its effects can be minimized. If the parents are combative and engage in continued hostilities after the divorce, the trauma for a child could be severe.

Any time an interviewee says that their childhood is something they are not comfortable discussing, it raises the possibility of abuse, whether sexual or physical. Screeners should always proceed cautiously when they hear the "comfort" phrase.

Possible questions:

1. "What was traumatic about your parents' divorce?"
2. "How do you think the divorce affected you later in life?" The screener should follow this line of questioning until he can transition into asking the interviewee about the length of time his prior romantic relationships lasted. Generally speaking, a child of divorce who has a difficult time sustaining significant-other relationships will have a difficult time sustaining a relationship with an adoptive or foster child. The screener should ask, "What is the longest relationship you had prior to getting married?"
3. "Why are you uncomfortable talking about your childhood?" If the interviewee avoids the question, ask him directly if he was ever abused as a child. If he answers yes, ask if he ever underwent counseling because of the abuse. If he answers yes, ask if he feels that it was helpful. Whatever his answer, you should ask for permission to talk to his therapist. For you to be able to approve him for an adoptive or foster child, you will need to see no lingering effects of the abuse in his behavior, and you will need an assessment of his mental health by a therapist.

Question 15:
Did Either of Your Parents Have Previous Marriages?
If So, Please Tell Me about Them and Explain Why and How the Marriages Ended.

Possible answers:

1. "No. It seems like they have been married forever."
2. "Yes. Both my parents had previous marriages. My Mom's first husband was killed in a car accident and my Dad was divorced from his first wife."
3. "I'm not sure about my Mom's first marriage. She never talked much about it."

Answer 1 is the preferred response, but with the American divorce rate exceeding 50 percent you are statistically more likely to receive a yes response to this question than you are to receive a no response. This is of importance only if the divorce had a lingering effect on the applicant. For example, if the applicant feels abandoned by a parent or feels hostility toward one or both parents, those feelings could have a negative effect on children placed with the applicant because they might be asked to "take sides" in marital disputes.

Answer 3 is a response that screams out for amplification. Why has the applicant never asked for an explanation from the mother? Why does the applicant *think* that her mother does not want to discuss her first marriage?

Question 16:
Have Your Parents Ever Had a Marital Separation?

Possible answers:

1. "Yes. They separated for a while when I was 10."
2. "No. I would have been crushed if something like that had happened."
3. "Not while I was growing up. They separated and then divorced after I went off to college. I was an only child. I felt like my world had been shattered."

Answer 1 could end up being positive or negative, depending on the applicant's reaction to the separation.

Answer 2 is preferable, but it opens the door on the applicant's admittedly fragile feelings about divorce and separation.

Answer 3 suggests a couple that stayed together for the benefit of their child. You would want to probe the applicant to determine if he or she feels they had a happy childhood or whether there was an awareness of the tension between the parents. The purpose of this question is to determine if the applicant experienced strong negative emotions about marriage.

Question 17:
How Were You Disciplined As a Child?

Possible answers:

1. "My daddy wore me out with a belt."
2. "Mother was in charge of that. She usually sent me to my room"
3. "Mother and Father both disciplined me. Mother handled the little things. Dad took care of the big things."

With this question you are seeking two types of information—how the applicant was disciplined and by whom. Answer 1 is of interest if the applicant intends to discipline a child the way he or she was disciplined, discipline that would run counter to the recommendations of most states and the National Association of Social Workers; it also is of interest if the applicant believes that discipline is the responsibility of one gender over the other.

Answers 2 and 3 are both acceptable, although 3 is preferred.

Question 18:
Were Your Parents Fair When Disciplining You?

Possible answers:

1. "No one wants to be disciplined, but, yes, I think they were fair."
2. "No way. I was blamed for everything."
3. "I think they thought they were fair. But the rules kept changing and I never knew what to expect."

Fairness is a major issue in discipline. An applicant who feels that he was unfairly disciplined may avoid a middle-of-the-road approach when disciplining his children and either be too lenient in an attempt to repudiate their past, or too strict, convinced that a strong hand is needed to establish "fairness." Answer 1 is indicative of a mature attitude. Answers 2 and 3 reflect the turmoil of growing up in a family in which discipline was neither predictable nor equitable.

Question 19:
Tell Me about Your Relationships with Your Siblings?

Possible answers:

1. "There's not much to tell. We were never close."
2. "We were like that television family, the *Waltons*. It was cozy."
3. "We love each other, but we don't especially like each other."
4. "We don't have a bad relationship, but they live a thousand miles away and we don't see each other often and that has created a strain in our relationship."

Answer 2 is the one you always want to hear, but you won't hear it nearly as often as you would like. Good relationships among siblings are calibrated by degrees, meaning there is a wide variance. Generally speaking, the stronger the relationship between siblings, the stronger the socialization skills exhibited by the siblings. Researchers have found that siblings learn all-important informal behaviors—school etiquette, street smarts, how to maintain friendships, overall socialization skills, and so forth—from sibling relationships (Kramer & Conger, 2009).

Good foster and adoptive applicants often report good sibling relationships.

Answers 1, 3, and 4 are not reason enough to disqualify an applicant, but they do raise concerns about possible abuse and unresolved issues that could surface in a parent–child relationship with adoptive or foster children. Answer 1 is acceptable if the siblings are 20 years apart in age.

Marital or Relationship Interviews

Sample Questions for Marital or Significant Other Interview

The first thing that a screener should be aware of when interviewing couples, whether heterosexual or gay, is that individuals who are experiencing relationship difficulties sometimes apply for adoptive or foster children in the belief that a child will bring them closer together. Sometimes couples who are experiencing sexual problems in their relationship will apply for children in the hope that the addition of a child will serve as a substitute for sex.

Neither scenario is acceptable. Children cannot "save" marriages, nor can they serve as a substitute for sex in a relationship that has shifted from sexual to platonic. Placement of children into homes in which either of these scenarios is present is tantamount to child neglect. For that reason, the most important questions that a screener will ask during the interview process are those that help define the current status of the relationship.

The areas of greatest concern are:

1. Conflict resolution (how they resolve disputes with each other)
2. Emotional compatibility (whether their personalities are a workable match)
3. Ethical/spiritual compatibility (do they share a common vision?)
4. Sexual compatibility (is the sexual relationship mutually satisfying?)

Question 20:
What Quality of Yours Do You Think Your Partner Most Appreciates?

Possible answers:

1. "My sense of humor."
2. "Good question. I've never been able to figure that out."
3. "My money. I had lots. He didn't have any."

The preferred answer is one that indicates the applicant has a grasp of what makes the relationship work. Answer 1 is an example of that. Other preferred answers would be, "Because we're interested in the same things" or "We have the same values" or "We seem to think alike on a lot of issues." Answer 2 could be an attempt at humor or it could reflect disappointment in the relationship. Answer 3 may be an accurate and realistic answer; if so, it probably does not bode well for the long-term prospects of the relationship.

Question 21:
What Do You Find Most Attractive About Your Partner?

Possible answers:

1. "The fact that he loves me."
2. "His smile."
3. "The way he always puts me first."

What you are looking for here is an indication of whether she sees the relationship in terms of herself or her partner. In other words, does she value the relationship based on the love that is given or the love that is received? Is she me-directed in the way she defines the relationship? Answers 1 and 3 are indicative of a person who values the relationship in terms of love received. Answer 2 may be accurate insofar as it goes, but it may be indicative of an applicant who is hesitant to reveal too much about her relationship.

Actually, this question is one in a category of important questions that have a bearing on the success of adoptive and foster placements. One of the most difficult experiences that adoptive and foster parents can have in a placement is when the child is unable to give as much love as he or she receives from the applicants. If an applicant is interested in adoptive or foster care because he or she is not receiving the love and affection that they expect in their significant-other relationship, they are likely to be disappointed if they do not receive love and affection from the child they have chosen as a substitute.

Question 22:
Who Are Your Partner's Best Friends?

Possible answers:

1. "I have no idea. He goes out with the boys from time to time, but he never invites them over to the house."
2. "He's got two good friends. He goes fishing with one, a man he works with— and he goes to ball games with the other, a man he's known since high school."
3. "He does things with the people he works with but they never invite me. Two of his friends are women. There is nothing wrong with that, I know, but I can't help but wonder about it sometimes, especially when they go out of town to conferences."

Answer 2 is the preferred answer—straightforward, understanding, and without a hint of suspicion. Answer 1 is troubling for several reasons. First, because the partner never invites his friends to his home where they can interact with his wife: Is it because he is jealous of his wife and is afraid for his male friends to meet her, or is it because he knows that his wife will not approve of his friends?

Answer 3 is a relationship train wreck waiting to happen. It is troubling that the respondent is not involved with her partner's relationships. The fact that two of his friends are women who he keeps isolated from his partner is bad judgment at best and suggestive of infidelity, at least in the respondent's eyes. See follow-up questions.

Follow-up questions. In strong marriages it is not uncommon for the partners to name each other as their best friend, although men are more likely than women to call their spouse their best friend. Like unmarried best friends, married best friends spend time together doing mutually pleasing activities. Research indicates that the correlation between fun and marital happiness is high, and significant (Markman & Stanley, 1996; see also, Jayson, 2008)). Couples who list individuals outside the marriage as their best friends run counter to that correlation and provide screeners with cause for concern. Not everyone who has a best friend outside the marriage is headed for divorce court, but it is not a practice that contributes to the strength of a marriage. Strong marriages can tolerate one partner having a best friend outside the marriage, but that may prove to be a problem for weak marriages.

Possible questions:

1. "How does it make you feel when your partner leaves home (or town) to do things with his friends and does not invite you?"
2. "Why do you not involve your spouse in your activities with your friends?"
3. "Do you ever socialize with your spouse's opposite-sex friends?"
4. "Have you ever accused your spouse of cheating on you with his opposite-sex friends?"

Question 23:
What Are Your Partner's Life Dreams?

Possible answers:

1. "I don't know because he never talks to me about things like that."
2. "Two things. He wants to own a business of his own, and he wants to have children."
3. "Oh, he's not much of a dreamer. He's a meat and potatoes guy."

Answer 2 is the type of answer you hope to hear. It is specific, optimistic, and provides you with a heads-up when you interview the husband. Answers 1 and 3 suggest relationships in which communication is at a minimum, with answer 1 more indicative of relationship problems than answer 3, which does not indicate whether the respondent is upset with her partner, in agreement with him, or simply resigned to his attitude. More questions are needed to determine which.

Follow-up questions. If one partner does not know the other partner's life dreams it may be indicative of a relationship with poor communication. In the case of the individual who does not talk to his spouse, it is important for the screener to probe the spouse's feelings about her partner-imposed isolation within the relationship. Has she resigned herself to her situation or does she hope he someday will change. In the case of the meat and potatoes guy, the screener should question how such an attitude affects the spouse.

Possible follow-up questions:

1. "When your spouse doesn't share his feelings with you, how does that make you feel?"
2. "Are there feelings that you don't share with your spouse?"
3. "(Regarding the "meat and potatoes" spouse) Does it concern you that your spouse has no dreams about the future?"
4. "How does your spouse react when you discuss your dreams with him?"

Question 24:
Does Your Partner Listen to You When You Talk?

Possible answers (from female applicant):

1. "I think so. At least he looks like he is listening. Doesn't say much though."
2. "He listens much more than some men."
3. "Never. He's always watching television."

An adoptive or foster parent who listens to his partner in all likelihood will listen to the children placed in his care. Answer 2 is the most acceptable of the three given, but you would want to probe more deeply into the couple's communication skills, beginning with additional questions that will provide you with more information regarding the respondent's expectations about communication within a relationship. The respondent who gave answer 1 may be engaged in wishful thinking that her partner may be listening to her. Answer 3 is the least acceptable of the three.

Possible answers (from male applicant):

1. "She talks more than she listens."
2. "Never. She's always in the kitchen or in the garden."

Possible follow-up questions:

1. (For the interviewee whose spouse talks more than she listens) "Do you feel that your spouse values your opinions? Do you ever feel angry that she won't allow you to express your opinions? Do you ever tell her that she talks too much? Have you ever left the room or the house because she won't listen to your opinions?"
2. (For the interviewee whose spouse who avoids situations in which she would have to talk to her spouse) "Do you like it when your spouse works in the kitchen or garden? Would you like for her to spend more time talking to you? Do you feel that she takes your advice when you offer it? Does she ever ask for your advice?"

Question 25:
Who Is Your Best Friend?

Possible answers:

1. "My husband, of course."
2. "This girl I work with. She's the best friend I've ever had."
3. "I don't really have any close friends. That's why I want to adopt/foster a child."

In a stable and loving relationship, you would expect each partner to say that the other partner is their best friend, so answer 1 is the most promising of the three given. Both answers 2 and 3 indicate a less-than-perfect relationship, with 3 giving cause for concern about the respondent's overall socialization skills. As needed as companionship may be for the respondent, adoptive and foster children can never be a substitute for a lack of adult friends. Respondent 3 should be considered a risky applicant. On those occasions when an applicant chooses someone other than their partner as best friend, you will want to inquire about the qualities that the friend has that the partner does not have. The answer will provide a revealing glimpse into the relationship. In other words, what qualities does a five-year-old foster child have, in the eyes of the respondent, that the husband lacks?

Follow-up questions. Of course, the answer you hoped to hear was "my spouse." As we have seen, research indicates that it is more troublesome if the husband names someone other than his spouse than if the wife names someone else as her best friend. Women typically have a more extensive social network than men. Follow-up questions should focus on the nature of any opposite-sex friendships outside the marriage, especially if they exclude the spouse.

The comment made by the interviewee that she wants to adopt or foster a child because of a lack of close friends is a cause for concern. Such a statement would be reason enough to deny an adoption application, because it may be indicative of a dysfunctional marriage and/or poor social skills.

Possible follow-up questions:

1. (If the male spouse says that his best friend is a woman that he works with) "What do you receive from the friendship that you do not receive from your wife?"
2. "What do you have in common with your friend?"
3. "Has your wife ever complained about the friendship? If yes, why have you pursued the friendship?"
4. (Regarding the interviewee who envisions children as a substitute for her lack of friends) "Did you have friends before marriage? If the answer is no, the screener should ask if she had friends as a child."
5. "Why do you feel that your spouse is not your best friend?"

Question 26:
When You Have Disagreements With Your Partner, How Do You Solve Them?

Possible answers:

1. "I go to the bedroom and cry and he leaves the house."
2. "We talk it out until it gets resolved."
3. "We yell at each other until we get tired. Then we both stomp around the house for a week or two until we more or less forget what we were arguing about."

If you want to know how a couple will deal with the problems associated with raising a child, look at how they resolve problems in their relationship, because the two will be the same. Answer 2 is the preferred answer because it allows for a healthy resolution of the problem. Parents who get angry with a child and leave the room without resolving the problem (answer 1) will have a difficult time being an effective parent to a child. Likewise, parents who yell at their children and allow the problem to fester while they angrily "stomp" about the house may, in time, forget why they are angry at a child, but the child will not forget.

Question 27:
What Is the Worst Argument You Ever Had
With Your Partner and How Was It Resolved?

Possible answers:

1. "We had a really bad fight one day over the checkbook. It showed we had $100 in the account and I wrote a check for $49 and the check bounced and the bank called my husband and he nearly had a stroke. We talked it over and figured out that my husband had written a check he had not notated in the checkbook. We considered various options and resolved the conflict by agreeing that I would write all the checks in the future."
2. "I think the worst fight we ever had was over this woman my husband works with. She calls him all the time and gives him expensive gifts. I asked him to tell her to stop calling and sending him gifts, but he said he didn't want to hurt her feelings. I packed my bags and went home to mother. I wasn't there two days before he showed up, hat in hand, and begged me to come back. He said that he had told the woman to go to hell."
3. "We have the same fight every year. I like to go home to visit my family every Christmas, but my husband doesn't want to go because he wants to see his family and we always end up having a terrible time. After three years of that we decided to visit my family every other Christmas and visit his family in the years between. He's much happier now, but I'm miserable in the off years."

When you interview applicants about their marital relationship, keep in mind that there are two areas that will concern you—how they resolve disputes and what they argue about. There are no unresolved disputes in a relationship (they may go underground for a time, but they are always there, ready to reappear during the next round of disagreements), so it is important for partners to know how to resolve conflict with words, instead of resorting to flight, sullen silence, or violence. Answer 3 is a good example of unresolved conflict. It took this couple three years to learn that they could resolve the problem with discussion and compromise, but better late than never. Hopefully, they learned a lesson that they will be able to apply to their next conflict. Answer 1 presents the kind of conflict resolution that you want to see in a couple. They identified the problem, considered solutions, and resolved the difficulty by concentrating responsibility for the checkbook with one person.

Answer 2 addresses two of the most persistent and troubling causes of conflict in a relationship—jealousy and the refusal of one partner to accept that appearances are important to stifle jealousy. This couple resolved nothing; they merely postponed resolution until another day. Jealousy in a relationship can be dealt with as long as the other partner does not insist that "It's what I do that counts, not what it looks like I've done." If one partner tends to be jealous, appearances are *everything*. Conversely, if one partner insists on doing as he or she pleases, regardless of the appearance of those actions to the partner, then the partner's jealousy will merely escalate until the relationship becomes unsustainable. This is a couple that could benefit from couples counseling prior to proceeding with their application to adopt or foster children.

Question 28:
Has Your Partner Ever Struck You During an Argument?

Possible answers (from female applicant):

1. "Define struck. He's slapped me a couple of times, but he's never hit me with his fist like so many men do. Is that what you mean?"
2. "That would never happen. We don't have that kind of relationship."
3. "Well, yes . . . but I deserved it."

If an applicant ever asks you to define "struck" or domestic violence in general, explain that it means, slaps, punches, chokes, kicks, pushes, or hair pulls. Answer 1 is indicative of relationships in which stress is handled with physicality. A slap is as bad as punch. A spouse who reacts to marital stress with violence, however slight, is likely to respond to stress with a child in the same manner. Answer 3 is consistent with domestic violence victims who undergo violence time and time again because they have been convinced by their partner that they deserve it. In such relationships violence tends to escalate until the relationship is terminated. It is important to remember that a partner who hits his or her partner is also capable of hitting a child if provoked. Answer 2 is the response you want to hear from an applicant. Domestic violence is incompatible with adoption or foster care.

Possible answers (from male applicant):

1. "Define struck. I slapped her a few times, but I never hit her with a doubled up fist. Is that what you mean? Did she say I hit her?"
2. "Well, yes . . . but she damned sure deserved it."

Possible follow-up questions:

1. (For the interviewee who slapped his wife "a few times") How often do you slap your wife? How does she react when you do? Has she ever filed a report with the police? If yes, when and what were the results? If no, why do you think she did not report you? Should you have been reported? How do you feel when you slap your wife?

2. (For the interviewee whose spouse "deserves" to be struck) Why do you say that she deserved it? Has she ever struck you? What are the things that a wife should be disciplined for? What would you do if your wife reported you to the authorities? Have you ever had an argument with your wife regarding your application to adopt/foster a child?

Question 29:
At What Age Did You Become Sexually Active?

Possible answers:

1. "14."
2. "17."
3. "24."

The median age at first intercourse for boys is 16.9 years and for girls it is 17.4 years (Alan Guttmacher Institute, 2002; data is based on unpublished tabulations), so if respondents report becoming sexually active between the ages of 17 and 19, they are within the "normal" range. Someone who reports the first sexual encounter at an early age (14) or an advanced age (24) may have a good explanation, but such deviations from the norm may suggest the possibility of sexual abuse from a stranger (rape) or family member (incest). The respondents who gave answers 1 and 3 should be questioned further about the person with whom they had sex and, in the case of the latter, why they waited so long to engage in sexual activity (there are many possibilities here: incest, physical abuse from a parent, gender confusion, religious commitment, and so forth).

Sex is an uncomfortable subject to bring up with an applicant, but it is essential that you do so because it is difficult to understand the relationship without understanding the sexual dynamics of the relationship. It is helpful to remember that you cannot place an adoptive or foster child in a home in which there is sexual dysfunction—in this context, defined as one in which one partner wants a sexual relationship and the other partner does not. If neither partner wants a sexual relationship, that does not necessarily disqualify them as adoptive or foster parents, depending upon the overall level of communication in the relationship.

Question 30:
How Often Do You and Your Partner Have Sex?

Possible answers (from female applicant):

1. "Every couple of months."
2. "Three or four times a month."
3. "Two or three times a week."

Your first task is to establish the couple's frequency of intercourse. One respected study found that 13 percent of married couples reported having sex a few times per year; 45 percent reported a few times per month; 34 percent reported 2 or 3 times per week; and 7 percent reported 4 or more times per week (Laumann, Gagnon, Michael, & Michaels, 1994; see also Michael, Gagnon, Laumann, & Kotate, 1994). Answers 2 and 3 are reflective of those that would be given by 79 percent of the couples in the United States.

Answer 1 falls in the 13 percent range and is a reason for concern. If a couple's frequency of sex is below average or extinct it will be necessary to further explore the reasons. It is possible for a couple with little or no sexual contact to properly raise a child, but only if both partners report no distress over such a relationship.

Possible answers (from male applicant):

1. "Every couple of months."
2. "Three or four times a month."
3. "Two or three times a week."

Possible follow-up questions:

1. (Every couple of months). Are you satisfied with the frequency of intercourse with your spouse? If yes, is the spouse satisfied? Has your spouse ever complained about your sex life? Have you ever been to counseling to discuss this issue?
2. (Three or four times a month) Who usually initiates sex, you or your spouse? Does your spouse seem satisfied with your frequency of intercourse? If not, what is your response?
3. (Two or three times a week) How would you rate your sex life? How would your spouse rate your sex life? Who enjoys sex more—you or your spouse? Do you think that your frequency level is right for you?

Question 31:
Does Your Partner Bear Any Grudges Because of Previous Sexual Relationships You Had?

Possible answers:

1. "Absolutely not."
2. "He brings it up all the time."
3. "Not really, but I sometimes feel guilty about it."

This question has less to do with sex than it does with communication within the relationship. Answer 1 is the one you hope to hear because it indicates an absence of obsessive jealousy and a capacity for forgiveness and relationship forgetfulness. No one likes to think about their partner having intimate encounters with other persons, but a functioning relationship requires persons to forgive and forget.

Answer 2 is suggestive of a dysfunctional relationship.

Answer 3 invites more in-depth questioning of the guilty partner's capacity to forgive herself for prior mistakes. An individual who cannot forgive herself is more likely to be subservient to her partner in a marital dispute and thereby build up resentment that is likely to erupt at a later date, thus creating a situation that the couple would be unable to resolve without professional help.

Question 32:
(For Males) Have You Ever Dressed as a Woman?

Possible answers:

1. "No. That has never entered my mind."
2. "Do you mean, like, for a college skit?"
3. "Well . . . (long pause) not really."

Answers 1 and 2 are what you would hope to hear.

Answer 3 is of concern because of the pause used by the applicant to adjust his thinking and because of his use of the phrase "not really." The applicant is obviously trying to decide how much to tell the screener. Your job is to pursue an interrogative line of questioning.

Follow-up questions:

"You sound like you are not certain. Have you ever dressed as a woman for a joke?"
"Maybe a few times."
"By 'a few' do you mean two or three?"
"Oh, I don't know . . . maybe more than that."
"What were the occasions?"
"It started out in high school when I dressed as Annie Oakley for a school play."
"You must have enjoyed it."
"I wouldn't say that."
"But you kept doing it?"
"It's exciting to be someone else."
"Have you ever been aroused while you were dressed as a woman?"
"Yes—is there anything wrong with that? I'm all man. Isn't it natural for a man to get excited in a situation like that? Men like women, right? They like everything associated with women, right?"

The applicant might be a transvestite, a type of fetish. Although some people will argue that it is a lifestyle, it is a diagnosable fetish. The *DSM-IV-TR* states that "Transvestic fetishism occurs in heterosexual (or bisexual) men for whom the cross-dressing behavior is for the purpose of sexual excitement." The *DSM-IV-TR* goes on to explain that transvestic fetishism "involves cross-dressing by a male in women's attire. In many or most cases, sexual arousal is produced by the accompanying thought or image of the person as a female (referred to as "autogynephilia") . . . Transvestic phenomena range from occasional solitary wearing of female clothes to extensive involvement in a transvestic subculture."

Why do we care if a male adoptive or foster parent dresses as a female?

Two researchers, N. Langstrom and K. J. Zucker, inform us that "transvestic fetishism may be associated with increased risks for sexual acting out that could injure the individual and victimize others" (Langstrom & Zucker, 2005, p. 88), and they cite Abel, Becker, Cummingham-Rathner, and Rouleau (1988) in their study of 561 male subjects that "up to 20 percent of individuals with transvestic fetishism also had been involved in the sexual molestation of children, and 36 percent had committed exhibitionistic acts." (p. 88).

Fetishism

Often when people think of someone having a fetish, they envision someone with a harmless affinity for pretty shoes or stylish clothing, but fetishism can be a significant mental health issue. Fetishism is one of several paraphilias including pedophilia, voyeurism, sexual masochism, and sadism that involve the use of a physical object for sexual arousal. Individuals often are unable to find sexual pleasure without the object (the fetish) being integrated into their sexual activity. Often this disorder starts at pre-puberty and continues throughout life. Typical behaviors include rubbing, smelling, or holding items such as other's underwear, high-heeled shoes, leather clothing, soft material, and rubber objects. These behaviors can be integrated into sexual activities with a partner, or they may completely replace sex with another person.

Transvestic fetishism involves men who are sexually gratified by wearing women's clothing. Typically they are not men who want to become a female. Although unusual, this behavior is not considered a mental disorder unless it creates undue stress that interferes with activities of daily living or compels the individual to take high risks or illegal actions to continue. Men engaged in tranvestic fetishism often feel overwhelming anxiety if they don't engage in the behavior, although some are equally overwhelmed by feeling of guilt and shame. Mental health services are more frequently associated with accompanying depression, anxiety, or alcohol abuse than the actual cross-dressing behaviors.

Contributing factors in the development of fetishism behaviors are thought to be associated with brain chemistry, reinforcement, imprinting, traumatic experience, or emotional attachment to transitional objects. Although the actual fetishism itself may not adversely interfere with family functioning, associated issues that contributed to the development of the behavior may prove to be quite destructive to family unity.

Question 33:
Does Your Partner Find It Difficult to Forgive You When You Make Mistakes— And Do You Find It Difficult to Forgive Yourself When You Make Mistakes?

Possible answers:

1. I don't think I've made a lot of mistakes that require forgiveness, but when I do make mistakes, my spouse is always understanding about it. If my spouse forgives me, I have no problem forgiving myself.

2. (sigh) I must admit that I am mistake prone. My spouse is a difficult person to please. He expects perfection—and I am not perfect. He seems more willing to forgive me than I am willing to forgive myself.

3. Sometimes I am afraid to say anything because my husband gets upset so easily. When I make mistakes he has a difficult time forgiving me because he says I should not have made the mistake in the first place. I don't have problems forgiving myself because I'm only human.

Answer 1 is the response you hope to hear. Both partners understand that mistakes are unavoidable. Both have the capacity to forgive, which bodes well for an adoptive or foster child placed in their home.

Answer 2 is suggestive of an obsessive partner who envisions the relationship as one that is built on certain rules that must be followed to prevent the relationship from collapsing. Unfortunately, the respondent has bought into that argument and has a difficult time forgiving herself for the mistakes that are inevitable in any relationship. Adoptive or foster children placed in this family are likely to become the source of frequent arguments.

Answer 3 is suggestive of partners who have opposing concepts of how a relationship should function. The husband has an obsessive view of the importance of "mistakes" in the maintenance of a relationship. The wife has a realistic view of the importance of mistakes. Children placed into this home would frequently find themselves caught in the middle.

Question 34:
Does Your Spouse Get Upset if You Don't Keep Him Advised of Where You Are at All Times—And Do You Ever Have Arguments About You Spending Time With People Your Spouse Does Not Approve of?

Possible answers:

1. He doesn't get upset because he knows that if I am going to be unusually late I will call to let him know. We don't have arguments about my friends because he seems to like them. There'd be something wrong if he didn't, right?

2. We do have arguments about my friends sometimes. I have a girlfriend that he thinks is a slut. He says that if I hang out with her, I will end up being a slut. I don't know. Maybe he has a point. Maybe I should be more careful.

3. I don't have to keep my husband advised because he calls me a hundred times a day. He doesn't like any of my friends, male or female. If I met a male friend for lunch, he calls every 10 minutes and asks how much longer I will be. He is very, very jealous. I guess that means he loves me a lot.

Answer 1 is the type of answer you want to hear from applicants. The interviewee seems considerate of the spouse's feelings, and the spouse is accepting of her right to have the friends of her choice. They would likely have the same attitudes with children placed in their home.

Answer 2 is suggestive of one obsessive partner and one partner who has self-esteem issues. Whether the friend is a person of low moral standards is not the issue (she, in fact, may be such a person). At issue is the husband's acceptance of the influence that "outside" people can have on his marriage. Any marriage that can be upended by the friends of one spouse is not a marriage that is built on mutual trust and respect. What the husband is really telling his wife—and indirectly telling the screener—is that he does not trust her with the relationship.

Answer 3 offers a good example of an obsessive husband and an enabler wife. She feeds his obsessions by accommodating them and feeling guilty over her so-called shortcomings. This relationship does not have a long-term future and therefore would be a poor risk for the placement of children.

Obsessive Love

Obsessive love is an insidious infliction on a relationship. Unfortunately symptoms are not always apparent early on. During the infatuation phase of a relationship, both parties often constantly think of one another. They talk to their friends about their new love, find all possible similarities with one another, and spend lots of time together, often to the neglect of their responsibilities. Their feelings are initially intense; both are very thoughtful of one another and seem to go out of the way to please.

Denise and Tom's love blossomed quickly, and they spent every available moment together. They couldn't get enough of each other. Tom enjoyed buying small gifts for Denise. After several months, his gift-giving intensified with more expensive, very personal gifts. He became increasingly involved in her schedule, wanting to know details of her day. He appeared hurt if she couldn't have lunch with him every day.

Tom defined his obsessive nature as overwhelming love for Denise. She often defended his probing inquiries and constant phone calls as caring concern for her. He claimed to worry if he didn't hear from her frequently or if she wasn't where she had told him she'd be. When Tom's behavior was confronted, he became very defensive and retorted that she must be hiding things from him, otherwise she'd be more open.

Denise tried to decrease her contact with him in an effort to establish reasonable limits, but all attempts failed. He responded intermittently with anger, mock understanding, contempt, and total frustration. Denise loved Tom, but over time his efforts to control her pushed her away.

Denise finally ended the relationship after Tom followed her to a meeting and created a scene in front of business acquaintances. Breaking away from Tom was not an easy task. For weeks, he sent flowers, gifts, e-mails, called Denise five or six times a day, and tried to see her. He sent her a message through a mutual friend that he was very sorry about his behavior and was seeking therapy. Tom wanted Denise to know that he was learning to control his jealousy and that his behavior had been precipitated by his overwhelming fear of losing her.

One day he explained that he needed to get in her house to get a razor that he had left. Denise agreed to leave the key out for him, thinking that under the circumstances, he would be on his best behavior. Much to her surprise, Tom took all the gifts he had ever given her, went through photographs, and collected phone numbers from an old cell phone. Soon afterward, he called several of her male friends and confronted them about their relationship with her.

One week later, Tom called Denise to apologize for his behavior and to offer the gifts back. Denise calmly but emphatically informed him to not call or contact her again. Denise continued to describe Tom as a very loving individual, but she clearly felt that he had sabotaged their chances and had led the relationship to destruction.

Had Denise not taken a firm stand with Tom, his obnoxious behavior would likely have escalated. It is at this point in a failing obsessive relationship that it is crucial for the injured party to resist the temptation to become an unwitting enabler, for to do so is usually an open invitation to escalate the obsessive behavior to stalking, physical abuse, or, in some incidences, homicide. It is often called obsessive love, but it is not a loving affliction.

Question 35:
Does Your Partner Know What Pleases You Sexually?

Possible answers (from female applicant):

1. "No—but he gets two out of three right, and that isn't bad, is it?"
2. "He doesn't have a clue. Never has."
3. "I have no complaints."

You don't approve or reject an applicant based on their response to this question, but you do use the answer to this question to evaluate satisfaction and communication within the relationship. Answer 3 is indicative of a healthy relationship, but answers 1 and 2 demonstrate a need for follow-up questions. If the relationship is sexually deficient why would the respondent not let the partner know what she needs to be fully satisfied—and why would the partner not want to fully satisfy his partner? This may be more of a communication issue than one that deals with sexual technique.

Possible answers (from male applicant):

1. "No, but I think that is probably my fault for not letting her know. I said something once and she cried, so I never brought the subject up again."
2. "Knowing and doing are two separate things."

Possible follow-up questions:

1. (This is probably my fault) Why did your spouse cry when you brought up the subject? Has she ever expressed dislike or disgust at your suggestions in bed? Why would you not tell her what you want? Has she ever made suggestions to you?

2. (Knowing and doing) Why would your spouse know what you want but not want to do it? Do you ever have arguments about sex? Do you know if she did things with other men before she met you that she refuses to do with you? If yes, can you accept the possibility that she may have done something once that she finds distasteful and therefore would not want to repeat?

Case History

Helen and Phillip T. were in their late twenties, an athletic and attractive couple who radiated high energy levels. Both worked as professionals and both had good incomes. When they came into the office for their first joint interview, they told the screener that they had been married for four years and despite their best efforts Helen had been unable to get pregnant. Their family physician ran tests and determined that there was no physical reason why Helen could not have children. (Reprinted with permission from Dickerson & Allen, 2007, pp. 127–128.)

Helen and Philip showed a great deal of enthusiasm about adoption. Helen said that she had wanted to have children for as long as she could remember. She was disappointed that she had been unable to conceive, but she felt that adoption was "the answer to a prayer." Helen was somewhat flirtatious during the interview, but it seemed to be consistent with her effusive personality. The screener concluded that she was probably the type of woman that flirts with everyone, men and women.

Helen and Philip related well to each other during the interview, and each was respectful of the other's opinions. They looked at each other often and exchanged smiles whenever the subject of children was brought up. By the time the screener went to the home for his individual interview with Helen he was optimistic about their chances for approval. That feeling continued through his discussions with her about her family life, leading him to believe that she had enjoyed a remarkably normal upbringing.

However, once the discussion turned to her relationship with Philip, the situation became more complex. She expressed great satisfaction with the relationship—"In many respects, I think we are soul mates"—but when their sex life was brought up she confided that she had been unhappy with the frequency of intercourse over the past two years. "He's just so tired when he comes home," she explained. "He works so hard. I just wish he would make more time for me."

Asked why they had no children of their own, she said they had been tested by doctors who told them that neither of them was infertile. They could find no reason why she could not become pregnant. "The doctor told me that a lot of times women like me get pregnant after they apply for adoption," she said. "Have you ever heard of that happening?"

"Yes," answered the screener. "Not often—but often enough to keep doctors talking about it."

By the time the screener left the house, he had grown very pessimistic about their potential as adoptive parents. The individual interview with Philip was conducted one week later at the agency office. The screener was eager to get to the critical points of the interview, but he knew from experience that it was better to pace the questions, beginning with the most routine and slowly building to the most critical. When Philip was asked about his relationship with Helen, he expressed agreement with her that the relationship was mutually satisfying . . . "Except for one thing," he added. "The sex."

"What do you mean?" asked the screener.

"No matter how much I make love to her, it is never enough," he said. "I just stay exhausted all the time. To me, sex is a great pleasure, but to her it's all tied in with her obsession with having a baby. Is that normal?"

The screener mumbled that normal probably didn't exist.

Philip thought about that for a moment and then dropped a bombshell. "You seem like a nice guy," he said. "Would you be interested in helping me out?"

Taken aback, the screener asked, "What do you mean?"

"You know, with the sex."

"Let me get this straight," said the screener, doodling on a notepad. "You are asking if I will have sex with your wife?"

"That's about it, yeah."

The screener told Philip that he was flattered to be asked, but would have to turn down his offer. As Philip left the office he turned and said, "I guess this conversation pretty much kills any chance we have of adopting, doesn't it?"

"Pretty much."

Helen and Philip were officially rejected as adoptive applicants two weeks later, but they did not contact the screener to ask why. The screener was never certain if Philip's "offer" was legitimate or merely an attempt to sabotage their application. Either way, the result was the same.

Philip's "offer" created a dilemma for the screener. He discussed the case with his supervisor, who agreed that the agency already had enough information and did not need to schedule additional interviews to reject the application, but he agonized over whether to write the incident up in the home study.

If he did, it would become part of the couple's permanent record and open the door to possible privacy abuses that, while within the law, hardly seemed fair. If he did not write it up, he risked exposing himself to legal action if the couple later changed their story out of vindictiveness and accused the screener of being the one who made the "offer."

Although he did not feel good about doing it, the screener decided to protect himself and write the incident up as it happened. It was yet another reason why he was glad he taped all his interviews and another reason why he was glad his agency had a policy against allowing anyone other than agency staffers to read home studies.

FIGURE 4.2

DISCUSSION QUESTIONS

What was the first sign of trouble in this interview? _____

_____

_____

_____

_____

_____

When Helen first brought up dissatisfaction about their sex life, should the screener have followed up with more in-depth questions? _____

_____

_____

_____

_____

_____

Bob raised the question of normalcy when he discussed their sex life. Which partner do you believe had a more realistic view of their sex life? _____

_____

_____

_____

_____

_____

If you were faced with this dilemma as a screener, would you write up the controversial aspects of the interview in the home study if you knew that there was a possibility the applicants would read your comments? _____

_____

_____

_____

_____

_____

Question 36:
Have You and Your Partner Ever Had a Marital Separation?

Possible answers:

1. "No."
2. "Yes, but we were able to work things out."
3. "Several. But we are still trying. Do we get points for that?"

With this question the separation is of less importance than the reason for the separation. Answer 1 is encouraging, but it does not eliminate the possibility that the couple has unresolved marital difficulties. Follow-up questions are needed.

Answer 2 will require follow-up questions to determine if the problems were resolved.

Answer 3 is of concern and will require follow-up questions. You can approve applicants who have had marital problems that were addressed and corrected, as long as you feel confident about their current relationship, but you cannot approve applicants who have unresolved marital problems.

Question 37:
Have You Ever Filed Charges against Your Partner for Assault or Have You Ever Had Reason to File Charges but Didn't?

Possible answers:

1. "No."
2. "Yes."
3. "I've never filed charges, but there was a time or two when I probably should have."

A "no" answer is what you would expect to hear. However, a "no" answer is not a ticket for a free ride; you must remain alert to the possibility of spousal abuse. A "yes" answer will require follow-up questions and perhaps a referral to a psychologist. Not many applicants who admit spousal abuse will be approved for adoptive or foster children. You will be surprised at the number of people who answer this question honestly. Sometimes a "yes" answer is actually a plea for help. It is not unheard of for individuals to apply for adoptive or foster children in the hope of obtaining help with serious marital problems or personality disorders.

Question 38:
Who Makes Most of the Decisions in Your Relationship, You or Your Partner?

Possible answers:

1. "I do."
2. "He does."
3. "We share It's probably 50-50."

The purpose of this question is to establish dominance in the relationship. Answer 3 is laudable and what you would like to hear, but you must keep in mind that very few relationships are based on 50-50 sharing because one partner is almost always more dominant, even if only slightly. If the applicant gives answer 1 or 2, you will want to look to the partner for verification. Establishing dominance is important because it helps identify motivation for adoption or foster care and illuminates decision making in the relationship.

Question 39:
Do You Ever Feel You Have to "Walk on Eggshells" around Your Partner?

Possible answers:

1. "Yes—I've never thought about it those terms, but that's the way I feel sometime."
2. "No, but my husband says that about me."
3. "No, I've never thought that at all."

The "walk on eggshells" reference is often made about people who can be diagnosed with BPD. In answer 1 the respondent clearly feels that her partner falls into that category. However, males are rarely diagnosed with BPD. If this is the response you receive about a male partner, you would want to pursue with additional questions. It could be that the person in question has a volatile personality, in which case the respondent almost certainly will have a variety of behaviors to describe.

Answer 2 clearly indicates a need for more in-depth questioning as to examples of behaviors that could be characterized in that manner. If you suspect a borderline personality, you should ask the applicants if they would be willing to undergo testing and evaluation by a psychologist to resolve questions you have about their relationship.

Answer 3 enables you to move on to other questions.

Question 40:
Do You and Your Partner Ever Have Disagreements about the Role of Religion in Your Relationship?

Possible answers:

1. "No, we never have fights about religion."
2. "Yes. He is a Protestant and I am a Catholic. He thinks we should both be of the same faith, but I don't think that is necessary."
3. "No, but my husband's family thinks that the entire family should be of the same faith and we sometimes have arguments with them about that."

The purpose of this question is to evaluate the applicants' ability to parent a child of a different religion. Answer 1 is the preferred response and indicates applicants that will be easy to work with on the subject of religion. Answers 2 and 3 suggest problem areas for the placement of a child of a different faith. It is not advisable to place a child into a home in which there will be a constant tug-of-war over religion.

Question 41:
Do You Ever See Yourself in Your Partner?

Possible answers:

1. "Funny you should ask that. We talk about that all the time. We don't look alike, but our friends all tell us that we are clones of each other in the way we think and behave."
2. "Oh, no. We are total opposites of each other."
3. "In many ways I do. Other ways I don't."

A relatively new relationship theory, advanced by five psychology professors— Sandra Murray, Gina Bellavia, John Holmes, Dan Dolderman and Dale Griffin— contends that couples in stable and durable relationships see themselves as mirror images of the other person. Conclude the authors: "People in satisfying and stable relationships assimilated their partners to themselves, perceiving similarities that were not evident in reality. Such egocentrism predicted greater feelings of being understood, and feeling understood mediated the link between egocentrism and satisfaction in marriage." Their research focused on the benefits of egocentrism in close relationships (Murray, Holmes, Griffin, Bellavia, & Dolderman, 2002). Respondent 1 clearly describes a "mirror image" relationship in which each partner shares the values, personality traits, and expectations felt and expressed by their significant other. The "mirror-image" concept of relationships is based on the belief that individuals tend to fall in love with themselves and when they look at their partners they see what they want to see. The reality may be that "mirror-image" couples are not clones of each other but see each other as clones, thus providing a basis for their mutual attraction. Just as beauty is in the eye of the beholder, so are loving, stable relationships. Mirror-image couples will tolerate negative behavior from their partner if they envision the behavior as potentially existing within themselves.

Respondent 3 indicates some evidence of a mirror-image relationship, but respondent 2 clearly does not. There has not been enough research on this theory to accept it as a definitive measurement of an applicant's relationship, but it is as good a marker as any to factor in assessments of the long-term survival of the relationship.

The Education Interview

Sample Questions to Determine Educational Attitudes

Minimum education standards for adoption or foster care run counter to this country's democratic tradition and therefore have not found acceptance among public or private agencies. There is another reason why those with graduate degrees have not received preferred consideration: There is no research that proves that a person's ability to be a loving and caring parent is in any way related to educational background. If that is the case, what is the point in making enquiries about educational background?

The main purpose is to gain insight into the applicants' attitudes about education. You do not want to place a child in the home of applicants who are antieducation because that would diminish opportunities for any child entrusted to them. For that reason, you want to know their attitudes toward education and more specifically toward teachers. Where do they rank education as a priority in a family's life? If they are adopting, do they intend to make financial plans for the child to pursue a college education—or are they opposed to higher education? What are their long-range educational plans? If they had an unhappy school experience, do they think that having a child will enable them to do a "makeover" on that experience?

Question 42:
How Would You Describe Your First Years in School? Did You Have Any Bad Experiences? Were You Able to Make Friends With the Other Students?

Possible answers:

1. "My experience with school was pretty much a nightmare. Everyone picked on me because of my red hair and it was really hard to make friends."
2. "My school days provided me with the best experiences of my life. It has been downhill ever since."
3. "I have really fond memories of grammar school, middle school, and high school. My teachers were very encouraging and I made friends that I have to this day."

Respondent 3 is a best-case scenario. Because she had good experiences at school she is likely to encourage her children to have good experiences. Respondent 2 had good experiences in school, so she is likely to be encouraging to any child placed with her, but you have to wonder what happened later in life to put her on the skids. Respondent 1 is convincing when she says that her school experience was nightmarish. The question is how does she feel about education now? Does she feel it is a waste of time? Does she feel that it sets people up for pain and failure later in life?

Question 43:
Tell Me About the Best Teacher You Ever Had. What Made Him or Her Special?

Possible answers:

1. "She had a way of teaching that didn't make me feel stupid."
2. "Miss Biddle was the best teacher ever. She let us do anything in class that we wanted to do."
3. "I still marvel at the things I learned from Mrs. Roberts, my eighth grade teacher. She was strict, but she taught us what we needed to enter high school."

This question and the following question are meant to provide information about an applicant's philosophy regarding education; but more importantly the questions provide a window into an applicant's capacity to accept supervision from the agency. Respondent 3's answer indicates that she did not feel stifled by authority and had a healthy appreciation of the academic process. Moreover, she does not appear to possess a me-directed personality. She is not likely to present problems during the supervisory period for adoption or foster care.

Respondent 1 obviously had issues as a child with her perception of her own capabilities, and she may be inclined to blame the teacher if her child ever comes home and says she feels "stupid." Likewise, she may blame the child care worker when she encounters problems with the child. Respondent 2 appears to have issues with authority and little understanding of the academic process. If she receives a foster child, she may have problems with a child care worker who asks her to use agency guidelines when parenting the child.

Question 44:
Tell Me About the Worst Teacher You Had. What Made Him or Her a Bad Teacher?

Possible answers (from female applicant):

1. "Oh, God—that would be Mr. Owens. He was such a prick. He never gave anyone credit for answering a question correctly."
2. "I had a teacher once who made everyone who made below a certain grade take the test over again. I never understood that."
3. "I had my own way of studying, but Miss Stone always insisted I do everything her way. She was not the boss of me and I made sure she understood that."

With this question you are looking for attitudes toward authority figures, particularly as those attitudes may relate to agency supervision, and attitudes toward the role of teachers in the classroom. Respondent 1 will probably side with her child in any dispute with a teacher and she is likely to become frustrated with a child care worker who does not ask her opinion on parenting issues. Respondent 2 may not believe in "do-overs" and may be resistant to a child care worker's suggestions that she rethink her approach to certain problems related to child rearing. Respondent 3 may prove to be difficult during the supervisory period, and if the child is of school age there may be a series of problems with teachers, which will necessitate the child care worker serving as a mediator between the two.

Possible answers (from male applicant):

1. "That would be Miss Barber. She had sex with one of the boys in the class and let him get away with murder. I asked her out once and she sent me to the principal's office."

2. "Mr. Jones never called on me when I knew the answer and raised my hand, but he always called on me when I didn't raise my hand. For some reason he just didn't like me."

3. "Mr. Stone was such a prick. Every assignment had to be done his way. He was not the boss of me and I made sure he understood that."

Possible questions:

1. (Miss Barber) If the teacher had a sexual relationship with a student, it is not entirely surprising that the interviewee asked her out on a date. His teacher's transgression and his subsequent punishment may have affected his perception of authority. That is the area in which the screener should focus. Were you ever sent to the principal's office for any other behaviors? Did your teacher's actions affect your relationships with other teachers? Do you think that most people in authority break rules on a consistent basis?

2. (Mr. Jones) Besides his history of calling on you when you did not know the answers, why do you think he did not like you? Did you ever treat him with disrespect? Were you ever disruptive in his class? Did you resent his authority? Was he not worthy of your respect?

3. (Mr. Stone) Why was Mr. Stone a prick? What did he ever do to you? Have you ever had similar problems with employers?

Question 45:
How Would You Describe Your High School Experiences?

Possible answers:

1. "In one word—nightmare! Nothing ever worked out for me in high school. I was never invited to anything. No one wanted me for a friend."

2. "I have found post high school life not much different than high school. Same rules. Same in-group. To the victor go the spoils."

3. "It was the high point of my life. I excelled at everything. As they say, I was a big fish in a small pond."

With this question, you want to identify social skills and isolation issues. Respondent 1 may be deficient in social skills and may want to adopt or foster to compensate for that deficiency. See follow-up questions.

Respondent 2 seems to have a realistic view of high school success, but her view of post-high school may be colored by negative life experiences. See follow-up questions.

Respondent 3 has not carried negative memories of school into adulthood, and that is a good thing; but you will want to know where she feels she now stands among her adult peers. See follow-up questions.

We all know people who excelled in high school, but later failed as adults (and vice versa). The point of asking applicants to describe their high school experiences is not to measure success or failure, but to have a reference point with which to evaluate an adult's social development. If an adoptive or foster applicant had no friends in high school, have they in the intervening years been able to develop adult friendships? If high school was the high point of their life, what is there about their adult life that does not measure up?

It is important for screeners to continue to remind themselves that adoptive or foster children can never be a substitute for social or emotional deficiencies in an adult's life.

Possible follow-up questions:

1. When you look back to the days when you had no friends in high school, are you able to understand why that was the case? Are you able to take responsibility for the way you communicated your opinions, dreams, and personality to your classmates?
2. You say that you see no difference in the social conventions prevalent in high school and those that define adult life. Do you feel any bitterness that adult life is not all that much different, at least in your opinion, from what you experienced in high school? How do you think that an adoptive or foster child will compensate for your feelings of being excluded from adult "in-groups?
3. You say that high school was the "high point" of your life. What is there about your life today that you find disappointing? What were you able to do in high school that you cannot do as an adult?

Question 46:
Did You Participate in Any Extracurricular Activities in High School?

Possible answers:

1. "Yes. I played in the band and I was editor of the school newspaper."
2. "No. I wasn't much of a joiner. I just put in my time and went home."
3. "I played basketball, but I think I enjoyed being in the Poet's Society more."

According to research, there is a correlation between participating in extracurricular school activities and success later in life. However, the findings suggest that greater educational attainment and income are associated more with sports and academic-related activities than with activities associated with fine arts activities. The reverse is the case if the individual is African American or Hispanic; for these individuals, activities associated with fine arts correlate more with success later in life (Lleras, 2008).

This has a bearing on applicants for adoptive or foster children in that it provides the screener with additional information with which to make recommendations for placement in an adoptive or foster home. The screener should take into account whether the child is heavily invested in extracurricular activities and whether the prospective parents are supportive of such interests, as indicated by their own past experiences. An applicant who gave an answer similar to answer 2 would not likely be the best choice for such a child. Likewise, an applicant who was heavily invested in extracurricular activities as a student would not be a good match for an older child that has no interests in that area.

Question 47:
How Many Books Do You Have in Your Home?

Possible answers:

1. "Do you count magazines? No—well, we've got a Bible and that's about it."
2. "Good question. Probably 500 or so."
3. "A couple dozen, I guess."

A recent study led by Richard Allington of the University of Tennessee, found that students who took books home with them had significantly higher reading scores than other students. Just taking 12 books home for the summer proved to be the equivalent of attending summer school insofar as increased reading skills are concerned. Researchers also found that low-income students lose about three months of ground each summer to their middle-class peers (Brooks, 2010).

Conversely, Jacob Vigdor and Helen Ladd of Duke University's Sanford School of Public Policy looked at computer use among 500,000 students, grades five through eight, and found that the spread of home computers and high-speed Internet access was associated with significant declines in math and reading scores (Toppo, 2010).

It should not come as a surprise to learn that books increase reading ability and the Internet decreases reading ability. The scope of Internet knowledge is vast, but the information is largely undocumented and unverified. The Internet is representative of mass opinion, a snapshot, if you will, of average intelligence. Books, on the other hand, are representative of society's greatest thinkers and teachers, and their writing undergoes a rigorous editing process. Such studies point to the need for social agencies to provide books to adoptive and foster children in addition to Internet access.

Answer 1 is obviously the least acceptable, while answers 2 and 3 offer promise. A screener would not want to place a child with great academic potential in the first home. Accordingly, a child of low academic potential might not be a good fit for the second and third homes. Counting the books in a home can provide you with more useful information about an applicant than any number of glowing testimonials from references.

Question 48:
Were You Ever Bullied by Other Students?

Possible answers:

1. "Yes. Especially in grammar school."
2. "No. I never had any problems along that line."
3. "If anything, I was the bully. I would never tolerate being bullied by anyone."

Some victims of bullying become isolated, experience low self-esteem, and become very pessimistic about their prospects in life (Garbarino, Espelage, & deLara, 2003; Nansel et al., 2001). Others internalize their hostility to the bully who torments them and resort to violence (firing a gun at school, starting fires, becoming a bully themselves) (Olweus, 1993). As for children who bully other children, a Finnish study has reported that boys who frequently bullied others at the age of 8 years were more likely to suffer from antisocial personality disorders (Sourander et al., 2007). As a screener your first task is to separate the bullies from victims, although in many cases victims respond to their victimization by becoming bullies themselves.

Any applicant who admits to being a school bully should be considered for evaluation by a psychologist for antisocial attitudes or behavior before proceeding with an application for adoption or foster care. Any applicant who admits to being bullied (respondent 1) should be questioned in more detail. See follow-up questions. Answer 2 is reflective of the answers you hope to hear from applicants.

Bullying

Whether you are the victim or the perpetrator, the effects of bullying are long lasting and often devastating. Although it happens to all age groups, bullying is actually more common in elementary school than in junior and senior high. Data suggest that about 20 percent of American children have been victims of bullying in elementary school, while another 20 percent admittedly has engaged in some form of bullying behavior. The likelihood of a victim of bullying occurs most frequently in second grade, by older children. As times goes on, bullying tends to be more of a male issue, and junior high bullies tend to pick on boys their same age.

When girls are bullies, they are more likely to use verbal attacks, whereas boys are often physical and verbally abusive. Professionals describe bullying as a specific type of aggressive behavior that is deliberate, with the purpose of gaining control over another person. Usually bullies attack without reason, other than the victim seems like an easy target.

Victims

Bullying is child abuse, perpetrated by a peer. It is often inflicted on those considered younger, weaker, or sicker by their peers. Most extreme victims report having few or no friends and being alone at recess and lunch early in their academic careers. Some do well in school and are able to make friends as they mature. If the proper support is offered, they are able to survive without significant long-term consequences of their trauma. Many victims can't ignore the physical and mental abuse and may start believing the perpetrator's opinion that they are weak, no good, worthless, pathetic, and incompetent. A growing body of research shows that later in life victims report high levels of anxiety, shame, depression, and relationship problems as adults, similar to survivors of other types of abuse. These thoughts, if they are combined with revenge fantasies, can lead to anger and rage feelings.

Bullies

Family environments that produce bullies are described as having little warmth or affection, characterized by parents who don't express positive feelings to one another and who are emotionally distant. Parents of bullies tend to use inconsistent discipline, often being very punitive, with physical punishment being very common. Some bullies seem to endorse the twisted values of evil film heroes who beat up and kill others and despise the weak and sick. Making friends may be difficult, but they do gain a certain level of popularity and peer status for their actions. It's been found that bullies are more popular with their peers than those who simply behave aggressively toward others. They often do not do well in school and have no connections with their teachers.

Bullying can be viewed as a first step to more serious problems such as delinquency and criminal activity. Bullies are also more likely to use drugs and alcohol as adolescents. Various studies indicate that between 20 to 40 percent of bullies grow into adult bullies, and of those, over half continue to be bullies at age 32. There is a strong relationship between bullying and later criminal convictions.

Follow-up questions:

Anyone who admits to either being bullied or bullying others is offering an invitation for further questioning. Research indicates that bullying victims tend to be more sensitive than their peers, physically smaller, socially isolated, nonassertive, and submissive to others (Beaty & Alexeyev, 2008).

Bullies tend to be louder and more assertive than their peers, although not necessarily larger. One study concluded that bullies may be the most popular and self-confident students in the school (Nudo, 2004). Outcomes often are devastating. Victims of bullying score lower on tests that measure social acceptance, scholastic competence, and self-worth (Mouttapa, 2001). Depression has been linked to bullies (Mouttapa, 2001).

Possible follow-up questions:

1. (Victims of bullying) Why do you think you attracted the attention of bullies? Did you have many friends in school? Do you have many friends now? Did you consider yourself to be a sensitive student? Do you now consider yourself to be a sensitive person? Did you make good grades in school? Do you now feel successful within your career? Did you have good self-esteem in school? Do you now have problems with self-esteem? The purpose of these questions is to determine emotional growth since the years of bullying in school. The screener should be more concerned with the responses pertaining to the present than to those pertaining to the past.

2. (Bullies) Were you popular as a student? Do you feel that you are popular today? Did you ever feel remorse when you bullied other students? Have you ever bullied anyone as an adult? How does it make you feel to do that? Were you ever depressed as a child? If yes, did you ever receive counseling? Are you ever depressed as an adult? The purpose of these follow-up questions is to determine whether the interviewee still has bullying tendencies. If so, that makes him a poor candidate for adoptive or foster children.

The Employment History Interview

Sample Questions to Determine Employment Attitudes

If the agency's application form does not provide enough space for the applicant to list all jobs, dates of employment, and reasons for leaving, the screener will need to do so for inclusion in the home study. Income will need to be documented for all current positions held by the applicants. Regardless of income the screener should inform the applicants of all financial assistance programs known to the screener. Several possibilities come to mind. The U.S. government offers an adoption tax credit of $10,000 that can be applied on qualifying expenses paid for a child's adoption. Various organizations offer grants and loans to individuals who adopt children with special needs. Some employers offer assistance to employees who adopt. The U.S. military will reimburse active-duty personnel up to $2,000 on adoption expenses for one child or $5,000 for siblings. The National Adoption Foundation has a $9 million fund from which it provides unsecured loans to adoptive families and grants that range from $500 to $2,500 per family. The program is open to all legal adoptions, whether public or private. There is no income requirement. The Hebrew Free Loan Association, a California-based organization, offers interest-free loans of up to $10,000 to qualifying Jewish families who have applied for adoption, but it requires that the money be repaid. All states offer financial assistance for "special needs" children as a result of the Adoption Assistance and Child Welfare Act of 1980. Children may receive a federally funded subsidy under Title IV-E or a state-funded subsidy as determined by each state's guidelines. The amount of money received is based on each state's foster home rate and varies from $325 to $1,283 per month (Mississippi rates, $325 to $500, depending on age; New York rates, $453 to $678, depending on age) (North American Council on Adoptable Children, n.d.).

Question 49:
Are You Happy With Your Current Job (Or Position)?

Possible answers:

1. "I've been with the same company for 8 years. I'm pretty content."
2. "It's all right, I suppose, but I'd like to find something better."
3. "I like the work all right, but I'm having problems with my supervisor."

Your first task is to determine employment stability. You would not want to place a child with someone who is contemplating changing jobs, nor would you want to place a child with someone who is about to be terminated. Applicants who are contemplating moving to another state should be advised to wait until they relocate to pursue adoption or foster care.

Respondent 1 has a stable employment record and expresses job satisfaction. Respondent 2 is expressing doubts about her work, but she is telegraphing a desire for change. Respondent 3 likes her work but not her supervisor. Does she have any plans to request a new supervisor, or is she locked into her current situation? See follow-up questions.

Follow-up questions. Sometimes individuals apply for adoptive or foster children when their lives are in a state of flux. They envision parenthood has having a steadying effect on their life. They see children as a life preserver. The answers to these follow-up questions will throw light on their employment stability.

Possible follow-up questions:

1. What do you dislike about your job?
2. Is your dissatisfaction due to the nature of the work or due to your relationship with your supervisor?
3. Why do you think you are having problems with your supervisor?
4. Have you ever had problems with supervisors at other jobs?
5. Describe the perfect job for you.

Question 50:
Do You See Yourself Staying There Until Retirement?

Possible answers:

1. "I'm only 28. I can't imagine staying there until retirement."
2. "It's the only job I've ever had. I wouldn't know how to get a job someplace else."
3. "I can't think that far ahead."

Respondents 1 and 3 are realistic about their employment future. A recent study by the U.S. Department of Labor found that individuals who were interviewed in 1979 between ages 14 to 22 and then subsequently interviewed in 2006 and 2007 held an average of 10.9 jobs during that 28-year period. Respondent 2 is a potentially riskier applicant than the other respondents because she might not possess the survival skills necessary to find work quickly if her employment was suddenly terminated.

Question 51:
How Would You Describe Your Relationship with Your Boss?

Possible answers:

1. "One of the best I've ever had. She never asks us to do anything she wouldn't do."

2. "Nonexistent. He doesn't even know my name. I'm just another face in the crowd."
3. "It's a love-hate relationship. He loves me and I hate him."

Respondent 1 has a fulfilling job and understands why it is special. She probably makes the most of any situation in which she finds herself, a good quality for a parent to have. Respondent 2 may have poor social skills. Certainly she does not have the skills necessary to make herself known to her employer.

Respondent 3 may "hate him" because of inappropriate demands he has made on her. If she is struggling to hold onto a job while fending off sexual harassment, it is a situation that should be explored by the screener because it could lead to an unstable work environment.

Follow-up. With these questions you will be probing for areas of instability. You cannot possibly place children with a family that is likely to experience an employment crisis in the near future. If the interviewees have a history of employment instability because of personality differences with supervisors, you cannot consider them for a placement until you are able to proceed with confidence. Remedial counseling may be a prerequisite to acceptance.

Possible follow-up questions:

1. Why do you think your contributions to your employer are not recognized by your supervisor? Have you ever been reprimanded? Have your deficiencies ever been pointed out to you? Has your sense of being ignored ever occurred at a previous job? Have you ever been passed over for promotion?
2. What is there about your boss that you hate? You said that he "loves" you. Why do you think that is the case? Why would you "hate" a boss that values you? What is there about you that he values? Have you ever experienced sexual harassment in the workplace? If yes, what happened? Did you file a complaint? If not, why?

Question 52:
How Often Do You Go to Work Early? How Often Do You Work Late?

Possible answers:

1. "I live twenty minutes from where I work, but I have it timed so that I arrive punctually at 10 till 9. I don't think I've ever been late. I've had to work late very few times because I get my work done in a timely manner."
2. "I arrive about an hour early every day so that I can get caught up on my work while the office is nice and quiet."
3. "I'm usually a minute or two late. But I work late quite a bit, which doesn't make my husband any too happy."

Some people have problems with tardiness all their life. Others don't display that behavior until adulthood, when they are under stress at work or at home. Individuals who are late on a consistent basis may be having problems at work and feel the need to overachieve simply to keep up with their coworkers, or they may have long-standing issues with self-esteem, or, if they are late coming home from work, they may be involved in a romantic affair.

Respondent 1 is punctual to the point of being obsessive about it, but she is obviously very well organized and allocates her time in a way that works for her. Most observers will probably see her as a very good parent who teaches responsibility to her children. However, her children may come to resent her dedication to timeliness and they may rebel by becoming the opposite person. See follow-up questions.

Respondent 2 may be having problems at work that need to be discussed in more detail. See follow-up questions.

Respondent 3 mentions working late and unhappiness on the part of her husband in the same breath so there may be a connection that needs closer scrutiny. See follow-up questions.

Possible follow-up questions:

1. (For the interviewee who is never late) You are to be commended for your punctuality. Do you feel that it is important for children to maintain a flawless record of punctuality? If yes, how would you handle a child who is chronically late for school? At what age do you think that a child is capable of understanding the importance of not being late?
2. (For the interviewee who arrives at work an hour early each day) Would you be able to be productive if you did not arrive an hour early? Do you feel that you have been given too much work? Do you feel that you are as good at your job as your coworkers? Do you ever worry about being fired or laid off?
3. (For the interviewee who often works late) How does your spouse feel about your late hours? Do you ever have arguments about working late? Has your spouse ever showed up at work to see you on days that you are working late? Has your spouse ever accused you of working late to cover up an affair?

Question 53:
Have You Ever Resigned from a Job without Having a Replacement Job?

Possible answers:

1. "No. I like to know where I'm going before I start out."
2. "Yes. I just couldn't take it any longer at my job. The people I worked with were so far beneath me."
3. "I did that once. But I had a good reason. This man I worked with was hitting on me nearly every day."

Respondent 1 appears very level-headed in her approach to job security.

Respondent 2 obviously has problems working with other people, not a good trait for someone who will be working with a social service agency that is responsible for supervising her parenting skills with adoptive or foster children. See follow-up questions.

Respondent 3 has a very good reason for resigning from her job, but her comment raises questions about whether she reported the harassment to her superiors. See follow-up questions.

Possible follow-up questions:

1. (For the interviewee who found her coworkers "beneath" her) What were the types of conflicts you had at your previous job that made it necessary for you to leave? How were your coworkers different from you? Have you ever resigned from another job because of differences of opinion with coworkers? What qualities do you have that make it easy for others to work with you?
2. (For the interviewee who was "hit on" at work) Did you report your problems to your employer? If no, why not? If yes, what was the reaction? Tell me the types of things that happened when you were being harassed. Was this the first time you had ever been harassed at work?

Question 54:
Have You Ever Been Fired?

Possible answers:

1. "No. That would be humiliating."
2. "Yes. That has happened to me twice. But it wasn't my fault."
3. "That happened to me once. But it was my fault."

Respondent 1 would obviously work very hard to keep from being fired from her job, not a bad trait for a would-be parent to have.

Respondent 2 may have problems working with other people. She also may have problems accepting responsibility for her mistakes. See follow-up questions.

Respondent 3 takes responsibility for her actions, an indication she may be able to work with the child care worker who will be supervising her home.

Possible follow-up questions:

1. (For the interviewee twice fired) What were the reasons you were fired? Why was it not your fault? Did you appeal to a higher authority? If not, why not? If yes, what was the outcome? Looking back, was there anything you could have done at work to keep from being fired?
2. (My fault) Why was it your fault? Why were you not able to keep your job?

Question 55:
Have You Ever Been the Target of a Conspiracy by Jealous Coworkers?

Possible answers:

1. "That's one job experience I've never had."
2. "Oh, yes. I have a target on my back. The other workers are all afraid of me."
3. "If there is a conspiracy, it is one of silence."

Respondent 1 provided a satisfactory answer.

Respondent 2 may have problems working with other people. See follow-up questions.

Respondent 3 has a sense of humor, but she also may be disliked at work. See follow-up questions. What you are looking for with questions like this is the applicant's capacity to take direction and accept criticism, mandatory requirements for working with a child care worker.

Possible follow-up questions:

1. (For the interviewee who has a target on his back) Why do you think your coworkers were afraid of you? Do you think that fear was justified? Do you want your coworkers to be afraid of you? Do you ever feel that your spouse is afraid of you? How do you feel when others criticize your work?
2. (For the interviewee with a conspiracy of silence) Do you feel that any of your coworkers are jealous of you? If yes, why do you think that is the case? Are your coworkers easy to work with? Have they ever criticized you at work? Do they ever invite you to attend gatherings outside work?

Question 56:
Have You Ever Been Reprimanded at Work for Losing Your Temper with Customers or Coworkers?

Possible answers (from female applicant):

1. "That happened once, but it wasn't my fault. I work with this woman who talks to her boyfriend constantly on the telephone, making it difficult to get my work done. One day I had enough and blessed her out. Unfortunately, she was on the phone with her minister and he complained to my boss."
2. "No, I've never been reprimanded at work for anything."
3. "I'm embarrassed to say, yes. It was totally my fault."

Respondent 1 may have a problem controlling herself during times of stress, not a good quality for a new parent. See follow-up questions.

Respondent 2 gave a satisfactory response that requires no follow-up.

Respondent 3 made a mistake at work, but she takes responsibility for what happened, a good quality for a new parent to have.

Possible follow-up questions:

1. (For the interviewee who "blessed out" a coworker) Before you blessed out your coworker did you ever ask her to stop talking on the telephone? If not, why? If yes, what was her response? How is your coworker different from you? What differences of opinion do you have, other than her use of the telephone? Is she of the same race? Is she better liked by your coworkers?
2. (For the interviewee who was at fault) Why was it your fault? Did you apologize? If yes, did she accept your apology? Have you ever lost your temper with other coworkers?

Possible answers (from male applicant):

1. "That happened once, but it wasn't my fault. I was with a customer who was very insulting about the way I dressed."
2. "I got into an actual fist fight with a coworker after he accused me of stealing money from his locker. That was a mistake and I will never do that again."

Possible follow-up questions:

1. (Happened once) What happened that day that made you do something you had never done before or since? Are you normally sensitive about the way you dress? If the interviewee provides a reasonable response, there is no reason for concern. Each of us is capable of making a mistake. If his response is not reasonable, then pursue by asking more questions. Have you ever been arrested as a result of losing your temper?
2. (Actual fist fight) How many fist fights have you participated in? Did the coworker who accused you ever apologize? If yes, did you accept the apology?

CHAPTER FIVE

Screening for Child Predators

Screening for child predators is one of the social worker's most important responsibilities when interviewing applicants for adoptive and foster children. It should be the first thought on the screener's mind when beginning the interview process and the last thought on the screener's mind before recommendations are made for approval or disapproval. The stakes are high because failure can result in the abuse or even death of an adoptive or foster child.

DSM-IV defines pedophile as a person with "recurrent, intense sexually arousing fantasies, sexual urges, or behaviors involving sexual activity with a prepubescent child or children (generally aged 13 years or younger)." (American Psychiatric Association, 2000). The diagnostic manual further stipulates that the person must have acted on these urges and be at least 16 years of age and at least 5 years older than the victim. Not included are individuals in late adolescence who are in ongoing sexual relationships with a 12- or 13-year-old. Also not included are individuals who have sexual relationships with adolescents ages 14 to 19 years.

Some law enforcement manuals use the term pedophile to describe an adult individual who has sexual relations with a minor, usually age 18 and younger, depending on the particular state in which the "consensual sex" legislation has been enacted. In those instances, pedophilia is not a diagnostic criteria but rather a description of a criminal activity. Some states such as Mississippi, North Carolina, and New Jersey have established the age of consent at 16; other states such as California, Florida, Tennessee, and North Dakota have set the age at 18. A few states, such as Massachusetts, have set different ages for men and women—in that state the age of consent is 16 for women and 18 for men. The practical implications of this are that social workers in different states have different standards to observe. For example, adult men in New Jersey who have sexual relations with a 16-year-old female cannot be classified as pedophiles, whereas adult men in Florida who have sexual relations with a 16-year-old female meet the legal (not diagnostic) criteria for being pedophiles and can be prosecuted.

Because foster care and adoption take place within a legal framework—and diagnosing pedophiles is not part of the screener's job description—the broader definition of pedophilia used by law enforcement may be more appropriate for screening adoptive and foster care applicants, even though it is not diagnostically correct. For that reason we will combine the two definitions of pedophile into the more practical *child predator*. Our interest will be in screening for any adult who has sexual relations with a minor. Adult–minor sexual behavior (vaginal penetration, oral sex, fondling) may not diagnostically meet the standards of pedophilic behavior—and it may not be illegal in all 50 states—but it may be classified as predatory behavior by social agencies and used as grounds for the rejection of adoptive or foster applicants who have exhibited such behavior.

It is relatively easy to identify individuals who suffer from depression, bipolar disorder, and borderline personality, but it is extremely difficult to identify child predators, primarily because they do not possess the visibly dampened spirits of someone with depression, or the manic episodes of someone with bipolar disorder, or the wide-eyed emotional eruptions of someone with borderline personality disorder. Contrary to public perceptions, child predators do not manifest their disorders with physically identifiable characteristics. Male child predators are seldom effeminate or "strange" looking. Female child predators are not masculine or "butch." They look exactly like the man and woman next door because that is who they are. They are likely married, with children in the home. Typically, they have responsible jobs and are perceived to be good citizens. It is not unusual for neighbors of child predators to exclaim, once the neighbor has been "outed" as a child predator, that they never "in a million years would have guessed it!"

Psychological Features of Pedophilia

Different psychological features give clues to the mechanisms underlying pedophilic behavior and offer potential treatment targets. More specifically, the person who sexually molests children has both impaired motivation and impaired inhibition. Possible motivational factors include social anxiety and the "abused-abuser theory." Possible inhibitory factors include impulsivity, cognitive distortions, and psychopathy. In addition, neurobiological abnormalities may pertain to either motivational or inhibitory dysfunction. All of these factors may come into play in any one person, but individual pedophiles may differ widely in their psychological profile (Cohen & Galynker, 2009).

One of the more horrific child abuse cases in American history occurred in the mid-1980s in Wakefield, Massachusetts, a bedroom community of Boston, where a sixth-grade science and math teacher used his position as a Scout leader to rape, torture, and photograph many of the young boys entrusted to him. They were stripped naked, blindfolded, handcuffed, and hung from ceiling hooks in the basement of his parents' house while the abuse took place. Often the children were punched and beaten with straps, always so that the abuse would not show. On one occasion, the boys were gang raped by several scout leaders at a scout jamboree held in a public park, where screaming boys was a normal occurrence. None of the boys reported the abuse because the scout leader told them he would kill their parents if they said anything.

From outward appearances, the scout leader was an outstanding member of the community. Not only was he a teacher and scout leader, he was chief of the firemen's auxiliary and a photographer for the local newspaper. Everyone liked him. When he was arrested and charged with raping young boys, posing them in the nude, and showing them obscene materials (*Boston Globe*, 1986), there was an outcry in the community over his arrest, with citizens holding meetings and writing letters in his support (*Boston Globe*, 1985).

However, that support disappeared quickly after his conviction. He was sentenced to 10 to 15 years in prison, but he died of natural causes before his sentence was completed.

Research indicates that people who molest children fall into distinct categories and have different motivations. (Lanning, 2001). Some molesters are opportunistic pedophiles who often can control their impulses. Others limit their behavior to incest. Others still are so-called true pedophiles who are motivated by uncontrollable sexual desires. It is the latter group that is considered the greatest public risk because it is characterized by repeated sexual encounters with or recurrent sexual urges toward children. Opportunistic pedophiles, according to researchers Lisa J. Cohen and Igor Galynker, have less attraction to children than true pedophiles, and their engagement with children may depend more on "circumstances, such as the availability of a child victim … or difficulty in connecting with an adult sexual partner" (Cohen & Galynker, 2009).

Word of Advice for Screeners

A good thing for social workers to remember is that pedophiles, whether they fall into the true, incest, or opportunistic category, are predators that are always alert to the acquisition of new victims. If you proudly display photographs of your children in your office, so that interviewees can see them, you may be setting your children up for potential abuse, especially if you have to reject an applicant for one reason or another. Keep photographs of your children facing you and not facing the interviewees seated in your office. Do not mention your children by name during interviews, even if the interviewees request their names. In addition, do not customize your license plates on your car, especially if you have an unusual name, because it will only make it easier for you to be tracked to your place of residence.

Warning Signs and Problem Areas
Consistent with Child Predator Leanings

Absence of a Significant Other

The scoutmaster mentioned in the previous story lived with his mother and father in a house across the street from one of the victim's churches. His torture chamber was in the basement. To the best of anyone's knowledge, he had never been married or sustained a long-term relationship with a woman or a man. That is typical of pedophiles, whether heterosexual or homosexual. From the data available for analysis in that particular case, it is difficult to know the extent of the scoutmaster's sexual attraction to boys. Because his homosexual adult friends were also often involved in the rapes and torture, it is possible that he was an opportunistic pedophile who used children to attract men, thereby forging adult relationships that he would not have otherwise have experienced.

There are millions of men in America who live with one or both or parents, and who are temporarily without significant others. Those two factors alone are not indicative of child predator tendencies. However, a lifetime history of failed adult relationships is reason enough to raise questions about an applicant's relationship skills. If the applicant has a history of failed relationships, it is necessary for you to determine why they failed. Were there problems with sexual or emotional compatibility? Were there problems with intimate communication? Was it because the individual was only attracted to children and simply could not sustain a relationship with an adult? If an applicant has no history of relationships with significant others, it is the responsibility of the screener to determine the reasons why.

Presence of Social Anxiety

Many child predators have been hypothesized to suffer from social anxiety disorder, which would explain why they prey on children who have low self-esteem and suffer from juvenile forms of social anxiety. They understand what a child with an anxiety disorder is going through because they have been through it themselves and, in fact, may still be going through it—and that provides them with insight into how to breech a child's defense mechanisms. There are two ways of looking at a child predator with a social anxiety disorder. One is that they display symptoms of social anxiety because of the shame and low self-esteem that they feel over their pedophilic urges. The other is that they turn to children because of existing social anxiety over their failure to connect with adults in meaningful relationships. They tend to be socially immature.

Your job as a screener is to identify any symptoms of social anxiety and then to determine if the disorder is related to child predator urges on the part of the applicant.

Social Anxiety

Social anxiety is not the nervousness most of us feel from time to time in situations where we have little control. It is a diagnosable mental condition that often goes undiagnosed, while sometimes causing a lifetime of suffering.

Social anxiety is the second most commonly diagnosed anxiety disorder. Anxiety disorders affect more than 18 percent of the adults in the United States each year, with 28 percent lifetime prevalence. Females are more likely to suffer from anxiety than males. The average age of onset is usually by 11 years of age, meaning that at least half the people with the disorder have their first episode of anxiety by that age.

In childhood, a shy child may fear being called on in class, taking tests, playing with peers, or being the center of attention. He may develop fears of being watched while doing something such as eating in public. It is not uncommon for a child with social anxiety to resist attending school. Later he may fear catastrophic results from attending a social event or going on a date. The fear of having to carry on a conversation is paralyzing. The possibility of embarrassment or humiliation outweighs any rational thoughts. He may worry for weeks or months in anticipation of an upcoming social event where attendance is mandatory.

The physical symptoms of social anxiety involve several body systems. The cardiovascular symptoms include pounding and rapid heartbeat, chest pain, and blushing. The respiratory system responds with shortness of breath or rapid breathing. One may feel dizzy, suffer headaches, and sweat profusely (neurological system). There is an interruption in the gastrointestinal system creating stomach pains, nausea, dry mouth, and sometimes even vomiting. A musculoskeletal response to the stress of social anxiety is tension, with muscle aches in the neck, back, and shoulders; tremors, and shaking. The psychological component involves excessive fear, feelings of impending danger, decreased concentration, restlessness, fatigue, negative self-judgment, sleep disturbance, and irritability. The behavioral consequences of social anxiety can be the purposeful avoidance of situations or events, compulsive behavior, extreme distress, or panic.

Without treatment, social anxiety can lead to depression. Adults suffering from social anxiety may engage in aberrant behavior to self-treat their unbearable pain. Many turn to alcohol and drugs, only to discover that self-medication only exacerbates the condition, sometimes leading to lifelong dysfunction.

A History of Sexual Abuse

Each applicant should be asked whether he or she was ever abused as a child. Not every adult who was sexually abused as a child will grow up to become a child predator, but the odds of that happening are high enough—30 percent, according to Dr. Gene Abel, medical director of the Behavioral Medicine Institute of Atlanta, and up to 60 percent, according to Lisa J. Cohen, PhD and Igor Galynker, MD—to cause concern if an applicant states that abuse occurred.[1] Some researchers believe that childhood abuse histories may be more characteristic of true pedophiles that opportunistic pedophiles (Cohen & Galynker, 2009).

Of interest to the screener will be whether the abuse was instigated by relatives or nonrelatives. Also important is how often the abuse occurred and how many partners participated in the abuse. A critical factor will be whether the applicant ever received counseling for the abuse and whether the counseling was effective in decreasing anxiety over the abuse (as determined by the therapist). Until recently, few therapists

---

1. See Arehart-Treichel, 2006, p. 37. The Jespersen and colleagues (2009) study concluded that "there is support for the sexually abused–sexual abuser hypothesis, in that sex offenders are more likely to have been sexually abused than non-sex offenders" (pp. 179–192).

were well trained to address child abuse and associated anxiety. As a result, many adults who were abused as children have not fully dealt with the abuse.

The screener must be alert to the fact that sometimes when an abuse victim applies for foster or adoptive children it is actually an attempt to receive help with child predator urges or actual predatory actions. It would be a grievous mistake for a screener to overlook the applicant's plea for help in that situation. If such a person is approved for children, the applicant may interpret that approval as the agency's tacit consent to satisfy his pedophilic urges.

If the issue of prior sexual abuse comes up during the interview, the screener should attempt to resolve the extent and effect of the abuse by asking the following questions:

- When did the abuse occur and who inflicted the abuse?
- Did the applicant receive therapy for the abuse? If no therapy was received, the applicant should be asked how he or she thinks they were affected by the abuse.
- The applicant should be asked pointblank whether they have ever been tempted to abuse a child. If yes, the applicant should be asked to explain.
- The applicant should be asked if they would mind being evaluated by a psychologist regarding the abuse.

Display of Inappropriate Symbols

There was a Canadian therapist of our acquaintance, now deceased unfortunately, who wore neckties with cartoon characters on them when he counseled children because he found that it increased their comfort level and lowered their resistance to his suggestions. It is a technique that is well known to both therapists and pedophiles. The therapist mentioned above was not a pedophile, of course, but he used the techniques perfected by pedophiles because he knew that the techniques would assist him in his counseling efforts with children.

Screeners should be alert to nontherapist men who wear neckties with cartoon characters on them, or who have displays of toys and stuffed animals in their home or office, or who have photographs of children not related to them on the wall. These symbols of childhood are used to attract victims to a web of false security and comfort: "I like the Cookie Monster. He likes the Cookie Monster. He must be just like me!"

Of course, not every man who displays such symbols is a child predator. Such displays should raise suspicion only if other factors are present, especially if the man suffers from social anxiety, does not have a history of relationships with significant others, or reports a history of childhood abuse.

Inappropriate Behavior toward Children

Some men are comfortable around children. Others are not. It can be endearing to see a father put his arm around his son buddy style while walking down the street, or muss his hair with a flourish and a big grin, or rough house with him, trading fake punches, or tickling him until he screams for him to stop, or dancing with his six-year-old daughter to her favorite song, or reading to his daughter while she sits on his lap. It's all part of the bonding experience. Not so endearing is witnessing a man doing those same things with a boy or girl to whom he is not related. It is off-putting because it is inappropriate.

Jackson, Mississippi once had a mayor who used his authority to stop a school bus so that he could hug the children on the bus, none of whom were related to him. His reason was that he loved all the children of the world and wanted to show his affection. His behavior made citizens uncomfortable because it was inappropriate. His position was that he was the mayor and, by definition, all his behavior was appropriate.

However, in human relationships appearances are everything. A man may be delighted that his female associate received a large commission, but if he touches her in too familiar a manner to show that delight his behavior is inappropriate, regardless of his good intentions. Pleas that he is "excited for her good fortune" will fall on deaf ears. Same thing with children. Good intentions are not a defense for inappropriate behavior. Perceptions matter.

The screener can initiate an investigation into this area by asking male interviewees to provide detailed examples of activities the interviewee likes to engage in with children. Do they think praise should be offered with words or with physical gestures? Ask them for examples of how they show affection to children. Take special note of physical activities or overnight trips with children who are not related to the applicant.

Discomfort Discussing Siblings

Male child predators are often reluctant to discuss their brothers and sisters—and usually with good reason. It is not unusual for a brother or sister to be aware of abuse in the home directed against a sibling. Likewise, it is not unusual for a brother to behave in an abusive manner toward a sister. In either case, an interviewee who has experience with abuse, either as victim or perpetrator, will be reluctant to direct an interviewer toward siblings who have knowledge of the abuse. To prevent that from happening, the interviewee may provide incorrect addresses and telephone numbers, or he may claim that he has lost touch with his siblings and has no idea where they can be reached. He may even claim that he cannot remember their names or the names of the cities where they reside. He may even lie about having siblings with an expectation that the screener will never discover the truth. On occasion, when asked for the names of siblings, a child predator may declare that he has such a bad relationship with his siblings that he would prefer they not be contacted because they would almost certainly lie to prevent him from receiving a foster or adoptive child. The authors are aware of one such case in which a brother denied the existence of siblings, only to have that falsehood revealed by an enterprising screener who investigated the brother's background and discovered three living sisters, one of whom stated that she was sexually abused by both her brother and their father.

This tendency for selective memory, or even deception, among adults who were abused as children can also be the result of abuse by grandparents, or aunts and uncles. Once, when responding to routine questioning about her grandparents, a young woman matter-of-factly declared that her maternal grandfather was no longer living. That misrepresentation was discovered by chance when the woman's mother off-handedly remarked to the authors during a reference telephone call that her father was in good health.

Questioned about her misrepresentation, the young woman broke down into tears, proclaiming, "No, he's not dead, but I wish he was dead! When I was ten he made me have oral sex with him and I hate him, I hate him, I hate him!"

Involvement as a Pastor, Youth Minister, or Church Music Director

Churches and youth groups offer child predators camouflage to mask their secret desires and behavior. They revel in wearing a protective cloak that suggests that they are "men of God" or of another world. They feel bulletproof as they walk among those who trust them the most. They rationalize that they would not be in positions of power if God did not sanction their behavior toward children.

Most of the men involved in youth ministries or organizations such as Boy Scouts and Little League are there for the right reasons and they contribute to the public good; but as news stories remind us each year there are a significant percentage of predators that pursue those affiliations as a cover for child abuse. Screeners should be concerned about men affiliated with youth ministries or other organizations who do not have a significant other or a history of satisfying relationships with adults. A personal relationship with God is not a substitute for a relationship with a significant other when it comes to screening for child abuse. A relationship with God by a youth minister or scout leader is certainly admirable, but if that relationship excludes close relationships with adults it should be of concern to a screener.

Unexplained Interview Hostility

If an interviewee displays anger and hostility during the interview for no apparent reason, it is a cause for concern. Child predators consider their sexual urges to be a sexual orientation or a lifestyle, not a psychological dysfunction, so they tend to become angry when those urges are challenged or if they feel threatened by an interviewer. Because they disagree with society's definition of inappropriate behavior, they sometimes feel righteous indignation over being singled out for engaging in behavior that they consider acceptable. They overcompensate by questioning the interviewer's knowledge and authority to "pass judgment" on them as potential parents. They may come across as being arrogant or condescending.

The source of the hostility, however slight, may be so oblique that the interviewer may have no idea why it is present. If the interviewer has self-esteem issues, he or she may feel that they are somehow to blame for the interviewee's anger. When faced with unexplained hostility during an interview, the screener should consider the following causes:

- Consciousness of guilt.
- A defensive mechanism used to discourage questions in sensitive areas.
- Self-loathing

Whatever the cause, interview hostility may indicate a level of intolerance that is incompatible with parenting adoptive or foster children.

Panic Attacks That Occur While Discussing Children

Internally, the pedophile may experience all the symptoms of a panic attack—accelerated heart rate, increased respiration, dizziness, tingling in the hands and fingers, chills, or excessive perspiration—but externally the panic attack may be identified by apparent blushing, red splotches where the neck joins the chest, avoidance of eye contact, and sudden shifts in posture (as in crossing and recrossing legs, or standing for no apparent reason).

Child predators sometimes experience panic attacks when interviewers discuss children. That occurs because the conversation leads the pedophile into thoughts that frighten and embarrass him, primarily because he is not absolutely certain that the interviewer does not know what he is thinking. The child predator may suddenly jump to his feet and ask to leave the room because he is not feeling well or because he says he needs a drink of water.

If this behavior occurs while you are interviewing a man about children, before you jump to conclusions that he is as child predator, consider whether you are discussing child sexual abuse or some other nonthreatening aspect of child rearing such as playtime or school issues.

If you are discussing child sexual abuse when such behavior occurs, you must consider the possibility that the interviewee is simply embarrassed by the conversation and feels discomfort about a subject that makes most people uncomfortable.

If you notice the above-mentioned behaviors, change the conversation to topics of a more general nature about parenting. The nonchild predator will become more relaxed. The child predator may not become more relaxed because he is reacting to his secret thoughts, not your words about a changed subject, and he is fearful of doing something that will reveal his secret thoughts.

Sex Abuse Statistics

- The average serial child molester has between 360 and 380 victims in his lifetime (see South Carolina Forcible Sex Crimes (1999).
- About 60 percent of male survivors surveyed report at least one of their molesters to be female (see Fritz, Stoll, & Wagner, 1981; Mendel, 1995).
- Young girls who are abused are three times more likely to develop psychiatric disorders or abuse alcohol and drugs as adults than girls who are not sexually abused (Kendler, Bulik, Silberg, Hetteman, Myer, & Prescott, 2000).
- Victims of child sexual abuse are 27.7 times more likely to be arrested for prostitution as adults than are nonvictims (see Widom, 1995). Despite the

fact that immediate family members have the most access to children, fewer than half of the sexual abuse perpetrators are family members or close relatives. Strangers make up only 10 percent to 30 percent of the cases, with the remainder identified as mothers' boyfriends, neighbors, teachers, coaches, religious leaders, and peers (Popenoe, 1996).

• Many child predators consider their behavior to be an expression of their sexual orientation. That belief is one reason why rehabilitation is seldom successful. They go to their graves convinced that their feelings toward children are appropriate and that they have done nothing wrong.

Case History

Malcolm and his wife, Sarah, came into the agency to apply for adoption, even though they had two birth children of their own. They said that they understood that couples who were unable to have birth children would have priority for infants, so they decided to apply for a girl age three to five.[2]

Malcolm and Sarah, both in their mid-thirties, made a good first impression. They were an attractive couple, friendly and outgoing. Malcolm worked as a police officer, and Sarah was the owner of a daycare center for preschool-age children. The screener used the first interview as an opportunity to explain agency policies and to probe the couple about their motivation for adoption.

"I just love children," explained Sarah.

"Kids that age are just so cute, we'd like to have more now that our children are in school," added Malcolm.

The screener scheduled the next interview for the office, with Malcolm soloing for his individual interview. He seemed more nervous for his individual interview than he had been for the first joint interview. The screener didn't think too much about it because that sometimes happens with overanxious couples.

The screener explained to Malcolm that he was going to talk about his childhood so that he could write up a family history for the home study. The screener used this approach to build a rapport with Malcolm. With his head down, avoiding eye contact that could be perceived as threatening, the screener wrote down detail after detail about Malcolm's early family life—early memories, school experiences, questions that did not break the rhythm of the interview. It was when the screener routinely asked him for the names and birthdates of his siblings that the interview slammed into a brick wall.

Malcolm said he had six sisters, but he couldn't remember their names. Asked if he could put them in birth order, youngest to oldest, and recall any of their birthdates, he answered that he could not. "We just weren't real close," he explained. "I don't even know where any of them live."

---

2. Dickerson and Allen, 2007, pp. 53–56. This case history was reprinted in altered form with permission.

Questioned about his memory—whether he had problems recalling other details about his childhood or recent events—he was adamant that he had no memory problems. To prove that he had a good memory, Malcolm told the screener about two little girls that his wife had babysat 10 years ago, during their first year of marriage. "They were beautiful little girls," he gushed. "Their names were Bette and Marcie. One was three, born on April 15, and the other was five, born on December 2."

That episode raised concerns for the screener. Male pedophiles who are attracted to females often have bad relationships with their sisters. Often their sexual experimentation begins at an early age with their younger sisters. Malcolm was correct about one thing—there was nothing wrong with his memory, as his detailed descriptions of Bette and Marcia proved. The screener also was bothered that Malcolm became so animated when he discussed the little girls.

Alerted to the possibility that he might be interviewing a pedophile, the screener became more aggressive with his questioning. His technique was to ask a series of innocuous questions, dutifully writing down his answers on a legal pad. He did that for 10 minutes, avoiding eye contact with Malcolm, building up Malcolm's confidence that he was controlling the interview. Then, abruptly, he put down his pen and looked Malcolm directly in the eye, shattering his composure with the question. "Do you know if any of your sisters were ever sexually abused?"

Malcolm was stunned. After a few awkward moments, during which he started and stopped a series of sentences, he asked if he could be excused to go to the bathroom. The screener excused him. As he was walking out the door, Malcolm turned and smiled. "I'll answer that question when I get back."

"No problem," said the screener.

Ten minutes later, Malcolm returned to the interview room, his face no longer showing the perspiration it had displayed when he left—an indication that he had washed his face. When he sat back down, he was composed. "To answer your question," he said. "No—sex was never discussed in my family."

Again, the screener asked a series of innocent questions, allowing Malcolm to relax. Then, as he had done before, he looked him directly in the eye and asked, "How have you prepared your daughters to deal with sexual abuse?"

Malcolm stared back at the screener, trying to break his gaze, but the screener held firm, looking him squarely in the eye. It was at that point that Malcolm experienced a panic attack. He rose to his feet and paced about the room, muttering, "Well, now . . . let me see." His newly washed face suddenly grew shiny. He sighed several times in rapid succession and then said, "I would tell them to beware of strangers."

After the interview, the screener went into his supervisor's office and told her that he had serious doubts about Malcolm's ability to be an adoptive parent. Said the screener, "I think he is a pedophile."

The supervisor asked why he felt that way, and he hit the high points of the interview. Noted the supervisor, "It sounds like he is afraid we will contact his sisters."

The screener agreed. Together, the interviewer and the supervisor decided to structure an aggressive interview for Sarah when she came in for her individual interview.

As it happened, Sarah's interview never took place. The following week, the agency learned that Malcolm had been arrested and charged with molesting two of the little girls enrolled in Sarah's daycare center. The agency further learned that the adoption application had been a ploy devised by Malcolm's lawyer, who thought that getting them approved for adoption would establish the agency as a source for "expert" witness testimony. He had coached Malcolm on how to respond in the interview and he had instructed him to list out-of-state references that would have no knowledge of his arrest.

This story ended with the agency preserving its integrity and protecting its adoptive children—and with Malcolm pleading guilty to child molestation.

Discussion

1. What was the first nonverbal signal that Malcolm offered that should have been of interest to the interviewer?
2. What was the first verbal signal that should have been of interest?
3. How many explanations can you think of to explain the incidence of a panic attack during an interview?
4. How many reasons can you think of that would explain Malcolm's memory lapses?

FIGURE 5.1

CHILD PREDATOR CHECKLIST	Yes	No
Does the applicant have a history of childhood abuse?	____	____
Does the applicant have a significant other?	____	____
Does the applicant have a history of significant others?	____	____
Does the applicant show any signs of social anxiety?	____	____
Does the applicant display any inappropriate symbols?	____	____
Has the applicant demonstrated inappropriate behavior?	____	____
Is the applicant comfortable discussing siblings?	____	____
Is the applicant involved in a leadership position with children or youths?	____	____
Did the applicant show hostility during interview?	____	____
Did the applicant have a panic attack during the interview?	____	____

CHAPTER SIX

Using Health and Reference Information as a Screening Device

A health questionnaire should be included in the initial application materials given to adoptive and foster parent applicants. The purpose is to gather enough general information directly from the applicants to ascertain whether they have any diseases or conditions that could be injurious to a child or which would affect their ability to care for a child's daily needs. The questionnaire also should query the applicants about their attitudes on certain health issues. A similar questionnaire should be sent to the applicants' physician to verify the information submitted by the applicants. The agency should ask the physician to complete the questionnaire and return it with letterhead stationary bearing his or her signature, in addition to the signature on the questionnaire (there have been cases in which applicants have forged physician signatures).

Obtaining information from the physician may be easier if the physician is not part of a corporate medical group or health maintenance organization (HMO), especially one that offers counseling as part of its services. Some HMO's may be reluctant to release counseling information because of a fear of litigation. For that reason social agencies should ask adoptive and foster care applicants to sign a confidentiality waiver to release the physician or HMO from legal liability if they provide requested information to the agency.

Typical questions on a health questionnaire include the following:

- Have you ever been diagnosed with heart disease, kidney disease, liver disease, digestive disease, bone disease, or blood disorders? If so, please provide dates and specific diagnoses.
- Have you ever been diagnosed with cancer? If so, please provide specific diagnoses and dates of treatment.
- Have you ever been diagnosed with any form of mental illness? If so, please provide specific diagnoses and dates of treatment.
- Have you ever been prescribed medication to calm your nerves? If so, please provide specific diagnoses and dates of treatment.

- Have you ever been diagnosed with alcoholism? If so, please provide specific diagnoses and dates of treatment.
- Have you ever been diagnosed with drug addiction? If so, please provide specific diagnoses and dates of treatment.
- Have you ever been diagnosed with HIV?

Most of the time medical reports are straightforward and require no follow up by the screener, but occasionally it will be necessary for the screener to make an appointment with the physician so that he or she can be interviewed in depth about the applicant. Such interviews can be tense because the last thing the physician wants is to be used as a reason for rejecting the application. The interview will go more smoothly if the screener focuses on specific health issues and avoids the appearance of "fishing" for non–health-related information. Know your questions in advance and ask the physician to amplify any answers you do not understand.

The current health of adoptive and foster care applicants is important only if it affects the care of children. If the applicant is battling a terminal illness or one that requires time consuming treatment, it is unlikely that the applicant could be accepted as either an adoptive or foster parent. Other conditions that could negatively affect the application are disabilities that require the use of a wheelchair or otherwise limit mobility (blindness); illnesses that pose a threat of infection or contagion (hepatitis B or C); intellectual disability (IQ less than 90); and mental illness that requires regular treatment, therapy, or both (bipolar, schizophrenia, or severe personality disorders).

As a social worker it is important for you to understand that the United States does not have national health standards for adoption and foster care. Each state determines its own health standards and those standards vary from state to state.

In addition to gathering health history information, it will be necessary for the screener to assess the health care attitudes possessed by the applicants that could affect the care of a child. Among the attitudes of primary interest are the following:

- Opposition to vaccination on the grounds that it is harmful
- Opposition to medical treatment on religious or political grounds (as in, "God will cure those who are worthy" or "the government wants me to do it, so I won't")
- Opposition to medical care in general on the grounds that they don't trust doctors
- Opposition to medical care by applicants who prefer herbal remedies
- A preference for faith healing

Health insurance is also an important issue. Do the applicants have adequate medical insurance? Does the insurance cover adopted children? It is a must that adoptive parents obtain health insurance for the child. Applicants should be encouraged during the home study process to find out all they can about changes in their insurance coverage if they adopt. Some insurance companies do not provide coverage to adopted children. Some physicians, with malpractice liability in mind, will not treat adopted children because it is often impossible to obtain a complete health history and physicians feel that puts them at increased liability for a lawsuit.

With foster care, the agency will provide for the health needs of the child, so health insurance for the child is not a factor; but it is necessary that foster parents have health insurance because a lack of coverage could disrupt the family in the event of serious illness and necessitate the removal of the foster child.

What Our Illnesses Say About us

Just as anger and hate can do damage to the human body by elevating blood pressure and putting stress on major organs such as the heart, so can the antithesis of those emotions—love—lower blood pressure and soften the impact of stress on the immune system.

Dr. Bernie Siegel, a New Haven, Connecticut, surgeon who has lectured extensively on the connection between emotions and disease writes: "I feel that all disease is ultimately related to a lack of love, or to love that is only conditional, for the exhaustion and depression of the immune system thus created leads to physical vulnerability. I also feel that all healing is related to the ability to give and accept unconditional love." (Dickerson & Allen, 2007, 122–123).

In agreement with Siegel is Leonard Laskow, a West Coast physician and the author of the book *Healing With Love*. "Through love, we can heal and become whole again," he writes. "With loving actions and felt awareness, we can experience our oneness, our universal relatedness" (Laskow, 1992).

Siegel and Laskow both link emotional wellness and overall happiness. "The simple truth is, happy people generally don't get sick," writes Siegel. "One's attitude toward oneself is the single most important factor in healing or staying well. Those who are peace with themselves and their immediate surroundings have far fewer serious illnesses than those who are not." (Siegel, 1990).

Scientific research leans in that direction. Studies show that individuals who are happy with their lives report one-tenth the rate of serious illness, as do those who are unhappy with their lives. Two Israeli researchers, Jack Medalie and Uri Goldbourt, studied 10 thousand men with risk factors for abnormal heart rhythms and high anxiety levels and discovered that the single question that most closely correlated with the development of chest pains was: "Does your wife show you her love?" Those men who answered "no" were found to be at a significant higher risk for heart disease (Medalie & Goldbourt, 1976).

The Medalie and Goldbourt (1976) study raises an interesting question: When we talk about the healing power of love, are we referring to an emotional and spiritual state, or are we also including the healing power of *touch?* Is love without touch mere lip service to an altruistic vision of how life should be in a perfect world?

No one is ever surprised when serial killers are described as "loners," for we have come to understand that isolation is a breeding ground for antisocial behavior. But is

FIGURE 6.1

SAMPLE REFERENCE LETTER (MEDICAL)

Dear Dr. _____:

Your patient, _____, has applied to us to adopt a child [to become a foster parent] and listed you as a medical reference.

We would appreciate it if you would take a few minutes to complete the following questionnaire and return it to us at your earliest convenience:

1) How long have you provided medical care to the applicant?_____

2) Applicant's Height _____ Weight _____ BP_____ Pulse _____

3) Are you treating the applicant for a chronic condition? ___ If yes, please explain

4) Has the applicant been tested or treated during the past 18 months for
  ❏ Hepatitis   Test Results _____
  ❏ Tuberculosis   Test Results _____
  ❏ HIV   Test results _____
  ❏ Other Sexually transmitted diseases   Please explain _____
  ❏ Infertility   Please explain_____
  ❏ Heart disease   Please explain _____
  ❏ Liver disease   Please explain_____
  ❏ Kidney disease   Please explain _____

5) Does the applicant have a medical condition that could interfere with his or her ability to effectively parent a child? _____ If yes, please explain _____
  _____

6) To the best of your knowledge, does the applicant have a problem with alcohol or drug use? _____

7) How would you rate the applicant's potential as an adoptive [foster] parent:
  ❏ poor, ❏ average, ❏ excellent, ❏ unknown.

_____   _____
            Physician   Date

Thank you for your help in this very important matter. Your responses to questions 6 and 7 are confidential and will not be shared with the applicants. If we have any questions about your responses, we will contact you.

Sincerely yours,

Department of Social and Family Services

Source: See Dickerson and Allen, 2007, 122–123. Reprinted with permission.

it the isolation per se that molds a serial killer or is it the lack of love expressed physically that makes a difference? Typically, serial killers engage the services of a prostitute prior to committing premeditated murder. That can be viewed as symptomatic of mental illness, or it can be viewed as a desperate attempt to self-medicate, through touch, a diseased and skin-starved psyche.

Much of the healing that took place in the New Testament occurred through the symbolic "laying on of hands." When songwriters and poets write about the effects of love, the words they use most convincingly are "touched" and "felt." Indeed, when people talk of "making love," they are not referring to some mystical manufacturing process; they are referring to the most intimate physical interaction that can be experienced by humans.

Husbands and wives who profess "love" for their mates, yet abstain from expressing those feelings in a physical context contribute nothing to their mate's good health. Love without touch is little more than prayer without conviction. To be successful as a healing agent, love must be accompanied by a "laying on" of hands.

Often when a marriage partner is diagnosed with a terminal illness, the first level of intimacy to disappear is sexual intercourse. The partner may justify withholding sex in a variety of ways—"it will make him/her feel worse" or "it will put a strain on his/her system"—but the hard reality is that withholding sex and physical affection is equivalent to watering down the patient's medications. Of course, sexual intimacy is not always appropriate. There may be physical reasons why the patient cannot engage in intercourse. In those cases, there are many other ways in which to physically express love—hugging, kissing, body massages, and hand holding, to name a few. When the Beatles proclaimed, "All You Need is Love," they were not far off the mark. Love promotes physical and emotional healing, it combats loneliness, it builds self-esteem, and it counters grief.

When reading a physician's report it will be helpful to keep the above-mentioned research in mind. Do the applicants go to the doctor often for ostensibly minor illnesses such as exhaustion, colds, aches, and pains? Do they have numerous illnesses that have to be treated with medications—sinus infections, vague stomach ailments, headaches, and so forth.

As screener you will be interested in whether the illnesses can be correlated with an unhappy marital relationship. If you suspect that the marriage is on shaky ground, you will want to schedule an appointment with the physician so that you can further inquire about the nature of the patient's illnesses. If he confirms that the applicants have a history of stress-related illnesses, you will want to question the applicants in more detail about their relationship.

What you may see discover is a likeable, motivated couple who are repressing their dissatisfaction with each other to the point where their frustrations are emerging as minor illnesses. Placing a child with them may "cure" their illnesses in the short term, but then escalate the illnesses once the stress of parenthood become evident to them.

Screeners should keep in mind that children are never a solution to stress. On the contrary, they can be a major source of stress.

References Are an Important Screening Tool

References can be a gold mine of valuable information to screeners. Not only do references provide validation from friends and relatives of an applicant's capacity to be a parent, but also they provide the screener with valuable insight into the applicants' judgment. Adoptive and foster parents make critical judgments on a daily basis about the children entrusted to them. The selection of references should be viewed as the first test of that judgment.

Because references are an important part of the application process—and can be controversial if improperly handled by the screener—it is essential that the agency establish the ground rules early in the procedure, preferably on the application section that asks for the names and addresses of references. It should be stated clearly on the application that negative information supplied by a reference will be investigated and, if found to be accurate, could be used as a reason to reject the application. However, it also should be made clear that although the identity of the reference will be protected by the agency, the allegations themselves will be shared with the applicants and they will be given the opportunity to rebut the allegations; and the agency may ask a reference for the names of other individuals who can confirm the allegations.

Because of the important role that references play in the process it is essential that an agency create clearly defined rules: "The agency's interest is the fullest, frank disclosure possible that results in a process fair to all concerned" (Schweitzer & Pollack, 2006).

Screeners should view references as tipsters, not as judge and jury. Negative information from a reference about an applicant must be independently confirmed by the screener. It is the first step in an investigative process that will involve additional sources. For example, if a reference provides a negative recommendation because the applicant once dropped their child off at daycare and got into a heated argument with daycare officials because of a lack of parking, the screener will be obligated to interview day care officials who witnessed the altercation.

References are accessible in four ways—by telephone, letter, face-to-face interview, and e-mail. Each medium has its own strengths and weaknesses. One of the positive benefits of obtaining references by telephone is that it allows the screener to ask follow-up questions; one of the negative aspects is that, unless the interview is recorded, the screener is faced with he said–she said information that the individual later can deny. E-mail references provide a written record of the interviewee's comments, a positive consideration; but the medium does not realistically allow real-time follow-up questions. Face-to-face interviews offer an excellent opportunity to ask follow-up questions, but if the interview is not recorded the information is subject to challenge at a later date. Letters are an excellent vehicle for obtaining reference information that is presented in the reference's own words and validated with a signature, but letters offer no immediate avenue for follow-up questions.

The best way to go about obtaining information is with letters that later can be followed up with telephone calls, face-to-face interviews, or emails as needed. There are several things a screener looks for when evaluating reference letters. Did the letter arrive in a timely manner? If not, is there any hint of hesitation in the wording used in the letter? If so, follow-up is required. Did a tardy reference letter have to be prompted by a telephone call? If so, a follow-up is required to determine whether the reference is reluctant to offer an opinion. Are the responses lengthy or short and to the point? If short and void of praise of any kind, a follow up is required.

The types of phrases that should prompt a follow-up contact:

- "I really don't know them well enough to say one way or the other."
- "I really don't know why they gave you my name."
- "I don't think they have what it takes to be parents."
- "They have overcome so much in their life that I think they deserve a chance."
- "I didn't know they were back together."
- "It depends on whether they want a girl or a boy."
- "I think they would be great parents if they have straightened out their financial situation."
- "I don't think their relationship is all that stable."

Follow-up interviews by telephone are usually more productive than e-mail or face-to-face interviews. It is a phenomenon that is well known to newspaper reporters who routinely conduct interviews by telephone. When you conduct an interview in person, the interviewee has many opportunities to control and direct the conversation. She can effectively divert a question or stall for time by lighting a cigarette, calling her cat, walking to the window to comment on the weather, standing to look for something across the room, knocking over a cup of coffee, asking the interviewer if she would like water or coffee, or pausing to call her assistant on the telephone to ostensibly ask for information. Not so with a telephone interview. It provides a direct ear-to-ear connection that is difficult to break. Body language is ineffective. Spatial diversions by the interviewee are meaningless because the interviewer cannot see what is taking place.

There are disadvantages to asking a reference to come to the office for a follow-up interview. It puts the interviewee on the spot, as if he were a child who has been summoned to the principal's office, and it provides less privacy than a home visit. The advantage to a home visit is that allows the interviewer to venture into the life of the interviewee and make observations that may prove revealing. A disadvantage is that it may make the interviewer feel threatened by his or her surroundings in the home. Explain Kadushin and Kadushin (1997):

> The interviewee, as host for the interview, gains a measure of control. The interviewee is in familiar friendly territory; the interviewer is in an unfamiliar setting. The interviewee controls seating arrangements and interruptions and can temporarily move out of the interview psychologically, or physically, by making

some household excuse for moving around. The interviewee can exercise a measure of self-protection by using "arranged distractions"—letting a radio or TV blare at full volume, giving a warm welcome to neighbors who drop in, or vigorously rattling pots and dishes while washing them during the interview (p. 83).

For the reasons cited above it is important that the interviewer always seek to control the interview. If the TV is too loud, ask the interviewee to turn it down or off entirely. If a neighbor drops by and it is obvious that the interviewee is not going to ask the neighbor to leave, then you have the option of politely informing the neighbor that a private interview is in progress, or you can suggest to the interviewee that another time be arranged for the interview. Under no circumstance should you proceed with an interview that you cannot control.

An angry reference letter that provides negative information about the applicants using words that typically apply to romantic relationships—"selfish," "uncaring," "untrustworthy," "unfaithful," and so forth—should be given close scrutiny to determine whether the negative reference is based on factual observations or emotional reactions to a perceived slight by the applicants. For example, it is one thing for the reference to report that the applicants handle children in a rough manner, such as jerking a child's arms when they don't obey instructions to leave the room, and another thing entirely if the reference bases his or her comments on the applicants being "selfish" or "uncaring." If the screener concludes, after a follow-up interview, that the reference's negative recommendation is not based on factual information—instances in which the applicants showed bad judgment in specific instances—the screener should carefully document his or her analysis of the reference's motivation for providing a negative reference.

Just as the screener must determine the motivations of applicants, so must the screener determine the motivations of individuals that provide negative recommendations. Sometimes friends feel threatened by their friends applying to adopt or foster children because they think that it will change their relationship in a negative way; sometimes the end result of that fear will be a negative recommendation. There are other reasons that individuals provide negative recommendations. It is not uncommon for prejudiced family members to make negative comments because they are opposed to the applicants bringing a child of a different race, ethnic background, or religion, into the family. If the screener suspects that to be the case, the screener should be alert to any reference to race, ethnic origin, or religion in the letter or follow-up interview. If the reference says "black child" instead of child, or uses descriptive language such as "Catholic child" or "Moslem child," the screener should probe the reference's racial and religious attitudes with questions such as:

- Do you have any friends that are black (Asian, Native American, white)?
- Have you ever had bad experiences with individuals of a different race?
- Are there any people of a different race or religion in your neighborhood?
- Do you approve of people adopting or fostering children of a different race?

Negative, noncommittal, or lukewarm recommendations from high-profile references raise questions about the applicants' judgment in choosing individual references. Did the applicants list well-known individuals because of their standing in the community or did they list them because they had long-term relationships with them? If it is the former, the references may be hesitant to recommend the applicants as foster or adoptive parents and provide cautious responses. Another thing to keep in mind is that adoptive and foster applicants may list high-profile individuals as references because they think that they will be attractive to the screener, or they may be afraid to list the names of long-term friends because they fear negative recommendations from the people who know them best. Also, keep in mind that it is not unheard of for an applicant who is opposed to his or her partner's desire for adoptive or foster children to list an individual for a reference that is certain to provide a negative recommendation.

If the references require follow-up calls or home visits, regardless of whether the information they provide is valid or not, the screener must evaluate the applicants' judgment in choosing the references. Bad judgment in choosing references may be consistent with a history of bad judgments in critical areas of child-rearing, education, finances, and significant-other relationships. In other words, applicants who take short-cuts in the adoption or foster care process may encourage the child to take short-cuts with homework assignments, tests, and other areas of schoolwork where honesty is a requirement. Applicants who do not possess the acumen to choose the best references possible may lack the skills to choose the best partner for a relationship or make good decisions regarding finances. Does an applicant with a negative reference have a history of mistaken judgments in other areas of his or her life? If not, it is incumbent upon the screener to delve deeper into the reference's motivations for giving a negative recommendation.

FIGURE 6.2

SAMPLE REFERENCE LETTER (FOR MARRIED APPLICANTS)

Dear _____:

Your friends, _____, have applied to us to adopt a child [to become foster parents] and they have listed you as a reference.

We would appreciate it if you would take a few minutes to complete the following questionnaire and return it to us at your earliest convenience:

How long have you known the applicants? _____

Would you describe the applicants as
❑ acquaintances, ❑ close friends, ❑ relatives,
❑ other (please explain)_____

How would you rate the applicants' parenting abilities:
❑ poor, ❑ average, ❑ excellent, ❑ unknown.

How would you describe the applicants' relationship with each other? _____

_____

_____

To the best of your knowledge, does either applicant have problems with alcohol or drug use? _____

_____

How would you rate the applicants' potential as adoptive [foster] parents?
Please explain_____

_____

_____

Thank you for your help in this very important matter. Your recommendations are strictly confidential and will not be shared with the applicants unless you make negative allegations. In that case, your identity will be protected but the information itself will be discussed with the applicants. If we have any questions about your responses, we will contact you.

Sincerely yours,

Department of Social and Family Services

Source: See Dickerson and Allen, 2007, 120–121. Reprinted with permission.

FIGURE 6.3

SAMPLE REFERENCE LETTER (FOR SINGLE APPLICANTS)

Dear _____:

Your friend, _____, has applied to us to adopt a child [to become a foster parent] and he/she has listed you as a reference.

We would appreciate it if you would take a few minutes to complete the following questionnaire and return it to us at your earliest convenience:

How long have you known the applicant? _____

Would you describe the applicant as
❑ acquaintances,   ❑ close friend,   ❑ relative,
❑ other (please explain)_____

How would you rate the applicant's parenting abilities:
❑ poor,   ❑ average,   ❑ excellent,   ❑ unknown.

How would you describe the applicant's relationship with members of the opposite sex? _____

_____

To the best of your knowledge, does the applicant have problems with alcohol or drug use? _____

_____

How would you rate the applicant's potential as an adoptive [foster] parent? Please explain _____

_____

_____

Thank you for your help in this very important matter. Your recommendations are strictly confidential and will not be shared with the applicants unless you make negative allegations. In that case, your identity will be protected but the information itself will be discussed with the applicants. If we have any questions about your responses we will contact you.

Sincerely yours,

Department of Social and Family Services

Source: See Dickerson and Allen, 2007, 120–121. Reprinted with permission.

FIGURE 6.4

REFERENCE CHECKLIST

Name of Personal Reference _____

Date mailed _____ Date received by agency _____

Recommendation ❏ yes   Noncommittal ❏ yes   ❏ no

Summary: _____

_____

_____

_____

Name of Personal Reference _____

Date mailed _____ Date received by agency _____

Recommendation ❏ yes   Noncommittal ❏ yes   ❏ no

Summary: _____

_____

_____

_____

Name of Personal Reference _____

Date mailed _____ Date received by agency _____

Recommendation ❏ yes   Noncommittal ❏ yes   ❏ no

Summary: _____

_____

_____

_____

Name of physician _____

Recommendation ❏ yes   ❏ no

Significant health problems _____

_____

CHAPTER SEVEN

Screening for Positive and Negative Parenting Attitudes

Parenting is not a democratic institution in which all parents are deemed to be created equal. Some individuals seemingly are born better parents than others. Some learn those skills through experience. The gap between good parenting and neglectful parenting is vast. In-between the two extremes is a vast gray wilderness that complicates the decision-making process for screeners, whose job it is to weed out individuals with negative parenting tendencies from parents with positive parenting tendencies. As you will see as you read through this chapter it is not a process that always lends itself to a black-and-white consensus. Parenting is a complicated subject that is characterized by many shades of gray.

Social workers usually begin this process with an optimistic belief that everyone has the potential to become a successful foster or adoptive parent, even though they know that statistically that is simply not the case. The screening process begins with an evaluation of the applicant's actual experience with children. If the application they completed does not list children in the household, the screener's first task is to evaluate their experience: "I see on your application that you have no children in the household. Have you ever had children in your household?"

If the answer is "no," then you will move on to a series of questions that will assess the applicant's experience with children and the applicant's potential as a parent. If the answer is yes, then you will have to establish the circumstances in which children were in the home.

Questions for Applicants Who Have Experience With Children

Question 1:
Under What Circumstances Were Children in Your Home?

1. We had a little girl, but she passed away when she was five.
2. We kept a neighbor's (or family member's) children while they dealt with the mother's hospitalization.

3. For a short time I had custody of a child from a previous marriage.
4. I operated a day care out of my home for two years.
5. We adopted a little boy, but it didn't work out.[1]

Answer 1 is a negative response only if the applicant has had a difficult time getting over the grief associated with his or her loss. To determine that ask if the applicant has experienced difficulty sleeping. Ask whether the loss has affected the applicant's social life. Ask if it has affected the applicant's relationship with a significant other. Ask if the applicant has been prescribed medication for depression or anxiety. In 1969, psychiatrist Elisabeth Kubler-Ross identified five stages of grief, which she hypothesized occurred in sequence: denial, anger, bargaining, depression, and acceptance. Kubler-Ross's earmarks were based on the study of patients with terminal illness and do not necessarily occur in the same sequence for someone who has experienced the death of a child. It may be useful to determine how many of these earmarks have been achieved by the applicant, but the determining factor for the applicant is whether he or she has adapted to life's day-to-day challenges in the wake of the loss. It is important for the social worker to understand that an adoptive or foster child is not an antidote for a broken heart. If an applicant is having a difficult time coping with life, his or her coping ability will not improve with the placement of an adoptive or foster child into the home. On the contrary, the applicant's maladaptive behaviors are more likely to worsen with the addition of a child into the home.

Answer 2 is the most promising because it raises no immediate questions about negative parenting behavior. An important follow-up question would whether the applicant was asked on subsequent occasions to keep the neighbor's children. If the answer is no, you will want to find out why, even if it involves interviewing the neighbors.

Answer 3 raises questions about why the applicant had custody for only a short time. If an applicant, male or female, states that they had custody of a child for a limited time you must consider the possibility, however remote, that abuse was either alleged or proved. You should begin your inquiry by asking the applicant for an explanation. If the explanation is inadequate, you should ask the applicant point-blank if there were any allegations of abuse.

Answer 4 is acceptable only if you determine from the licensing authority the reasons for the day care closing and if there is no reason to suspect neglect or abuse.

Answer 5 is troublesome at first glance, but you should withhold judgment until you know all the facts. The obvious first step is to ask for an explanation about why the adoption did not work out. For starters, you must ascertain who placed the child with the applicant, the dates of the placement and removal, and the current status of

---

1. Dickerson and Allen, 2007, p. 136. Some of the questions in this section were reprinted with permission. All answers and discussions are original to *How to Screen Adoptive or Foster Parents.*

the child. There are acceptable reasons for the termination of an adoption—a court order based on the request of a parent who had not been notified of the proceedings, the emergence of previously unknown emotional or health problems too severe for the applicant to address, or some other occurrence not the fault of the applicant. Unacceptable reasons include dissatisfaction with the placement, significant other opposition that developed after the placement, or serious health conditions involving the applicants that were not evident at the time of placement. Of course, any applicants who were involved in a failed placement must be thoroughly vetted for potential problems if approved for a second placement. There are second chances in adoption and foster care, but they are not offered lightly and they must be closely scrutinized for any potential for subsequent failure.

Question 2:
What Would You Want to Do Differently with Foster or Adoptive Children That You Didn't Do with Your Birth Children or Children That You Cared for on a Regular Basis?

1. I'd be more patient and understanding.
2. Nothing. I'd treat them all the same.
3. I wouldn't let them get away with so much devilishness.
4. I'd correct the mistakes I made with my birth children.

Answers 1 and 4 indicate that the applicants learned lessons from their previous parenting experiences—comments that indicate growth, maturity, and even temperament. These are lessons that would correlate with success as adoptive or foster parents. Answers 2 and 3 indicate that the applicants did not learn much from their earlier parenting experiences and would probably prove to be mediocre adoptive or foster parents at best.

Question 3 (For Applicants With Children in the Home):
Have Your Children Ever Been Referred to Undergo Counseling at School for Behavioral Problems?

1. No. School has been a positive experience for them.
2. To the best of my knowledge, no.
3. Yes. The school insisted, but I don't think it did any good.
4. Yes. My son was having some problems with a bully, and I think the counseling helped. My son and the boy who tormented him ended up being best friends.

Answers 1 and 4 are consistent with good parenting. In both instances the applicants were positive in their attitudes about their children's capacity to adapt to change, and they were not resistant to the mention of counseling as a tool for solving problems. Answer 2 is typical of individuals who are being evasive to the question or negative to the interviewer.

Answer 3 indicates hostility to counseling as a problem solver. You will want to question the applicant in more detail to determine why he or she feels that counseling was not successful, and you will want to determine why the applicant had a difference of opinion with the school on the need for counseling.

Question 4:
Have Your Children Ever Run away from Home?

1. No. Never had that problem.
2. Yes, but we no longer discuss that in our family.
3. Yes. It happened during a difficult time. My father was dying and I tried to care for him, but my children did not understand and felt rejected by me.

Answer 1 is what you would hope to hear from a promising applicant.

Answer 2 lets the screener know that the applicant experienced a serious problem with an issue that was never resolved. The screener must identify the problem through direct questioning and determine whether it is a present threat to family unity.

Answer 3 is reflective of a family that undergoes a problem for which there is no easy solution. The applicant's situation is certainly understandable. The question that must be addressed is whether the applicant did everything possible to keep his or her children from feeling rejected during a very stressful time for the family.

Question 5:
Have Your Children Ever Had Encounters with the Police?

1. No. They've never even come close.
2. Yes. But it wasn't their fault.
3. Yes. They were caught at a friend's house setting off fireworks. I don't think that will ever happen again.

Answer 1 is the best choice. Most children grow into adulthood without ever being arrested or cautioned by police officers. Adoptive and foster applicants should be drawn from a pool characterized by successful parenting.

Answer 2 is a source of concern. Your first duty is to research the incident with the police and learn the facts of the case. It is admirable for a parent to defend his or her children, but only if they are demonstrably innocent of wrongdoing. It may well turn out that the parent's defense of wrongdoing is more troubling than the wrongdoing itself. Depending on the facts of the case, this statement could be reason for rejection.

Answer 3 should not disqualify an applicant from receiving adoptive or foster children. There are no perfect children or parents. You should not be overly concerned about a fireworks violation unless the fireworks were being used to deliberately injure another person.

Question 6:
How Do You Discipline Your Children?

1. We use time out and withhold privileges.
2. We just give them a good talking to.
3. My parents had it right—spare the rod and spoil the child. Despite what the liberal media says, we've found spanking to be very effective.

Answer 1 is the preferable response. Time out and negative reinforcement have proved to be effective disciplinary tools. However, the applicant also should be educated on the usefulness of positive reinforcement when setting disciplinary standards (see Clark, 1985). A combination of the three techniques presents the most effective approach available to parents.

Answer 2 is acceptable as long as the "talking to" is not verbally abusive, but, even when used appropriately, it is too limited to be the sole disciplinary technique used to modify a child's negative behavior.

Answer 3 is totally unacceptable. Many of the children who come into the care of a social welfare agency have been physically abused. Placing those children in foster or adoptive homes where there is a possibility they could be further struck, slapped, or otherwise physically punished is not a conscionable option for a social agency. The admitted use of corporal punishment by adoptive and foster care applicants is reason enough for the rejection of the application.

Spanking

The National Association of Social Workers has a clear-cut policy on the use of corporal punishment: The use of physical force against people, especially children, is antithetical to the best values of a democratic society and of the social work profession. Thus, NASW opposes the use of physical punishment in homes, schools, and all other institutions, both public and private, where children are cared for and educated.

Dr. Alan E. Kazdin, the 2008 president of the American Psychological Association and author of numerous books on child psychology, considers spanking to be an ineffective strategy for controlling behavior: "It does not teach children new behaviors or what to do in place of the problem behavior. It is also not useful in suppressing the problematic behavior beyond the moment. Research indicates the rate of misbehavior does not decline, in fact, the problem behavior returns, even if the parent escalates the punishment" (American Psychological Association, 2010).

The most definitive study yet on the subject was undertaken by researchers at Tulane University. The study found that children who are spanked at the age of three are more likely to be aggressive by age five. Wrote Professor Catherine Taylor, who led the research: "The odds of a child being more aggressive at age five increased by 50 percent if he had been spanked more than twice in the month before the study began." (Taylor & Manganello, 2010).

The study further concluded that spanking sets a bad example, teaching children that aggressive behavior is a reasonable problem-solving alternative.

Question 7:
Did Your Parents Spank You on a Regular Basis? If So, Do You Feel That It Had the Desired Results?

1. Yes, they did. I think I turned out all right.
2. Yes, but I refuse to spank my own children.
3. No, they did not spank me. If the desired result was for me to grow up to be a nonviolent person, I think they succeeded.

Answer 1 is of concern because it suggests that the applicant seeks to justify spanking, in which case he or she may be a "closet" advocate of corporal punishment. This response would be of special interest if the applicant has already denied using spanking as a behavior management technique because it could be an indicator of deceit. Screeners must always be alert to the possibility that applicants will tell them what they think the screener wants to hear.

Answers 2 and 3 are both appropriate for applicants for adoptive and foster children. In one instance the applicant seeks to emulate his or her parents' positive behavior and in the other the applicant seeks to repudiate the parents' negative behavior.

Question 8:
Do You Consider Scolding and Statements of Disapproval to Be Appropriate Parenting Techniques?

1. Yes, it is better than spanking. I find it very effective.
2. I don't have anything against those techniques, but I have not found them very effective.
3. No. Every time I scold my son, he scolds me back. If I counterscold him, he has a temper tantrum. Sometimes it escalates into all-out war.

Answer 1 is the most appropriate response of the three given. However, parents should only resort to negative reinforcement if positive reinforcement fails. The determining factor in whether to use scolding and disapproval should be effectiveness. Therefore, Answer 2 is appropriate based on the applicant's declaration of ineffectiveness.

Answer 3 is a clear indication that the techniques should not be used with that particular child. Other signs of ineffectiveness are indicated by children who smile or ignore the parent when the techniques are used. In addition, a child who argues with a parent who scolds or expresses disapproval is making a clear statement about the technique's ineffectiveness.

In general, scolding and disapproval should be used only in serious situations in which the child's safety is at issue. For example, scolding would be appropriate to dissuade a child from running out into traffic or playing with fire. Minor infractions such as folding a newspaper incorrectly or brushing one's teeth incorrectly would require a lighter touch.

It goes without saying that applicants who have had experience parenting children have knowledge that applicants who have never parented children do not possess; but that does not mean that the screener should discriminate based solely on experience, because some experience may be related to inappropriate parenting. Whatever the applicants' experience with children, it is the screener's job to assess current or potential parenting abilities. To accomplish that, the screener must look for both positive and negative parenting attitudes and hope that the positive attitudes outweigh the negative attitudes.

If the applicants already have children in the home, or have grown children who have left the home, it is important for the screener to interview the children. Do they support their parents' desire for more children? Do they feel rejected by their parents' decision? Do they feel that they will be able to accept adoptive or foster children in the home?

Questions for Applicants Who Have No Experience With Children

Question 9:
Have You Ever Kept Other People's Children in
Your Home Overnight or for an Extended Period of Time?
If Yes, How Did You Feel When They Returned to Their Parents?

1. I often keep my niece and nephew when my sister goes on vacation or on overnight business trips. I'm always sorry to see them leave because we have so much fun.
2. No. I've never been asked to keep children.
3. Yes, I keep my brother's children from time to time when he and his wife go out of town, and on several occasions I keep children for my coworkers when they have medical issues that require them to be admitted to the hospital. Depending on how long they stay, it is sometimes hard on me when they leave. I cry for days.

Answers 1 and 3 are both acceptable. However, the individual who gave Answer 3 is more suited to adoption than to foster care by virtue of his or her stated anxiety about giving the child up at the end of the stay. As we have learned, one of the important characteristics of a successful foster parent is the ability to relinquish children without emotional turmoil.

Answer 2 is a cause for concern. Are there reasons why friends and relatives would not want their children staying with the applicants? Are the applicants antisocial individuals who like to keep to themselves? Is one applicant's spouse hostile to the idea of having children in the house?

Question 10:
As an Adult, Have You Ever Had a Dog or a Cat?
If So, How Did You Correct Your Pet When It Displayed Bad Behavior?

1. We smacked him with a rolled up newspaper.
2. We scold her and she usually gets the message.
3. We started out moving them away from whatever they did that we didn't like, while saying no in a very firm voice—and it worked. Now we just say no.

Individuals may discipline their children the same way they discipline their pets. If they hit their pets, they may hit their children. If they jerk their pet's leash, they may jerk the arms of a child. Answer 3 is the one that offers the most potential for parenting an adoptive or foster child, but Answer 2 is acceptable. Answer 1 suggests that the applicant is accustomed to using violence, however slight, to get what he or she wants. When a screener hears an admission of "smacking" a pet with a rolled-up newspaper, he should question the applicant closely about whether he or she favors spanking children who have misbehaved.

Why Pets Are Important

If you want to know how an adoptive or foster parent applicant will treat a child placed into their home, take a close look at the way they handle their pet. Someone who disciplines pets by hitting them, shouting at them, or otherwise displaying aggression toward them when they misbehave, almost certainly will display the same behavior to a child. Likewise, someone who is nurturing and affectionate toward a pet is likely to treat children with the same consideration.

Pets are also a good barometer for measuring abuse in the home. Research indicates that there is a connection between animal abuse, domestic violence, and child abuse. Actually, it is a vicious circle, with one category of abuse leading to another category. Thus, the abused child becomes the animal abuser and then subsequently the wife or husband abuser. Likewise the abused wife becomes the animal abuser and then the child abuser.

In one study, 38 women seeking shelter at a safe house for battered women voluntarily completed a survey that addressed pet ownership and violence to pets (Ascione, 1998). Of the women who reported current or past per ownership, 71 percent said that their partner had threatened or actually hurt or killed one of more of their pets. Fifty-eight percent of the women had children, and 31 percent of the women reported that one or more of their children had hurt or killed pet animals. Study author, Frank R. Ascione, a developmental psychologist and professor at Utah State University, concludes that "the research is pretty clear that there are connections between animal abuse and domestic violence and child abuse."

In another study of psychiatric patients who had repeatedly tortured dogs and cats, it was found that all of them had high levels of aggression toward people as well (Felthous, 1980; Felthous & Lockwood, 1998), and we are all familiar with the research conducted on serial murderers and their history of animal abuse.

Questions about pet care are important considerations for screeners. The goal is not to seek out serial killers, but to identify patterns of negative and positive behavior toward pets that may be indicative of behavior toward humans. You would never want to reject an applicant solely because they grew tired of a pet and gave it away or because they abused pets as a child, but those instances of abuse and emotional detachment can be used as investigative guides to pursue additional information applicable to a history of abuse and emotional detachment toward humans.

Question 11:
Have You Ever Had to Leave Work to Take Care of Your Pet? If So, Did You Get in Trouble with Your Boss?

1. Yes, but my boss was very understanding.
2. No, my employer has a firm rule about leaving the office without prior approval. It would take a lot for me to leave work.
3. Yes. I received a telephone call that my dog, Lucky, was hit by a car and rushed to the vet. I left in a rush and got there just in time to say goodbye. When I returned to work, my boss chewed me out and said that if anything like that ever happened again I would be fired.

Answer 1 is what you hope to hear because it indicates an employer that is likely to be understanding with a parent who needs to leave work on occasion to care for an ailing child.

Answers 2 and 3 raise questions about the applicant's ability to care for a child placed in his or her care, although it is entirely possible that an employer who would not allow an employee to go home to care for a pet would be agreeable to an employee leaving work to care for a child. It is not enough to be sympathetic to the applicant for having such a negative employer; the screener must consider the welfare of any child placed in such a situation. If the applicant cannot make acceptable arrangements for the care of a child during times of illness or injury (for both parent and child), the screener will be hard pressed to justify approval of the application. Of course, the screener will not reject applicants based on child unfriendly employment policies, but rather on the failure of the applicants to compensate for those policies with a well-thought-out plan for emergency care.

Question 12:
Have You Ever Given Away a Pet That You No Longer Had Time For?

1. No. Every pet I've ever had has been like a member of the family.
2. Yes. I hated doing it, but my new job was too demanding. The dog was better off being with someone who could spend time with him and provide responsible care.

3. Yes. I don't know where you're going with that question, but dogs aren't people. If having one becomes an inconvenience, you do what you have to do.

Answer 1 is the best response for an applicant that wants an adoptive or foster child. Generally, people who become deeply attached to pets are more likely to become deeply attached to adoptive and foster children.

Answers 2 and 3 are both flashing caution lights. Respondent 2 displays an ability to rationalize making painful decisions on an ill-defined altruistic goal. It is a small step from saying "the pet is better off without me," to saying "the child is better off without me." This individual may have a long history of taking the easy way out of difficult relationships. Respondent 3 is an individual that is opinionated and draws qualitative distinctions on life issues. It is easy for such an individual to make the leap from "dogs aren't people" to "it's not like the child is blood kin—she'll do just fine somewhere else."

Question 13 (If the Applicants Have Siblings with Children): *If Something Happened to Your Siblings, Would You Want to Raise Their Children?*

1. Yes. I would love to raise them if something happened to my sister and her husband.
2. Yes, I would be glad to do it. However, my husband would be against it since he thinks the children have been spoiled.
3. No, I don't think so. I was never that close to my brother.

Answer 1 is the response you would expect from a well-adjusted individual with strong nurturing instincts. Answer 2 is troublesome because it indicates that the husband is judgmental about certain behaviors and would not hesitate to deny care to family members. He would likely be quick to deny love and attention to adoptive or foster children who did not meet his expectations. Answer 3 raises questions about the applicant's motivation for wanting children in the home and the applicant's ability to maintain family relationships. The obvious follow-up question is why the applicant is not close to his or her brother.

Question 14: *Do You and Your Spouse Agree on How Children Should Be Disciplined? If Not, How Do You Differ?*

1. Yes. We were raised by parents who had similar views on discipline. We plan to raise our children the way we were raised.
2. Not exactly. He's a lot stricter than I am.
3. No, but we've got that worked out. I will discipline the children and he will decide what schools they attend and choose the organizations they are allowed to join.

On the surface, Answer 1 is the most appropriate. However, before the screener can proceed with satisfaction it must be determined exactly how the applicants were raised. How were they disciplined? How were they educated? The applicants' answer raises more questions than it answers.

Answers 2 and 3 are flashing warning lights on the subject of discipline. To move past this answer, the screener should establish the specifics of the conflicts that now exist. If the applicants disagree over the methods that should be used to discipline children (for example, if one partner believes that a belt or leather strap should be used to discipline children and the other prefers spanking their hands) it is of more concern than if they disagree over the issues that merit discipline because there is usually more room for compromise on issues than methods.

General Questions for Applicants With or Without Experience With Children

Question 15:
Do You Think That Children Have a Good
Understanding of a Parent's Need for Love?

1. Yes. They have an innate knowledge of a parent's need for love.
2. Depends on the child. Some children just naturally understand what their mother and father need and expect of them.
3. No. I think they have to learn that as they go along.

Answer 3 is the most appropriate response.

Research suggests that battered children often have parents who believe that children have an adult's awareness of what does and does not satisfy adult needs. Parents who abuse their children attribute adult qualities to them. In a four-year study of the parents of abused children, Brandt Steele (1966) identified a common denominator characterized by a demand for high performance and the satisfaction of parental needs. "In all our patients who have attacked children, we have seen a breakdown in the ability to mother," Steele concluded. "There is no great difference between men or women in this breakdown. By 'mothering' we don't mean the superficial technique of care, but the deep, sensitive, intuitive awareness of, and response to, the infant's condition and needs, as well as consideration of the infant's capacity to perform according to his age" (Steele, as quoted in Gill, 1973, p. 35).

Answers 1 and 2 are consistent with answers that potentially abusive parents might give. If the applicant indicates that he or she believes that children should understand their emotional needs, the screener should revisit the pet issue and ask if they think that pets that ignore an owner's needs should be punished. Generally, people with abusive tendencies believe that all living creatures, people as well as animals, "misbehave" because they care more about their needs than they do the needs of their masters (parents). That is an accurate assessment, of course; but the abusive personality takes it personally and believes that they should be punished, while a nurturing personality understands that there is no way for pets and children to understand the needs of an adult and they pursue corrective action with that in mind.

Question 16:
Have You Ever Been Shown Disrespect by a Child and Not Understood Why?

1. Yes—and it makes me furious!
2. No. I've been around children who ignored me when I asked them to do something, but I don't think it was disrespect. I think they just had other priorities.
3. No—and that's a good thing since disrespect is something I won't tolerate.

Respondent 2 has a good understanding of child psychology and displays a positive parenting attitude. Before a child is capable of disrespect he or she must be capable of understanding the concept of respect and its relationship to self-esteem. That is a concept that develops slowly in children. Typically, if an adult accuses a five-year-old child of showing disrespect simply because the child disobeys or "talks back," the problem is rooted more in the adult's faulty self-esteem than in the child's behavior.

Answers 1 and 3 are indicative of self-esteem issues, perhaps related to abuse experienced by the respondent as a child. If a respondent offers either of these responses, the screener should ask the respondent why they are deserving of respect. If the respondent becomes angry over being questioned about the issue, the screener will gain valuable insight into the respondent's potential as a parent.

Question 17:
From Your Experience, What Is the Best Way to Get a Child to Stop Doing Something You Don't Want Them to Do?

1. Spank their hands or buttocks
2. Send them to time out
3. Withdraw privileges
4. Put the object of conflict (a particular toy, television, and so forth) in time out
5. Allow the consequence of the misbehavior to naturally occur (such as when a child holds a cat too tightly and is scratched by the cat)
6. Scold them in a loud voice that lets them know you mean business

Answer 1 is the least desirable of the choices offered, followed by Answer 6. Spanking generates aggressive behavior in the child and scolding teaches children that shouting is an acceptable way of communication during times of stress. If you ever see a child shout at his or her parent, you can be reasonably sure that the child has been shouted at by the parent. Shouting and scolding are preferable to spanking, but the most productive alternatives are Answers 2–5. Of course, natural consequence discipline (Answer 5) has its limits. Although it is acceptable for the natural consequence of not doing homework to occur (a poor grade and perhaps staying after school), it is not acceptable to allow the natural consequence of riding a bicycle too close to the street to occur (a serious injury). The most difficult skill a parent has to learn is how to match the punishment to the misbehavior. Through trial and error, each parent learns what works best in a given situation. The purpose of screening is to determine exactly where the applicant falls on the learning curve.

Practical Parenting Issues

One of the first parenting issues that must be resolved from an adoptive couple is which partner will be the primary parent. Will either be a stay-at-home parent? If both parents plan to work outside the home, the screener must determine in specific terms their plans for physically caring for the child. Do they plan to hire a nanny? Do they have a relative who will help care for the child? There is nothing wrong with both parents working, but if their schedules are such that their child-care plan is to let someone else raise the child, the parents must demonstrate that they have an adequate plan that has a backup for unexpected problems.

If both parents plan to work outside the home, it is crucial that one parent take a leave of absence from work to stay at home with the child to be the primary caregiver. Different agencies have different policies on how long that should be and the time can vary from one month to six months, or possibly longer in some instances. The screener should make inquiries about what the applicants have worked out with their employers and then reconcile that with agency policy.

For foster parents, agency policy on whether mothers should have jobs outside the home varies according to the age of the children involved. It is unlikely that an agency would allow a foster mother to care for an infant or preschooler and hold a full-time job outside the home because children that age need stable, consistent care-giving from the caregiver who is the bonding target, but the policy may differ for individuals who want to care for school-age children. Agencies want foster care to reflect, as accurately as possible, the parenting norm in society as a whole and because most families find it necessary for both parents to work that reality is reflected in the foster parenting programs set up by most agencies.

Whether they are foster or adoptive parents, single or married, they should be questioned about their plans for alternative care in the event of illness or family emergencies. Who will care for the child if they have to stay overnight in a hospital or if they have to leave town for several days on business? If the applicant is single, they should be able to describe not only a plan for alternative care, but also a back-up plan in the event the first plan does not work.

It is not necessary for foster parents to articulate a long-term plan for the child because their involvement is, by definition, for the short term, but it is essential that adoptive parents be able to discuss their plans for long-term care. Have they chosen a guardian for the child in the event of their deaths? Have they purchased life insurance policies that are sufficient to provide for the child's financial needs?

Once an interviewer has determined that an applicant possesses none of the negative characteristics that would make him or her risky as an adoptive or foster parent, it is time to shift the focus onto those characteristics that make the applicant a good risk.

Children are egocentric in that they take love more easily than they give love. That characteristic is heightened in adoption for the simple reason that child–parent bonding fails in a higher percentage of cases involving adoptive children than with natural children. A good adoptive parent is one who will be able to accept the possibility that he or she may go through a lifetime in which they give more love than they receive. It takes a parent with a good self-image to be able to adjust to a one-way relationship with a child who frustrated friends and relatives might depict as "unappreciative."

Characteristics that adoptive and foster parents need to make them good parents to an adoptive or foster child include (Dickerson & Allen, 2007, pp. 138–139. Reprinted with permission):

- Optimism in the face of adversity. Adoptive and foster parents typically experience more problems associated with bonding and attachment than do birth parents. One measure of a parent's ability to deal with bonding and attachment problems is his or her ability to function in a family without frequent confirmation of the parent's contribution to the family. Parents that are able to navigate through the minefield associated with bonding and attachment disorders typically are optimistic, able to accept personal criticism, and able to demonstrate patience while dealing with situations that are not quickly resolved.
- Strong self-image. Good adoptive and foster parents will be able to deal with the likelihood that their child will one day want to locate his or her natural mother and father, and perhaps want to maintain a relationship with them as well. This is an area where the screener will want to engage in direct questioning and offer numerous "what if" scenarios to the applicants and be prepared to talk to them about their feelings.
- Positive attitudes about adoption. When and how to tell children that they are adopted is a gradual process that begins around or before age five and continues until the child is old enough to understand the more obvious implications of adoption. It is essential for the screener to determine an applicant's feelings about this very important issue. If the parent has negative attitudes about adoption, such as a belief that it represents a failure for the parent that she cannot have children of "her own," then those negative attitudes will influence the child's view of adoption.
- Flexibility (if an open adoption is involved). In open adoptions the child's contact with her birth parent may take the form of personal visits, or it may be limited to telephone calls and letters. This is becoming increasingly common with private agencies in situations in which birth mothers relinquish their children only on the condition that they are allowed contact with the child as he or she is growing up. If the applicant says that they can accept an open adoption, it is important for the screener to provide them with numerous hypothetical

situations and evaluate their response. If the applicant says that they cannot accept an open adoption, the screener should accept their answer and not pressure the applicant to change his or her mind.

- Ability to accept things as they are. Many adopted children enter adolescence with a deep sense of loss concerning their birth parents. It is not unusual to hear adopted teens describe that feeling as a "hole in my soul." It is important for the screener to look 10 or 15 years down the road into an adoption and discuss issues that are certain to arise. The only way that an interviewer can do that is with hypothetical questions: "How would you feel if a child you adopted as an infant and raised to adolescence spent her teens complaining that she had a "hole in her heart" over the loss of her birth mother? Would you feel you had failed?"

- Problem solving ability. Adopted children experience problems that other children do not have to face, such as pain-causing prejudice among other students and teachers, especially if it is a biracial adoption. Difficulties can arise out of routine assignments—writing an autobiography, for example. The screener needs to present hypothetical problems that the applicant can "solve." There are no pass-fail scores here, merely a greater understanding of the applicant's parenting potential.

- Ability to accept delayed gratification. Most adoptions and foster home placements provide parents with great joy, but those good feelings do not always arrive in a timely manner. It is not unusual for adoptive and foster parents to seek counseling over their perception that the love they receive from their children does not equal the love they give. The screener wants to be alert to comments that indicate an applicant's ability to be productive in delayed gratification situations. Hedonistic individuals seldom make good adoptive or foster parents.

Sample Questions for Interview About Adoptive and Foster Parenting Issues

Question 18 (For Open Adoptions):
If You Told Your 14-Year-Old Adopted Daughter That She Could Not Smoke,
and the Birth Mother Told Her That She Could Smoke,
How Would You Handle the Situation?

1. I would let her know that she will be punished each time she smokes.
2. I would let the social worker know so that she can reach an understanding with the birth mother.
3. I would have a face-to-face with the birth mother and suggest that we work together for the good of the child.

The appropriate response is Answer 2. The situation calls for a mediator, and the social worker is in the best position to serve that role. Answer 3 would be appropriate only if the two mothers have developed a working relationship in which they can speak freely to each other. Answer 1 is the wrong solution to the wrong problem.

Smoking is not the main issue here. The issue is the birth mother's bad judgment. Punishing the child for the birth mother's bad judgment will confuse the child and put a strain on the relationship.

Question 19:
If You Had Negative Information about Your Child's Birth Parents, at What Point Would You Share It with Your Child?

1. Probably never. Why burden the child with a parent's wrongdoing?
2. I would tell the child everything that I know. The worse the birth parent looks, the better I look.
3. I wouldn't tell unless the information was important to the child's development and I had been advised by a social worker that I should share the information.

Adoptive and foster parents often become aware of confidential information of a negative nature about the child's birth parents. There are not many situations in which it would be appropriate for the adoptive or foster parent to share that information with the child, especially if the child is of a young age. In foster care, information sharing is the responsibility of the social worker. In adoptions, parents have no right to disclose information to the child until the adoption is finalized, and, even then, they should use discretion about sharing the information. In most instances, the only time that adoptive parents should share information is if the child has heard rumors from individuals outside the home and the child is emotionally distressed about the rumors and the parent feels that the truth will be helpful.

Answer 3 is the most appropriate response, but answer 1 is not inappropriate in that it mirrors the Hippocratic Oath insofar as not taking action that could cause emotional harm to the child. Answer 2 is totally inappropriate and suggests an adoptive or foster parent who has a hostile attitude toward the birth parents, an attitude that could be destructive to the child.

Question 20:
Do You Think It Is Possible for a Child to Love Two Parents Equally?

1. Yes—I love my parents equally. I would expect an adopted child to love her mother and father equally.
2. No. It's human nature for a child to love one parent more than the other.
3. I would hope that an adoptive or foster child would love my partner and myself equally, but I think that depends on the level of bonding that has taken place.

All three answers are correct, even though that may seem contradictory. Birth children often love both parents equally, but that is not always the case, especially if one parent has been emotionally distant or abusive. The odds of adoptive or foster children bonding with both parents equally are more remote than they are for birth children. It is not uncommon for an adoptive or foster child to be closer to one parent than the other. It is important for adoptive and foster parents to understand that possibility in advance of receiving a child because not understanding it could result in tensions that could escalate to the breakdown of the placement.

Adoptive and foster parents sometimes experience an emotional letdown once they receive children. Adoptive and foster children don't always react to their new parents with undying love and devotion. With infants the odds of successful bonding are much greater than they are for older children. Sometimes bonding is a struggle that when it fails can lead to depression among adoptive or foster parents who have unrealistic expectations about the process. It is important during the interview process for the screener to have a frank discussion about this issue with the applicants.[2]

Question 21:
What Do You Think Is the Biggest Disappointment That a Parent Can Have with a Child?

1. If the child becomes seriously ill.
2. Children who don't love their parents.
3. Children who do poorly in school.

Parents have varying degrees of expectations when it comes to children. The screener's challenge is to determine the parameters of those expectations. Can the applicants cope with a seriously ill child? Can they deal with children that don't love them in return? Can they handle being the parents of children who have the worst grades in their class? The above question will help open that discussion.

Answer 1 is of concern only if the respondent feels disappointed with the child. If the respondent feels disappointed with life for delivering such a blow to the child, that is understandable and not of great concern.

Answer 2 is troubling because the respondent is broadcasting disappointment if their adoptive or foster child does not bond with her.

Answer 3 is of concern only if the respondent, upon further questioning, suggests that a poorly performing student would affect her feelings toward the child.

Question 22:
Do You Think That You Are Responsible for Whether Your Child Loves You?

1. No. That has to come from the child.
2. That's an odd question. Is anyone ever responsible for love?
3. Yes. If my child did not love me, I would probably blame myself for doing something wrong. Children naturally love their parents, don't they?

---

2. Karen J. Foli, an assistant professor of nursing and an adoptive mother, conducted an interesting study of postpartum depression among adoptive parents in *The Post-Adoption Blues: Overcoming the Unforeseen Challenges of Adoption* (Foli & Thompson, 2004). In the study, Foli concludes that some parents experience depression on the dual discovery that bonding with the child is sometimes a struggle and the realization that birth parents often enjoy a level of support from family and friends that does not always accompany adoptions.

Answers 1 and 3 are incorrect. If the respondent answers yes, it may indicate that she has low self-esteem over a series of events in her own childhood and feels hostility toward a parent that she feels should have done something to facilitate a loving relationship with her. She rationalizes that if it is not her fault, it must be the parent's fault. If the respondent answers no, she is putting blame on the child for something that is beyond the child's capacity to deliver.

Answer 2 is closer to the truth, but its acceptance as truth does take the parent off the hook for doing her best to promote bonding with the child.

Is anyone ever responsible for love? Yes, the parents are responsible for offering love and all its emotional trappings, even when it is not immediately offered in return by the child.

Sample Questions to Determine Capacity to Nurture Adoptive and Foster Children

There are many qualities that are essential to be good adoptive and foster parents. However, the single most important quality is the ability to nurture other human beings because it sets the standards for everything else that happens in a family. Some people have that ability; others do not. There is probably not a day that goes by that a parent somewhere does not warn a child that if he does such and such he is "no longer a child of mine." It is a type of emotional bullying that stems from the inability to be a nurturing parent. Adoptive and foster children, by virtue of their often stressful prior experiences at home or in foster care, need parents of above-average nurturing ability. It is not essential for both husband and wife to have strong nurturing abilities, but it is important for at least one of them to demonstrate above-average nurturing abilities. Unfortunately, there are no reliable tests to measure a person's ability to nurture others. The best measure of present and future nurturing ability can be found in past and present behavior.

Question 23:
If You Are Ill, Who Takes Care of You?

1. I take care of myself. I'm pretty independent.
2. My spouse does a pretty good job of taking care of me.
3. My mother mostly. My spouse doesn't have a great bedside manner.

Answer 2 is the preferred response. It lets the screener know that there is at least one partner who has nurturing abilities. Answer 1 is not necessarily a negative response, but it does raise questions about whether the applicant would expect a child to take care of himself. A follow-up question should address that issue. Answer 3 is disturbing in that it suggests that the applicant is more dependent on the mother than on the spouse. Would that dependence extend to situations that arise with adoptive and foster children?

Possible follow-up questions. If you are sick, who will take care of the child? If the interviewee says that a spouse, family member, or neighbor would take care of the child, ask if they have been approached about doing so. Advise the interviewee that you will need the names of neighbors or family members who would be agreeable to taking care of the child. Talk to the spouse during the individual interview to determine if both interviewees are in agreement on this issue.

Question 24:
If Your Pets Are Ill, Who Takes Care of Them?

1. My spouse and I do that together, or we take turns.
2. That's my job. My husband says that if I want a dog I have to take care of it.
3. I'm not sure what you mean by that, but we don't go out of our way. We certainly don't hold their paw when they're sick. We're talking about cats, not people.

Answer 1 indicates that the applicants have a well-thought-out plan to care for their pets when special care is required. They are likely to do the same with a child.

Answer 2 should make the screener wonder if the husband would have the same attitude toward an adoptive or foster child.

Answer 3 indicates that the respondent has the capacity to compartmentalize issues related to nurturing, thus making it possible for the respondent to justify a lack of nurturing abilities in a given situation. For example, "I'm sorry you have a stomach ache, but you should have washed your hands before eating. I can't stay home with you. You'll have to go to school and report to the sick room."

Question 25:
Tell Me about the Last Time You Nursed Your Partner When He or She Was Ill?

1. Last week. She stayed home with the flu and I left work several times to make certain that she was eating and drinking the way she should. She did the same for me last year when I took a nasty fall and was laid up for a week.
2. I don't think I've ever done that. We are both pretty independent.
3. I'm much better at that than my husband. He's a germ freak. He won't come near me when I'm sick.

Answer 1 demonstrates a couple with above-average nurturing abilities.

Answer 2 may suggest a couple with a nurturing deficit.

Answer 3 suggests that the partner's nurturing ability is hampered by a fear of disease. If he won't help his ailing wife, is he likely to help an ailing child? Would the nurture-reluctant husband be willing to accompany the screener and the spouse to a children's hospital and volunteer to socially interact with ill children? If the screener is skeptical of the applicants' ability to nurture an adoptive or foster child, a hospital trip could be helpful in making a decision.

Question 26:
When Was the Last Time You Made Dinner for Your Partner?

1. That would be . . . let's see . . . every day.
2. I'm not much of a cook. We mostly eat out.
3. We take turns.

What the screener is looking for here is a sense of the applicants' nurturing skills. Cooking for one's partner is a very nurturing enterprise. Do both partners exhibit the same skill and inclination, or does one partner dominant that area of the relationship?

Answer 1 demonstrates at least one nurturing partner, while Answer 2 is indicative of a couple that either has below-average nurturing skills or one in which both partners are so distant from the relationship that neither partner is willing to be giving. In that case, the screener must be alert to the possibility that one partner feels stifled by the relationship and is seeking a child for suppressed nurturing skills to be expressed. The other partner may be a coconspirator in that endeavor.

Question 27:
If You Hurt Your Partner's Feeling, Whether Intentionally or Unintentionally, How Do You Handle the Fallout?

1. I say, "I'm sorry."
2. I would say I'm sorry, but that only makes things worse. Better just to move on.
3. There's a big blow up. Then I have to be careful what I say for several weeks.

Nurturing gestures and arguments cannot occupy the same space at the same time. One excludes the other. This question is important because couples generally react to children the same way they react to each other. A family in which it is difficult for one partner to say "I'm sorry" to the other partner is one in which it will be difficult for children to say that they are sorry when they break the rules. It is a household in which children would grow up never hearing a parent say "I'm sorry," thus handicapping the children's relationships with their peers, teachers, and, ultimately, employers.

Answer 1 is what a screener should expect from a well-adjusted applicant. Answers 2 and 3 are indicative of relationships in which there are serious communication problems and very little nurturance from either partner.

Question 28:
When Your Partner Is Not Feeling Well, Do You Inquire about Him or Her During the Day?

1. Yes—several times.
2. No, it only irritates her. She thinks I am checking up on her because I don't trust her.
3. Depends on how busy I am at work. I always check in once or twice. I don't call a lot because she might be asleep and I wouldn't want to awaken her.

Answers 1 and 3 are both adequate to demonstrate nurturance, but the "several times" mentioned in answer 1 could be indicative of obsessive behavior. Three times a day may fall within the normal range of nurturance; 10 or more times a day raises questions about the nature of the relationship. Answer 2 is indicative of issues more serious than a lack of nurturance. It suggests that there may be trust issues in the relationship.

For Single Parents: Questions Related to Male–Female Bonding and Role Modeling

Question 29 (For Single Applicants Who Want Opposite-Sex Children):
Do You Have Friends or Family Members of the Opposite Sex Who Can Serve as Same-Sex Role Models for an Opposite-Sex Child Placed with You?

1. Yes. I have two siblings who live nearby and I have opposite-sex friends that I have maintained friendships with for years.
2. What does that have to do with anything?
3. No. I don't get along too well with members of the opposite sex.

Answer 1 is the preferred answer.

Answer 2 is an invitation for follow-up questions to determine the applicant's relationship with members of the opposite sex.

Answer 3 is indicative of an applicant who will have a difficult time providing a same-sex role model for a child placed in his or her care.

What Opposite-Sex Single Parents Should Know about Raising Children

Most parents understand the need for children to have contact with both sexes, but many ignore that need. Children need both sexes to contribute equally, but differently, in their lives. Before a mother can know how to take the place of an absent father, she must first understand the role that men play in her child's life. Before a father can know how to take the place of an absent mother, he must understand the role that women play in his child's life. Most parents find the truth about gender responsibility surprising, which is why so many of them make the same mistakes over and over again (Dickerson & Allen, 2006).

Children need attention, physical presence, affection, and guidance from both sexes. They need to feel protected and assured by the adults in their life that they are capable of taking control when necessary. A boy needs to be in the presence of a man who will be available to encourage him, take him places, talk to him, and guide him. The most qualified teacher for a boy is his male role model. Men can teach boys a value system, coping strategies, self-control, and self-reliance. Even when there is limited contact with a man, boys will find themselves becoming their male role models over time (Dickerson & Allen, 2006).

Mothers teach sons different skills. They teach them how to maintain relationships without exerting dominance. They teach them important social skills such as communication and self-expression. They teach them table manners. They teach them study habits. Mothers are reservoirs of love and understanding that children depend on for stability.

For the first year of life, daughters are more responsive to women than men. That is because during the first few months it is usually the mother who feeds her, talks to her the most, and holds her. At birth, daughters will recognize and prefer the sound of their female caregiver's voice to all others; but toward the end of the first year, daughters show a preference to being held by their primary male caregiver. That is because men hold them with more authority and tend to toss them around more aggressively during play, creating breathtaking sensations that are not soon forgotten by the daughter.

Men teach male children things that often are not taught by women: self-control and empathy, math skills, and respect for women. If that latter trait—"respect for women"—comes as a surprise, you are not alone because the myth is that mothers teach sons to respect women. In truth, boys learn to respect women from other boys or men.

Boys who grow up in families with strong male role models do not have the same need to dominate women and create exclusionary, all-male activities, as do boys who grow up in families with absent or uninvolved fathers. Statistically, the first group also leads happier lives. When happy and successful adult men are asked by researchers why they are happy and successful, they usually attribute it to happy and successful male role models.

It has long been understood that fathers teach their children math (Goldstein, 1982) and sports skills, but only recently have researchers learned that men are instrumental in teaching their children self-control and empathy, two critical skills associated with success and happiness. A 26-year study that focused on the relationship between parenting and empathy levels in adults found that the most important correlation between parenting and empathy was a man's involvement in child care (Koestner, Franz, & Weinberger, 1990).

That finding astonished mental health professionals, for in the absence of any existing research, they had assumed that empathy was a product of good mothering. To some people, empathy may sound like one of those throwaway concepts that have no bearing on the real world, but nothing could be further from the truth: Empathy is what enables people to be law-abiding and compassionate citizens (Popenoe, 1996).

FIGURE 7.1

PARENTING CHECKLIST

Do the applicants have experience with children?   ❑ yes   ❑ no.
If yes, what are their strong points?_____

_____

_____

If no, in what areas do they show potential?_____

_____

_____

What are the applicants' strengths as parents?_____

_____

_____

_____

What are the applicants' weaknesses as parents?_____

_____

_____

_____

Do you have any concerns about the applicants' ability to be good parents?

❑ yes   ❑ no.   If yes, explain _____

_____

_____

Would you be comfortable leaving your children (or pets) with the applicants
overnight?   ❑ yes   ❑ no.   If no, explain _____

_____

_____

How would you rate the applicants' nurturing ability?
❑ high   ❑ average   ❑ low

How would you rate the applicants' acceptance of agency policies?
❑ accepting   ❑ skeptical   ❑ oppositional

CHAPTER EIGHT

Applying the
Foster Parent Syndrome

Children seldom come into protective care for the express purpose of being placed in an adoptive or foster home (the main exception being children whose parents have died). For the most part when children enter foster care it is usually part of a comprehensive plan by a social service agency to provide for the child's short-term needs while professionals attempt to resolve the family problems that made a foster home placement necessary. Everyone's goal is to return the child to his or her birth family.

Each year over 300,000 children enter foster care in the United States. Combined with the children already in foster care, that brings the total number of children in care at any given moment to around 550,000.[1] About 84 percent of those children ultimately are removed from foster care and reunited with their birth parents, placed with relatives or nonrelated guardians, or emancipated, leaving about 16 percent that are placed on adoption (of those about 10 percent are adopted by foster parents.) (U.S. Department of Health and Human Services, 2001).

Clearly, being a foster parent is not a high-percentage shortcut to adoption.

The capacity to love a child on a temporary basis and then relinquish the child runs counter to the instincts that make good adoptive parents. It is largely for that reason that foster parent applicants should be viewed differently from adoption applicants. They have different needs, different aspirations, and different motivations.

Those differences were first noted in comprehensive studies by two researchers, Martin Wolins and David Fanshel, who while working a continent apart in the early to mid-1960s arrived at similar conclusions. Wolins was associate professor of social welfare at the University of California at Berkeley and Fanshel was director of the Child Welfare Research Program at Columbia University School of Social Work. Both sought to gather research to establish a baseline of data that could be used for improved selection of foster parents. Among their separate findings were that foster

---

1. See "Numbers of children in, entering and exiting foster care. (FY 2000) exhibit 1. www.childwelfare. gov/factsheets/fosterexhibit1 and FY 2006. U.S. Department of Health and Human Services.

parent applicants were primarily motivated by (1) a hope of financial gain;[2] (2) a desire by the husband to please his wife; (3) a need to put religious beliefs into action; and (4) a need to feel a general warmth for children. By contract, adoptive parents are motivated by a different set of considerations, beginning with the most common motivating factor—the inability to have biological children.[3] Other factors include the desire to build a permanent family, a desire by one partner to please the other, and because they feel a general warmth for children. Adoptive and foster parents share some characteristics (desire to please the partner and a general warmth for children), but they are unlike in the major characteristics such as a hope of financial gain, the inability to have birth children, and the desire to put religious beliefs into action (adoptive parents rarely cite that as a reason for adoption).

The findings of the Fanshel and Wolins studies were of great interest to James L. Dickerson, the coauthor of this book, because their publication preceded his employment as an adoptive and foster parent screener and served as a beacon. He viewed the research as fresh and innovative and he used their research to develop practical applications for the screening of foster and adoptive parents. In October 1972, Dickerson published an article in the *Journal of the Ontario Association of Children's Aid Societies* entitled "A Casework Approach to Foster Homes" in which he first introduced the concept of the "foster parent syndrome":

> With little research, the information that was available seemed to suggest that foster homes could be utilized as neutral territories for the child, freeing the social worker to venture into battle to combat poverty, injustice and a host of assorted psycho-social maladies. Since foster homes were considered to be 'cool' situations, casework was usually directed entirely toward the 'hot' situations as defined by protection caseloads. As a result, child care workers, usually the only workers to have contact with the foster parents, were each assigned dozens of children and encouraged, if not forced by their caseloads, to devote little of their time to the foster family as a unit . . . My experience has led me to think that there is in existence a foster parent syndrome which can be identified and documented as falling within the boundaries of distinct behavioral patterns. If these patterns are identified and catalogued prior to the placement of a foster child, the home accepted as existing within a framework of special needs, and the placement of a child into the home viewed as a problem instead of a solution, then the success probabilities of such a placement can be greatly extended, as long as there is constant casework being directed toward the family as a unit (Dickerson, 1972).

---

2. "A financial incentive was seen to be operating as a motivational factor for a third of the foster mothers and for two out of ten foster fathers" (Fanshel, 1966, p. 144).

3. Findings indicate that more than 80 percent of those adopting did so because of their inability to have birth children (Berry et al., 1996, p. 166.).

The foster parent syndrome is a motivational marker that allows screeners to group applicants in acceptable or unacceptable categories based on the basic needs that they seek to address by becoming foster parents. The satisfaction of some needs is consistent with being a good foster parent, while the satisfaction of other needs is not acceptable for a variety of reasons. The first challenge for the screener is to cleanse his or her intellectual palate of any notion that the applicants he or she is interviewing will prove to be neutral copartners in the agency's mission to care for children in need. Foster parents are individuals with special needs, and the measure of their effectiveness will be determined by whether those needs are addressed by having foster children in the home. The screener's job is to: (1) identify those needs, (2) determine if they are of a type that pose an acceptable risk for the agency, and (3) formulate a casework approach to working with the foster family once they have a child in their care (Dickerson & Allen, 2007).

Applying the Foster Parent Syndrome to Selection

When faced with screening foster parent applicants, the screener has two tasks:

- To determine the applicants' motivation
- To determine whether the applicants' motivation is in the agency's best interests

To perform those tasks, the screener should begin with the stated Goal (to receive foster children) and then work backward through a tangled obstacle course of Intrinsic and Extrinsic Motivations to reach the Basic Needs of the applicants. Intrinsic motivations are those that come from within the individual; extrinsic motivations are those that are imposed from outside the individual. Generally speaking, intrinsic motivations are more closely related to positive outcomes than extrinsic motivations.

The screener should begin the assessment process with the assumption that the applicants have well-defined reasons for wanting to be foster parents. The screener's job is to catalog the stated reasons and then determine the motivations so that he can isolate the basic needs that would be met by giving the applicants a foster child. You might call this process separating the wheat from the chaff. Common reasons include encouragement from religious leaders who recommend foster parenting; a need to put religious beliefs into practice; news stories; public speakers that present programs of foster children; a desire for increased income; the death of a child, pet, or close relative; to obtain a playmate for a birth child already in the home; because they identify with people having hard times; because it offers prestige within the community; to "undo" bad parenting experienced as a child; because the applicants cannot have a biological child; because the stay-at-home partner needs something to do during the day; because they believe it will make their marriage stronger; because of a strong paternal drive; because of poor social skills among adults; because of sexual, physical, or emotional abuse experienced as a child; peer pressure from neighbors or work associates; fascination with watching children grow up; to have close physical contact with "cuddly" babies; a general warmth for children; to help the less fortunate; to

FIGURE 8.1

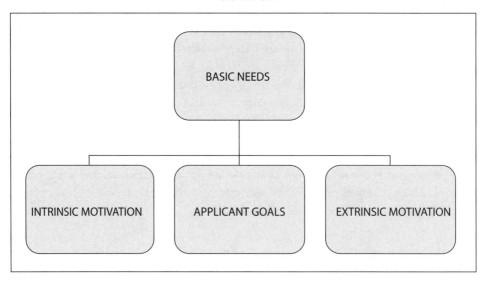

meet the expectations of domineering parents; for women, to have "something of my own"; lack of sexual intimacy in the relationship; and because the applicants enjoy the challenge of a difficult task.

The foster parent syndrome defines successful foster parent applicants as those whose basic needs are compatible with the basic needs of existing foster children, as identified and defined by their social workers. With that in mind let us examine the aforementioned reasons to determine acceptability.

- Encouragement from religious leaders who recommend foster parenting (extrinsic motivation)
- To put religious beliefs into action (intrinsic motivation)
- News stories (extrinsic motivation)
- Public speakers that present programs of foster children (extrinsic motivation)
- A desire for increased income (extrinsic motivation)
- The death of a child, pet or close relative (intrinsic motivation)
- To obtain a playmate for a birth child already in the home (extrinsic motivation)
- Because they identify with people having hard times (intrinsic motivation)
- Because it offers prestige within the community (extrinsic motivation)
- To "undo" bad parenting experienced as a child (intrinsic motivation)
- Because the applicants cannot have a biological child and would like to adopt (intrinsic motivation)
- Because the stay-at-home partner wife needs something to do during the day (intrinsic motivation)
- Because they believe it will make their marriage stronger (intrinsic motivation)
- Because the applicants enjoy the challenge of a difficult task (intrinsic motivation)

- Because of a strong paternal or maternal drive (intrinsic motivation)
- Because of poor social skills among adults (intrinsic motivation)
- Because of sexual, physical, or emotional abuse experienced as a child (extrinsic motivation)
- Peer pressure from neighbors or work associates (extrinsic motivation)
- Because birth or adopted children left the home because of college, marriage, and so forth (extrinsic motivation)
- To meet the expectations of domineering parents (extrinsic motivation)
- To have a close physical contact with "cuddly" babies (intrinsic motivation)
- To help the less fortunate (intrinsic motivation)
- Because of a general warmth for children (intrinsic motivation)
- Fascination with watching children grow up (intrinsic motivation)
- For women, to have "something of my own." (intrinsic motivation)
- Lack of sexual intimacy in the relationship (intrinsic motivation)

There are no nationwide "best practice" standards for acceptable motivations for foster parents. Each state has its own standards, resulting in wide variance from state to state; some states have no established standards, resulting in uncertainty within local jurisdictions. One reason for that may be the complexity of human decision making. It will be helpful to keep in mind that not all intrinsic motivations are acceptable and not all extrinsic motivations are unacceptable. In lieu of any enforceable practice standards for screeners, we recommend that screeners make decisions about application of the foster parent syndrome based on the aggregate wisdom of the social workers who approved the foster parents studied by Fanshel and Wolins, as defined by the frequency with which socials workers assigned identifiable motivations to approved foster parents. Based on that baseline (acceptable motivations are those that occurred with a 50 percent or greater frequency in the research group) we classify the above-mentioned motivations as acceptable, conditionally acceptable (acceptable as long as the applicants present some motivations from the acceptable list), or unacceptable.

Motivations Associated With the Foster Parent Syndrome

Acceptable

- To put religious beliefs in action
- Because they identify with people having hard times
- Because it offers prestige within the community
- Because the applicants enjoy the challenge of a difficult task
- Because of a strong paternal or maternal drive
- Because birth or adopted children left the home because of college, marriage, and so forth
- Because of a need to care for infants
- Because of a general warmth for children

Unacceptable

- To compensate for a nonsexual marital relationship
- Peer pressure from neighbors or work associates
- Because of sexual, physical or emotional abuse experienced as a child
- Because of poor social skills among adults
- Because they believe it will make their marriage stronger
- Because the applicants cannot have a biological child and would like to adopt
- To obtain a playmate for a birth child already in the home
- The death of a child, pet or close relative

Conditionally Acceptable
(If Applicants Display Two or More Acceptable Motivations)

- News stories
- Public speakers that present programs of foster children
- A desire for increased income
- To compensate for inadequate parenting experienced as a child
- Because the stay-at-home partner needs something to do during the day

Caseworking the Syndrome

In cases in which the applicants have experienced the death of a child, loved one, or cherished pet, the temptation is to ask, isn't it reasonable to give such an applicant a foster child to lessen the pain they feel over their loss? It would be reasonable if it was the social worker's job to lessen their pain. However, that is not the case. The social worker's job is to find the best homes possible for the children in the agency's care. From that perspective the worst thing that a screener could do would be to give a temporary child to someone who has experienced a painful loss, for they are likely to find it very difficult and painful to give up children placed in their care. Instead of being considered for foster children, the applicants should be encouraged to pursue adoption, whether they have lost a significant person in their life or a significant pet (a foster child is not a suitable replacement for a pet).

Likewise, any applicants who apply for foster children because they cannot have a biological child and would like to adopt should be encouraged to apply for adoption, not foster children. Individuals who have a motivation to adopt would be poor risks as foster parents because they may have a difficult time returning a child to his or her birth parents after caring for the child. Indeed, they may attempt to sabotage the child's relationship with the birth parents. Even if they demonstrated a willingness and an ability to return children to birth parents, is it fair to place foster children into homes in which the parents wish to "test drive" children in an effort to find the one that is right for them? Social agencies are not in the "rent-a-child" business.

A desire for increased income is listed as a Conditionally Acceptable motivation in situations in which the applicants also possess several motivations from the

Acceptable list. However, a financial motivation is unacceptable if it is the primary motivation. It strikes us as overly idealistic for social workers to entirely discount the appropriateness of financial motive for foster parents, when the social workers themselves are financially benefiting from their efforts on behalf of the children. Foster care requires teamwork—and that is difficult to achieve when some team members are deemed worthy of compensation and others are not.

Once the screener has explored the motivations attached to the foster parent syndrome and secured the approval of applicants who meet the criteria as foster parents, it is important that the screener apply that data when decisions are made about each placement. Foster parents should receive children that address their needs as defined during the home study process. That information should also be made available to the child-care worker supervising the placement. If the foster parents' basic needs are met, the odds of a successful placement greatly improve.

Case History

Mary B. was one of the agency's favorite foster mothers. In her mid-50s, she and her husband, Bob, had raised two children of their own. A third child, Bob Jr., had died of cancer at the age of three. Mary and Bob blamed themselves for Bob Jr.'s death, convinced that they should have been able to prevent their son from getting cancer.[4]

After Bob Jr.'s death, the tensions between husband and wife grew so strong that they separated for six months after the funeral. They reunited once they realized that their two surviving children needed them to work together as a family. Once Bob and Mary focused on their other children, they were able to rediscover the common bond that had defined their marriage and they forged a new relationships based on realistic expectations;.

The timing of Mary and Bob's application to be foster parents coincided with the departure from the home of their youngest child, who enrolled in an out-of-state college. By that point, Mary and Bob had reconciled their differences and come to understand that they were happier together than they were apart. They loved each other, but they were not in love with each other, as they had been when they began their family.

Mary and Bob were transparent in their motivation. Mary had a need to give hands-on care to a child whom she could hold and cuddle and whisper sweet nothings to—a child whom she could give a second chance for life, and Bob had a need to make up for his abandonment of his wife and children at their time of greatest need. Bob also had a need to please Mary and a need to prove his belief in her on a daily basis.

Mary and Bob were not a good risk for older children for several reasons. The screener felt that they would become attached to the point of dysfunction to older children that stayed longer than six months in their home and he felt that they would experience parenting disagreements based on unresolved conflicts rooted in the loss

---

4. Dickerson and Allen, 2007, pp. 39–40. This case history is reprinted with permission.

of their son. However, the screener felt that they would make good foster parents for infants who would be in their home no longer than three to six months, and they were approved for infants only.

The results were spectacular.

Mary was a rosy-cheeked woman who beamed whenever she saw an infant. Her initial interaction with them was a fascinating thing to witness. Each time the screener entered her home with an infant, her eyes locked onto the child with laser efficiency and her arms automatically extended to take the child. At that moment there was no one else on the planet except that child.

The warmth that the screener could see in Mary's face was felt by each infant that entered her home. She cared for three to four infants a year for 10 years and gave each child a wonderful new start in life. She cried with sadness each time the infants left her home, and she cried with happiness each time a new one came into her life. It was a type of stress that she and Bob could live with.

Mary and Bob were successful foster parents because the screener was able to get an accurate reading on their motivation, which made it possible for him to address their needs in a manner that posed minimum risk to the foster child and the agency. Equally important was the screener's ability to set perimeters for their use as foster parents by establishing a casework approach to their supervision.

Mary and Bob are good examples of the foster parent syndrome at work. They applied for children because they had separate, well-defined needs that could be met with children in the home. The screener could have rejected them because of their past marital problems, but he was convinced that they had something positive to offer to infants on a short-term basis. By taking a casework approach to supervising this couple, based on identifiable needs, the agency was able to help the couple come to terms with their grief by allowing them to receive altruistic reinforcement for their service as foster parents. Supervision of the home was based on an active casework approach. Mary and Bob were counseled on a regular basis about their relationship and the care of the children in their home. As problems arose over the years, they were worked out to everyone's satisfaction.

FIGURE 8.2

DISCUSSION

1. Are the applicants' needs to deal with grief involving the death of a child ever a good reason to approve them as foster or adoptive parents? _____

_____

_____

_____

_____

2. Under what circumstances would a marital separation exclude applicants from consideration as adoptive or foster parents?_____

_____

_____

_____

_____

3. Why were Mary and Bob not good risks to care for older children? _____

_____

_____

_____

_____

4. Why were infants acceptable for placement in this home?_____

_____

_____

_____

_____

5. Do you think this couple would have been as successful without active casework supervision?_____

CHAPTER NINE

_____

_____

_____

Understanding Your
Legal Obligations

Foster and adoptive homes must meet various requirements to become licensed. Sadly, in spite of the law and regulations, abuse of foster and adoptive children continues to be a serious problem. Concerns over different facets of foster and adoptive parent selection and recruitment have lead to an increasing trend in liability issues facing departments of human service agencies, and foster and adoptive parents. The single most popular alleged infraction is negligence.

Negligence is not the same as carelessness. Negligence is a legal term; carelessness is not. Negligence is the failure to exercise the type of care that a reasonable person in society would exercise under the same circumstances. Negligence can be an overt act or an omission of an act that results in harm. In a civil case, such as an abuse or wrongful death, frequently referred to as a personal injury case, there are specific elements that must be established. These elements are duty, breach, causation, and damages.

Duty

A duty is breached when a defendant knowingly exposes another person to potential damage. It is generally agreed that a person has a responsibility or "duty" to exercise reasonable care regarding foreseeable risks of harm that may rise from their conduct. Therefore, courts will look at a number of factors to determine exactly what a person's or agency's duty is. This may involve balancing a number of different factors such as the connection between the conduct that caused the injury and the injury suffered. Once a legal duty has been established, the next element is viewed: Was that duty breached?

Breach

The second element of negligence is breach. A breach occurs when a person's or agency's conduct creates a foreseeable chance of harm or an unreasonable risk of harm. In other words, a foster or adoptive parent, or an agency worker, must live up to a standard of care, to act as a reasonable person would under the same or similar circumstances to not cause harm. If there was a duty to behave in a certain way, and the parent or agency failed to behave reasonably, then a breach occurred. Although customs in a community or locale will not define the reasonable person standard, courts frequently will consider them in determining whether a person acted reasonably in a specific situation. In terms of supervision of a child by a foster parent, "every moment a youth is in a residential setting he or she must be 'supervised.' This may or may not mean they need to be in constant eyesight. It does mean that policies, procedures, and programs must be designed to minimize the possibility of "negligent supervision" (Pollack, 2007b) and thereby minimize the possibilities for negligent behavior.

Causation

The third element of negligence is causation. Causation may be viewed as having two parts: actual causation, and proximate causation. Actual causation can be determined through a "but for" test. For example: "But for the door to the swimming pool not being locked, the two-year-old would not have drowned." Actual causation is also commonly referred to as cause in fact. If actual cause can be established, then the next step is to determine whether the negligent conduct was the proximate cause of the injury. Was the harm resulting from an action reasonably able to be predicted? For example, was it foreseeable that leaving a 17-year-old child in charge of an eight-year-old foster child roasting marshmallows over a fire might result in the child getting his hand severely burned because he took the hot marshmallow off the stick?

An act may cause an injury to a plaintiff, but perhaps it was not reasonably foreseeable that the plaintiff would be injured. When an act starts a sequence of events that ultimately injures the plaintiff, but the plaintiff is significantly removed from the original act, the act may be the factual cause but not the legal cause of the resulting damages, in which case there would not be liability on the part of the defendant.

Damages

The fourth element of negligence is damages. To recover damages, legally recognized harm must have occurred. General damages involve pain and suffering. These kinds of damages cover injuries that cannot be given an exact dollar amount. Compensatory damages usually include medical expenses and lost income and wages. The purpose in awarding damages is to put the injured person in the position he or she was in prior to the injury. Courts generally award money to a successful litigant, with the exact dollar amount always in dispute. For this reason testimony will be offered by experts representing the plaintiff and the defendant as to the extent of pain and suffering caused by the negligence of the defendant.

Generally, cases involving complex child placement issues present issues that are not well known by members of a jury, and so testimony by expert witnesses can help

FIGURE 9.1

WHAT IS GROSS NEGLIGENCE?

A general definition of *gross negligence* is conduct or a failure to act that is so reckless that it demonstrates a substantial indifference, lack of concern, or disregard for whether an injury will result. Another aspect to the definition of gross negligence is that it constitutes a deviation from the professional standards so egregious that it demonstrates a conscious indifference to a professional duty. Determination of gross negligence is an issue of fact properly decided by a jury. An example of gross negligence might be when a Department of Human Services (DHS) worker places a severely asthmatic child in a home with foster parents who are heavy smokers and have numerous long-haired pets; in addition, the DHS worker fails to send the child's asthma medicine along with the child. Frequently, for a plaintiff to prevail, it may be necessary to establish gross negligence rather than ordinary negligence to overcome a legal impediment to a lawsuit. For instance, a state or county government employee who works for DHS may be immune from liability for ordinary negligence but may be liable for gross negligence.

Source: See Rothschild and Pollack, 2008.

clarify what happened. These experts offer testimony to assist the court and the jury in determining liability. In some states, to find liability, a court would need to find that gross negligence occurred.

Are Social Workers Immune to Prosecution?

It is well known that there is a severe shortage of foster and adoptive homes. For that reason, there sometimes is a temptation for screeners to overlook deficiencies in the prospective parents or placement. This is a temptation that must be avoided even though screeners for public agencies usually have some level of immunity from prosecution.[1] When individuals who work for government are sued for monetary

---

1. See, for example, *Abdouch v. Burger* (426 F.3d 982 [8th Cir. 2005]) and *Babcock v. Tyler* (884 F.2d 497 [9th Cir. 1989]; absolute immunity shields social workers to the extent that their role is functionally equivalent to that of a prosecutor); but see *Burton v. Richmond* (276 F.3d 973 [2002]; when a state department of human services affirmatively places children in an abusive foster care setting, the state may be liable for damages); and *Gray v. Poole* (275 F.3d 1113 [D.C. Cir. 2002]; qualified immunity covers social service workers acting as investigators, but when testifying as witnesses they are protected by absolute immunity). Qualified immunity is often afforded if the social work is involved in a "discretionary function" unless his or her conduct is clearly a violation of a statute or constitutional principle as with *Snell v. Tunnell* (698 F. Supp. 1542 [W.D. Okla. 1988]).

damages they generally are granted either absolute or qualified immunity. The U.S. Supreme Court has stated that qualified immunity is the norm, with absolute immunity the exception.[2]

That is not necessarily the case with social workers who work for private agencies. They may receive special consideration from a court because of the historical trustworthiness of their profession, but they do not have qualified immunity from prosecution because they work for private entities, whether their agencies are church-based or secular. If a screener for a private agency makes a negligent error, he or she can be held accountable in a court of law.

Abuse and death of children in foster care and adoptive homes can devastate the victims and their families. Ensuring that those responsible are held accountable, plaintiff attorneys try to secure for the victims and the estate of the victims the compensation and care they deserve. Sadly, in spite of the law and regulations, abuse of foster and adoptive children continues to be a serious problem. Concerns over different facets of foster and adoptive parent selection and recruitment have led to an increasing trend in liability issues facing departments of human services, and foster and adoptive parents. When a standard of care is not complied with, and there is a resultant injury to the child, a lawsuit may result. The allegation against the department and/or the worker will usually be an allegation of negligence.

The term "contributory negligence" is often used to describe the actions of an injured person that may have also caused or contributed to that person's injury. Where contributory negligence law is in force, if the plaintiff in any way contributed to his or her own injury, the plaintiff is barred from recovering damages. The extreme consequence of this approach has led to its being severely limited or abandoned in many jurisdictions.

The general increase in litigation has substantially changed the liability environment in which social workers operate. This environment has changed the fundamental structure of the child welfare profession. Today social workers may face greater risks for performing the same tasks they performed in previous years without difficulty. No longer are social workers viewed simply as good-hearted people. The more stringent standards and practices expected of social workers are being enforced through lawsuits. These changes might seem disheartening at first. But there is a bright side. Being sensitive to potential liability often leads to improved agency policies, controls, and procedures. Like it or not, higher expectations of social workers are here to stay. It is hoped that these expectations will lead to a greater emphasis on following legal and ethical behaviors. In doing so, we will hope to prevent unnecessary harm to children.

---

2. See *Harlow v. Fitzgerald* (457 U.S. 800 [1982]; absolute immunity is appropriate in limited circumstances—judicial, prosecutorial, and legislative functions—whereas executive officials usually receive qualified immunity.)

Social Workers Do Not Exist in a Legal Vacuum

Social workers sometimes get so caught up in the day-to-day stresses and emotional highs and lows that accompany the profession that they sometimes forget that they can be held accountable for their professional decisions, just as doctors, lawyers, and many other professionals can be held accountable. Whether a screener approves an application or rejects an application always has the potential of becoming a court case.

Experienced social workers understand that they are never more than one decision away from being called to a witness stand. The fear of that possibility has occasionally prompted social workers to misrepresent their decisions or camouflage their actions by creating false evidence. Social workers should understand the difference between misrepresentation of physical or verbal evidence and the actual creation of false evidence. Misrepresentation involves the willful giving of a misleading representation of the facts. Creation of false evidence involves the act of improperly causing a "fact" to exist. More often, critics and attorneys accuse workers of a willingness to misrepresent, selectively quote, and misconstrue information to support their claims and therefore to present an entirely misleading case. Rather than sticking to agency protocols and training, the workers sensationalize their documentation and findings in a misleading fashion.

To what extent are such allegations true? Do workers consciously or unconsciously misrepresent evidence, and selectively engage in systematic distortion? How often do they make deliberate efforts to mislead, deceive, or confuse their own supervisor or the court to promote their own personal or ideological objectives? How frequently are workers omitting or concealing material facts?

From a social work, legal, or judicial perspective, making a knowing misrepresentation is a serious ethical breach. The NASW (2008) *Code of Ethics* notes that "Social workers should base practice on recognized knowledge, including empirically based knowledge, relevant to social work and social work ethics" (p. 22). The *Code of Ethics* goes on to state that "Social workers should not participate in, condone, or be associated with dishonesty, fraud, or deception" (p. 23).

Dishonesty, shading the truth, or a lack of candor cannot be tolerated in child welfare services, a field of endeavor built upon trust and respect for the law. Whether or not child welfare workers deserve immunity from prosecution when they misrepresent or fabricate evidence is a question each state's courts are dealing with. A worker's misrepresentation or fabrication of evidence is particularly pernicious because it puts the whole field of child welfare in a negative light. There is simply no excuse for this kind of willful and egregious conduct.

Ten Things to Do to Avoid Being Named in a Lawsuit

- Adhere strictly to the standard of care.
- Be familiar with your state's laws and regulations.

- Do not do anything outside the scope of your expertise.
- Ask questions if you think your supervisor or administrator is asking you to do something you believe may be improper.
- Communicate effectively across the child welfare spectrum.
- Keep abreast of evidenced-based practice.
- Be aware of changing trends in child welfare practice through continuing education.
- Educate yourself regarding child welfare/legal issues.
- Make reasoned, safe judgments.
- Appropriately document your judgments and decisions.

What Should You Do If You Are Sued?

Courts, government agencies, administrative law judges, hearing examiners, and attorneys have the authority to issue subpoenas under certain circumstances. Upon receipt of a subpoena, social workers should contact their own attorney to discuss an appropriate response. Your attorney may be able to narrow the scope of the subpoena and make the timing of the response less burdensome. If you are sued, it is normal to feel angry and disappointed that your judgment is being challenged and the legal system is scrutinizing everything you did connected with a particular case. There is a temptation to discuss the case with lots of people. Resist this temptation! Do not talk with anyone unless your attorney approves. Talking with someone else about your case could inadvertently damage your defense.

What To Do About Your Notes and Records

The child welfare profession generates volumes of paper. Each state decides the point at which a legal duty arises to retain documents that might otherwise be discarded. You should familiarize yourself with these regulations. Although social work records are the summaries of discussions, exchanges, and agreements between nonlawyers, these records may be forced to be interpreted in an exclusively legal manner, something neither the writer nor any of the interested parties may have intended. This is not a shortcoming of human services, but a consequence of the "legalization" of the profession.

Recognizing this mandates that records be viewed as having human services and legal value, while acknowledging that ultimately it is the legal interpretation that may prevail. Thus, as long as records are subject to judicial review, social workers must attempt to conform their retention of those records to sensible legal standards (see Pollack, 2003).

Under no circumstances should a record be destroyed if it is presently or will soon be sought for litigation purposes. Even though the agency may have the "right" to destroy a document upon reaching the final retention date, it cannot do so if the intent is to deliberately and knowingly impede a lawsuit. Many states consider such action to be an obstruction of justice, usually a felony (see Pollack, 2003). However you choose to track records, you should keep them all in a single, convenient location. Keeping track of your contacts may seem awkward at first, but it is not hard to do. If you can get in the habit of being your own record keeper, you will never be sorry.

FIGURE 9.2

LEGAL CHECKLIST

(1) Are you comfortable with everything that you have written in your home study? Have you written anything that you will not be able to defend in court?

❏ yes   ❏ no

List any reservations you have here: _____

_____

(2) Have you been careful not to attribute to an applicant negative motives that are not based on fact?   ❏ yes   ❏ no.

For example, have you given the applicants a label (criminal, liar, cheater, etc.)

that you cannot prove? _____

_____

(3) Do you have a conflict of interest when it comes to processing an applicant's application? For example, did you have a prior relationship with the applicant? Have you ever had an intimate relationship with a member of the applicant's family? Is the applicant a friend of a friend? Have you ever had business dealings with the applicant? Yes answers to any of the above indicate that you should withdraw from the case and ask your supervisor to assign another screener to the case.

(4) If your decision is to reject an applicant, have you withheld any information of a positive nature about the applicants? _____

_____

_____

❏ yes   ❏ no

(5) Do you need to ask for a conference with the agency's attorney before making your recommendations to your supervisor?   ❏ yes   ❏ no.

If yes, please explain: _____

CHAPTER TEN

_____

_____

How to Make Recommendations to a Supervisor

Once you have completed your interviews and assembled your information, you must come to a reasoned conclusion about your findings. Do you want the applicants approved for adoptive and foster children? Or do you want to reject their application? If it is the former, do you want to attach any qualifications to your recommendation? If it is the latter, what are the reasons for rejecting the application? Can you back up your recommendation with facts?

Before you submit your home study to your supervisor for consideration, it is advisable to go through a checklist to determine if you have assembled all the needed parts:

- Have you done both individual and joint interviews with the applicants?
- Have you received replies from all the applicants' references?
- Do you have a report from the applicants' physician?
- Have you written an analysis of the applicants' relationship characteristics?
- Do you have a clear understanding of the applicants' parenting abilities?
- Have you ruled out any possibility of abusive tendencies?
- When you wrote the home study, did you describe the applicants' behavior or did you label it for convenience? If you presented your interviewees with labels—loving, hateful, psychotic, suicidal, and so forth—it is time to go back and start over again. Write about the behavior or the history of behavior that led you to make your conclusions, don't label.
- If the applicants have specified older children, have you explained that love is seldom enough to parent a child and that they should prepare themselves for possible counseling sessions at different stages of the child's development?

Before you attempt to convince your supervisor of the conclusions that you have reached about a particular applicant, take the time to carefully review your work, weighing every sentence for its potential as a spark for litigation. An error in judgment at this juncture can be damaging to both yourself and your agency. Words do matter. Start the self-evaluation process by asking yourself three important questions:

- Have you written anything that will put you or your agency in a position to defend a lawsuit that alleges negligence on your part?
- Have you overlooked anything in the applicants' history that would indicate a potential for negligence?
- Can you explain and defend everything you wrote in the home study?

Screener Recommendations

The vehicle in which the screener communicates with his or her supervisor is the home study. Once it is completed and the screener has made the case for approval or rejection and evaluated the legal risks, especially in the areas of negligence and invasion of privacy (usually defined as disclosure of embarrassing private information or intrusion into one's private affairs), thought should be given to how the applicant will react to portions of the assessment if the agency is one that allows applicants access to the home study. If that is the situation, the agency should have a policy on how sensitive portions of the home study will be handled. Applicants have the right to know why they were rejected or approved, but they do not have the right to read what others have said about them, including their spouse, family members, or physician, all of whom provided information to the agency on conditions of confidentiality.

If your agency allows applicants to read their home study, there should be a protocol for dealing with the confidentiality issue. It has been our experience that agencies that do not allow applicants to read their home studies are more professional in their evaluation and more successful in their placements. The reason for that is because screeners tend to be more honest in their evaluations when they do not feel pressured to withhold information that might be considered by the applicant to be unflattering or critical.

The problem with "editing" home studies for content is that can open the door to fibbing of a more general nature. Of course, there is a difference between misrepresentation of a piece of physical or verbal evidence and the actual creation of false evidence.

When the number of children who require care far exceeds the number of available foster parents, there is a tendency for screeners and their supervisors to lower their standards in response to pressure to approve more homes. Screeners sometimes broaden the range of acceptance in the belief that a foster home that presents some minor problems is better than no foster home at all. Martin Wolins calls this the "skimming" effect. He writes: "When the ratio of applicants to children is low (as in foster care), the agency is forced closer to the threshold and must often invade the risk area of the continuum, where poor homes may be numerous. The emphasis then changes from completely eliminating risk to reducing it as much as possible." (Wolins, 1963).

That is seldom the case in adoption because the ratio usually is reversed, with demand exceeding supply.

If Approval Is in Order

The approval of applicants for foster or adoptive care is a positive affirmation of their abilities to be good parents; it is not the absence of negative characteristics. If your attitude as a screener is that the applicants should be approved because you cannot think of any reasons why they should not be approved, you have failed your responsibility. There must be positive reasons for approving someone for foster or adoptive care and you must be able to articulate those reasons to your supervisor. When you describe the applicants, you should be as objective as possible and choose words that can be validated. For example, don't tell your supervisor that you would like to see the applicants approved because of "the great love they have for children." Social work does not currently have a statistically reliable measurement for love. If you use the "L" word, back it up with facts. For example, can you provide documentation that the applicants love children? Have the applicants spent time with children's organizations, donated money and time for children's projects, written articles or letters-to-the-editor in support of causes that affect children, or do they have documentation of instances in which they have put the needs of neighborhood children above their own? The only accurate measurement you have of the future is the history contained in the past; present affirmations of good intentions toward children have no scientific validity.

If you feel that the applicants should be approved, then you must describe in detail the parenting skills that qualify them for acceptance. Equally important to your ability to describe the applicants' parenting skills is your assessment of what kind of child should be placed with them. A screener who cannot articulate an applicant's qualifications for a particular type of child has not done his or her homework. Among the characteristics that a screener should have formed judgments about are:

- Gender—are the applicants better suited for a male or female child? Does one partner have a preference for one gender and the other partner a preference for the opposite gender? Are the applicants convincing if they say they can accept a child of either gender?
- Race—will the applicants accept a child of any race, or do they have restrictions?
- Religion—have the applicants specified a preference for a child of one religion, or are they accepting of any religion?
- Temperament—which personalities would be a good fit and which would be a bad fit?
- Emotional problems—what reason do you have to recommend that the applicants can be effective parents to a child with behavioral problems? Do they understand that older children may have a history of emotional or physical abuse that may require years of professional counseling?

Approved Applicants

Different agencies have different procedures for approving applicants for foster care or adoption. Sometimes approval or rejection is based solely on the screener's meeting with the supervisor. Other times agencies may have a placement committee whose responsibility is to approve or reject applicants. The committee may consist of the screener, the supervisor, and professionals from other departments within the agency.

If the applicants are approved, the screener will notify them by telephone and send them a congratulatory letter. It is useful for the screener to remember that the jubilation felt by the applicants will soon be tempered by the realization that adoption or foster care is not an instant gratification process. For that reason, the screener should stay in regular contact with the applicants during the waiting period so that they do not become discouraged as time goes by.

Grounds for Rejection

The screener is more than a mere collector of information; he is a psychosocial profiler who is expected to evaluate the sensitive data that he gathers. The screener must always be aware that an incorrect evaluation can result in the abuse or neglect of a child. It is important that every possibility for both positive and negative behavior be considered by the screener before a final judgment is made about the suitability of the applicants.

Because it is the responsibility of the screener to find the best adoptive and foster homes possible, his first responsibility is always for the welfare of the children who are dependent on him for protection. That responsibility frequently requires the screener to reject applicants who are not a good match for the children in the agency's care. Sometimes the applicants have personal problems that make them an unacceptable risk. Other times their rejection may be based on a history of poor decision making. It is seldom that one or more of the applicants does not have redeeming personal qualities that cause the screener to feel distress over the agency's decision. When it comes to adoption and foster care, few things are ever black and white.

Rejecting applicants for adoption or foster care is not a simple matter since the legal system requires the agency to presume that the applicants are capable of being good foster or adoptive parents unless it is proved otherwise. You cannot reject an applicant simply because you don't like them, or because you don't approve of their religious beliefs or their ethnic heritage. Before applicants can be rejected, the screener must demonstrate that he or she has examined the applicants as individuals and as a couple (if they have a significant other) and has weighed their strengths and weaknesses and can make an argument that their weaknesses overshadow their strengths. It is important to remember that no applicant is ever without redeeming qualities. In all likelihood you will be asking your supervisor or a consulting board to reject applicants who have positive qualities as well as negative qualities.

Checklist for Rejection

- Lack of financial resources
- Sexual abuse in the applicant's past that has gone unresolved
- Screener concerns about potential pedophilia
- Alcoholism or drug addiction
- History of spousal abuse, either as victim or abuser
- Inadequate socialization

- Alienation from family members
- Membership in a radical organization that advocates violence against minorities
- A history of unresolved relationship difficulties (individuals who make the same bad relationship choices over and over again)
- Hostile statements or attitudes toward the country of origin of a prospective adopted child
- Arrests or convictions for assault, substance abuse, or drug trafficking
- Poor health prognosis
- History of serious mental illness
- Poor parenting skills

The above list is one of *possible* reasons for rejection. Some of the individual items on the list are cause for outright rejection, but other items should be considered part of an accumulative pattern of behavior and evaluated accordingly.

Sometimes there is an element of bonding that takes place between the screener and the applicants. They may be of similar age and background, or they may have compelling life narratives that resonate with the screener. In those instances it is important for the screener to remember that his or her primary job is to select the best possible adoptive and foster parents for children who cannot make those decisions themselves. We have known screeners who looked the other way to disturbing flaws because they liked the applicants so much, or because they made an attractive couple, or because they shared the same social and religious values as the screener. Experienced supervisors know that can happen, which is why they sometimes pressure a screener to explain his conclusions about individual applicants.

Rejection Procedures

When rejection is necessary the most appropriate way to notify the applicants is by mail. Telephone rejections, especially if they arrive at an awkward moment when family members or friends are visiting, can be especially painful for the applicants. A written notification serves several purposes. First, it eliminates confusion about the agency's decision, as can sometimes happen in a telephone conversation. Second, it allows the applicants time to adjust emotionally to the rejection, time to collect their thoughts, especially if they are the type of individuals who would want a more thorough explanation from the screener.

Notifications in person are the least desirable way to reject an application. Not only does it open the screener up to possible verbal or physical abuse, but it also puts the applicants in the embarrassing position of trying to be gracious to someone who has dealt them an emotional setback, and it may set them up to say things they would never consider saying if they had time to give it thought.

The rejection letter should notify the applicants of the agency's decision, but the screener should choose only the most general reasons possible for the rejection. That is not conflict avoidance; it is a means of providing the applicants with space to discuss the letter with each other or with family members. If the applicants want more information they will request a face-to-face meeting with the screener. If that happens, the screener should prepare for one of the most difficult interviews that he or she will ever experience.

Few social workers are trained in the art of rejection. They are taught to be supportive, reasonably optimistic, and empathetic to an individual's emotional pain. For that reason, rejection interviews require a great deal of preparation. If the rejection was based on confidential information received from a reference, the screener must be very careful about what he or she says to the applicants. That's a nice way of saying you can't tell the truth, the whole truth, and nothing but the truth. You have an obligation to protect the individuals who went out on a limb to provide you with information critical to your decision making. You also have an obligation to help the applicants understand why their application was not approved. Your challenge is to conduct an interview in which everyone's rights are respected, including your own.

Unfortunately, you cannot do what individuals do when they break up with a significant other. You cannot say, "It's not you—it's me," as a way of gently letting them down. It most certainly is *them*. You cannot tell them, "It's nothing you have done." It *is* something they have done, something that the issue of confidentiality prohibits you from explaining. You have to explain your reasons for rejecting them without being so specific that you betray the confidential source that provided information to you.

The applicants may be combative or they may be tearful or they may have baffled expressions on their faces. Regardless of the applicants' demeanor, the screener should be polite and professional. He should avoid the temptation to be overly friendly to compensate for the rejection. No one who has had their hopes dashed wants to be greeted by a grinning glad-hander. The screener's coworkers who work in protection or child care seldom have to reject individuals who have approached the agency for help. Rejection itself runs counter to every instinct that a social worker possesses.

There is a line from a well-known movie that goes, "When you kill someone, you take away everything they have and everything they ever will have." So it is with adoptive and foster parent rejections. When you take away an applicant's dream of adopting or fostering children, you take away their vision for the future. Unlike job rejections, when the applicant can be encouraged to continue searching, adoptive and foster parent rejections are often the end of the line. If the applicants are rejected by a private agency, it is unlikely that they will be approved by a public agency, and vice versa. Research indicates that while rejection lowers mood and self-esteem, the primary cause of hurt and distress is the loss of control that is felt by the persons rejected.[1] That is the major reason the applicants have come to the office for a face-to-face interview with you: To find a means of gaining control of a very painful situation.

---

1. Jonathan Gerber, a PhD candidate at Macquarie University in Australia, analyzed 88 existing rejection research studies to arrive at his conclusion that loss of control is the factor that most affects those who have been rejected for one reason or another. His unpublished research was promoted by the university.

If the applicants are unhappy with your explanation for their rejection, you should explain the options they have for appeal. One option is for them to talk to the supervisor and ask for reconsideration. Often such a meeting will satisfy the applicants' desire to know that the rejection was based on something other than the screener's personal opinion. Another option is an appeal to the agency's governing board. All those considerations aside, the screener has an obligation to the applicants not to destroy their relationship with each other or with family members or close friends. There will be instances in which the screener can take the pressure off himself by pointing a finger at the spouse or a relative or a friend, but he must resist the temptation to do so.

Of course, it is essential for screeners to remember that the applicants have a right to file a lawsuit if they feel that they have been unfairly treated during the application process. There is no constitutional right to adopt or be a foster parent, but there are legal issues associated with the process itself that may attract the attention of the court system: for example, racial or gender discrimination, or professional negligence, or, if the screener has been careless or malicious with home study descriptions of the applicants, creating an invasion of privacy.

Writing home studies of individuals who have applied for adoptive or foster children is a serious undertaking that can make or break the lives of the individuals who have submitted to the process—and put at risk the lives of innocent children for whom the screener is responsible, both morally and legally. Screeners should always view that process with the respect and seriousness that it demands. Lives hang in the balance.

PART TWO

Psychological Assessment

The Power of the Question: When to Consult Psychologists During the Home Study Process

Social workers are typically the interviewers responsible for screening adoptive and foster home applicants in the home study process. Chapters 1 through 10 of this book prepare screeners for this task. If the social worker adheres to this process, informed decisions can be made in most cases without need of further consultation. However, some cases will need further assessment to delve deeper into relevant psychological issues. By adding the informed opinions of a consulting psychologist who provides expertise from a different perspective, screening and placement decisions can be strengthened.

Test Your Decision-Making Skills

If a Screener Finds Ambiguity in the Data, He or She Should Always

1. err on the side of safety and deny the applicant.
2. schedule the applicants for additional interviews.
3. refer for psychological consult.
4. give the applicant the benefit if the doubt and approve placement.

Answers 2 and 3 are the best response. We recommend a psychological consult in any case where behavioral ambiguity exists and data does not clearly dictate approval or denial. Although a psychological assessment adds time and expense, it yields better predictive value to the overall evaluation of the parents.

A Psychological Consult Is Helpful When Placing Children with Behavioral Problems

1. in making initial placement decisions
2. in making preplacement training recommendations
3. in making postplacement recommendations
4. in all of the above situations

Answer 4 is best. Social agencies have multiple responsibilities in the foster and adoptive process. Social workers not only conduct the screening to determine if an applicant will be approved for placement of a child, but also they prepare the parent for receiving a child and then later are responsible for evaluating parenting abilities after placement.

Psychological consultations are beneficial for identifying any specific focus of training needed by adoptive and foster parents after placement. Some parents who are approved to have a foster or adoptive child often need to address troublesome behavioral issues that arise during the placement. Since psychological consultations are designed to provide solutions to behavioral problems, the evaluation results can be invaluable. Being willing to acknowledge the need for assistance is the most responsible and ethical action for a screener. Even if the agency denies the screener's recommendation for a psychological consultation, the screener should document the recommendation.

To Get the Best Evaluation from a Psychologist, a Screener Should

1. be vague so as not to bias the psychologist
2. tell the psychologist exactly what test should be administered to the applicant
3. have the psychologist perform a parallel evaluation as a test of the veracity of the applicant's responses
4. none of the above

Answer 4 is the best choice. Any psychological consultation that is a part of the screening process is always undertaken in collaboration. The psychologist should never work without all the data gathered by the screener prior to the referral. The psychologist is called in to add psychological expertise only. The screener should feel comfortable suggesting particular tests that they have found helpful in making placement decisions. The psychologist has different expertise and is not assessing the screener's skills. They must feel comfortable with their partnership or it will be a disservice to the applicant.

It is important for the screener to frame the referral question in a way that will guide a psychological consult to provide the most valuable data most efficiently. Later we will discuss the type of assessments that may be needed, what style of reporting is best, and how to increase the likelihood the psychologist will make relevant recommendations.

When More is Needed

Only the screener has spent hours with the applicants and has the benefit of the information obtained during the interview process. In earlier chapters, screeners learned how to assess applicant responses to direct questions, learned how to evaluate information offered without questioning, learned what to look for during naturalistic home environment visits, and learned how to sort through conflicting information obtained from applicants or collateral sources. These tools are critical in determining approval, denial, or whether further evaluation is needed.

Most applicants are eager to know if they are approved for adoptive and foster children, even if they must adjust to specific caveats such as limiting the age range of children that they are approved for, or requiring psychotherapy, or parenting training. No matter how eager or genuine the applicant may be, screeners must not hesitate to ask an applicant to cooperate in seeing a consulting psychologist if warranted. Anytime there is the slightest suspicion of uncovered data that could influence agency decisions, it is in the best interest of all parties for the applicants to be referred for further evaluation.

Agencies should vigilantly guard against influencing their screeners to not recommend further evaluation for fear of losing an applicant. Understandably, agencies often have limited financial resources, and the added expense of a psychological consultation can be troublesome. The applicants' unwillingness to cooperate with a psychological consultation may, by the refusal itself, provide valuable data that may negatively impact approval and placement decisions.

Telling What You Already Know

A screener should not ask a psychologist to gather the same information that was gathered during the home study interviews. The purpose of consultation is to fill in the gaps in the evaluation, not to provide reliability to the screener's opinion.

The screener should provide all relevant background history of the applicant, including education, work history, health, current mental status, and significant relationships with children and others to the psychologist. The screener should provide a brief description of the applicant's family history of mental illness, trauma, cognitive deficits, neglect, and sexual or physical abuse.

List any standardized tests or questionnaires that were administered and the results. Describe the applicant's affect, general appearance, speech patterns, self-awareness, and any other specific features of the applicant. Offer the screener's insight into the applicant's level of comfort with the home study process and if that comfort level changed in the presence of others. Rate the applicant's social skills and provide examples of strengths and weaknesses as applicable. Include as many clinical observations and impressions as possible. Do not hesitate to include conflicting information; just be sure to identify it as such. In fact, conflicting information is a major reason for referrals.

The most important aspect of making a good referral is stating information in behavioral terms. Sharing what the applicant does in terms that are easily visualized, avoiding excessive descriptions about how he feels or thinks. As mentioned earlier, terms that evoke different definitions for different people such as emotional problems, poor attitude, sloppy, and inconsiderate, may create different expectations for the screener and psychologist. Seek professional uniformity in describing the applicant. In addition to describing the "what" in behavioral terms, provide the psychologist the "when," how frequently, and under what circumstances.

The screener should provide the psychologist with their professional impressions that may explain the behaviors of concern. A referral may evolve out of a lack of plausible explanations for behaviors. Usually the screener and agency have formulated possible hypotheses about the applicants before a referral but may not have sufficient evidence to approve or reject an applicant.

Asking the Questions

You get what you ask for. Unfortunately, most psychologists are only asked to do a "psychological evaluation." So, the psychologist who submits a two-, six-, or 10-page document that adds nothing, or goes in the wrong direction, or only repeats already gathered data, under the guise of a "psychological evaluation," has not contributed defining data to the agency that has requested the evaluation.

It is the screener or agency's responsibility to ask the psychologist clear questions at the time of a referral. Be specific as to what has been found and what is being asked of the consultant. The applicant deserves a comprehensive assessment if there are issues that may impact the placement decision. Being vague and encouraging the consultant to "fish around or see what you think" is not an appropriate referral. When a screener gives little, they receive little in return. Worthless details and ideas that are poorly formulated only contribute to agencies spending time and money to pay for a psychological evaluation that misses the mark. Basically, the strength of a psychological consultation is dependant on the thoroughness of the referral from the screener or agency (Dickerson & Allen, 2007, p. 172).

Asking a psychologist to determine the etiology or actual cause of a behavior is an inappropriate referral question. Usually, psychological evaluations are most helpful in determining current mental functioning rather than determining causation. Of course, as a result of a psychological evaluation psychologists can attribute specific behavioral symptoms to specific mental diagnoses. This does not determine etiology, but can help understand the "why" of behaviors. There are usually far too many contributing factors to actually determine causation. In addition, seeking answers to the etiology of behaviors is not within the realm of responsibilities for screening foster and adoptive parents.

Screeners would delight in having answers to exactly what will happen in the future. Asking for a prognosis is typical and appropriate. However, no psychological procedure can guarantee exactly what will happen in the future. Psychological tests, skilled clinicians, along with familiarity with relevant research, can offer a good idea of what to expect. Because most of us respond or react in a similar manner, studying how others have responded to similar situations has offered professionals a fairly reliable blueprint of what to expect in similar circumstances. This level of predictability can help inform pre- and postplacement decisions.

Channing has been married 12 years and has tried unsuccessfully to get pregnant for the past 10 years. She says she is ready to let go of her desire to get pregnant and feels adoption is what life has for her. She smiles frequently and repeats that adoption is a wonderful opportunity to give love to a child. She describes herself as someone who has a lot of love to give and someone who is ready to get on with her life. During the screening Channing tears up frequently but quickly controls it and smiles. Her husband, Matt stated that his wife seems obsessed with how an adoptive child may look, wanting the child to physically resemble one of them. Matt is just ready to have a baby in the house to put his wife out of what he calls "her misery."

1. Do you feel a psychological consultation is warranted?
2. Why?
3. If so, what might be the referral question be?

Yes, a referral is warranted if the screener suspects pathology in Channing's responses and in Matt's use of the word "obsessed." The psychologist will need to determine whether Channing is depressed and is still grieving the news that she cannot have a biological child. The evaluation will need to address how realistic both applicants' expectations are for dealing with the challenges of adoption.

The referral question may be similar to: "Please offer your professional opinion concerning the applicant's personal grief process, plus any psychological diagnoses and applicable recommendations to pre or post placement."

Brandon and Allie, an unmarried couple who applied to adopt an infant, appear to have a good time together and seem very much in love. They have lived together for over a year and have strong ties to both families. Brandon's family is described as laid back and has few rules or limits. He and his family drink nightly, allowing the teenagers in the family to have a beer from time to time. Brandon and his family lived a comfortable life, although money was not plentiful. Allie and her family are supporters of many community and church events. She attends church each week with her parents and feels that her values are rooted in her religious affiliation. Brandon teases her about being emotionally dependent on her parents. The couple seems to have found middle ground for both to have their separate lives but to be happy together. Upon further inquiry, it is revealed that Allie's parents are recovered alcoholics. Her father has a history of gambling and abusive behavior, but her parents both stopped drinking two years ago. She is unusually protective of her father and claims he is a changed man and will be a wonderful example for her child. The couple insists they respect one another's feelings and don't believe their differences will now become a problem after adoption.

1. Do you feel a psychological consultation is warranted?
2. Why?
3. If so, what might be the referral question be?

Yes, a psychological consultation is warranted for two reasons: (1) if Allie denied physical or sexual abuse by her father during interviews with the screener, and (2) if the screener is unable to resolve concerns about Brandon's problems with alcohol and Allie's acceptance of his drinking. Brandon and Allie's different values are being ignored now but may fester and later emerge under the pressure of parenting a child. Allie's immediate unconditional acceptance of her father does not seem to have a healthy basis. Her choice of a partner who is a heavy drinker is a red flag and must be explored. A referral to a psychologist may be similar to: "Please offer your professional opinion of the readiness of this couple to parent an infant, addressing issues associated with possible sexual abuse and alcoholism, plus your assessment of any mental health challenges that should be considered in evaluating the applicants."

> Jennifer is a 37-year-old, well educated, single female. She was divorced 4 years ago and has dated off and on. Her home study revealed a seemingly well-adjusted adult who has a good understanding of the commitment and challenges associated with parenting foster children. She does not want to consider adoption at this time because she would like to find the right man, get married, and let that relationship dictate their future. She has a close relationship with her three nieces and has been left in charge of them for days at a time. She seemed to have realistic expectations of childhood behavior and skills in applying positive discipline. She was willing to only give brief responses about her marriage and divorce. She repeated that it was a mistake from the beginning and that she'd fallen in love in college when all the other girls were getting engaged. All of her references were exceptional. Everyone seems to describe her as "almost too perfect." The screener's concern is with Jennifer's potential stability as a foster home. Is she capable of maintaining the status quo for the duration of a child's need for care, say 10 years? Does she have the relationship skills to choose a partner who will be accepting of a foster child in the home? If forced to choose between a new partner and the child, will she choose the child?
>
> 1. Do you feel a psychological consultation is warranted?
> 2. Why?
> 3. If so, what might be the referral question be?

No, a psychological consult does not seem warranted, given this information. Psychologists do not have access to crystal balls. In this instance, the screener should schedule follow-up interviews that can gather sufficient data to establish a pattern of relationship choices by the applicant. Does the screener think that Jennifer will remain single for the duration of the need for foster care? Does Jennifer have a history of relationship choices that demonstrate her willingness to stand up for what she believes is right—in this case, the foster child who has been entrusted to her? Will she choose a partner who will support her decision to have a foster child in the home? There are no tests that a psychologist can administer that will answer those questions? The answers must be derived from a careful analysis of Jennifer's relationship history.

> Austin reported several traumatic losses early in his life. None of his responses seemed unusual or created any doubt in his potential to provide a strong and

supportive family for adoptive or foster children. He reported that he has never talked to anyone about his near-death experiences and the loss of both parents at an early age. He stated that he is better off leaving all of that in the past and making a new life. Austin has never been married and has no close relatives. He appears to be somewhat of a loner, but makes a good impression. He has held the same job for 15 years.

1. Do you feel a psychological consultation is warranted?
2. Why?
3. If so, what might be the referral question be?

Yes, a referral is warranted. The signs and symptoms of isolation, no close relationships, and refusal to deal with his past trauma are not consistent with a mentally healthy individual. Austin apparently can hold himself together for extended periods of time (that is, at work, during interviews), but there are some disturbing elements in his behavior that suggest the need for further evaluation.

A referral may be similar to the following: "Please offer your professional opinion on what effect the applicant's past trauma may have on his ability to handle the parenting challenges of foster or adoptive children and applicable recommendations for pre- or post-placement."

Chelsea appeared to be a charming mother of two. She and her husband, Scott, have been married five years. During their home study they freely discussed having some ups and downs in their marriage, including once being separated. Scott declared his love for Chelsea and described her as a mother who is defined by her children. He suggested that Chelsea can be intense and a perfectionist. She frets over everything about the girls. Nothing is good enough, clean enough, or safe enough for them.

With a nervous laugh, Scott describes his wife as, "too perfect, but no one can be too perfect when it comes to being a mother." The screener has exhausted all avenues of examining the applicants without obtaining enough data to make an informed placement decision. While conducting the home study with Chelsea, the screener felt that she tried to befriend the screener, became too dependent, and needed the screener to cross professional lines to validate her. She seemed to be fragile, yet harshly rigid.

1. Do you feel a psychological consultation is warranted?
2. Why?
3. If so, what might be the referral question be?

Yes, a psychological consultation is warranted. Chelsea's behavior is confusing for many, but it could be symptomatic of a personality disorder. Her husband's behavior is rather typical of a spouse living with an individual with borderline personality disorder. A referral may be similar to the following: "Please offer your diagnostic impressions of the applicants and your professional opinion of the effects on the family if approved for placement of a foster or adoptive child. Please include applicable recommendations for pre- or post-placement."

The Evaluation

This book is primarily written for social workers, but it would benefit psychologists who provide consultations for social agencies to become familiar with the content. The consulting psychologist needs to understand the model presented and the expectations for a psychological evaluation. They must know how the home study process works, the responsibilities of a screener, and when a referral is appropriate. Psychologists will appreciate the contributions they can make to foster and adoptive children by providing relevant evaluation and reports.

After receiving a referral the consulting psychologist should clarify any misleading or conflicting requests of the screener. Asking for specificity can help minimize errors. Most psychologists use professionally recognized tests for assessments. The tests are standardized and evaluated for the appropriateness for use with specific demographics. Using these well-accepted and researched tests increases the confidence screeners will have in the results. Psychologists follow the guidelines for administration and interpretation of psychological tests from the *Standards for Educational and Psychological Tests* published by the American Psychological Association (2002).

This document informs the psychologists not only on the appropriate administration of tests, but also on setting standards for standardization, reliability, and validity of tests. Well-respected psychology training programs clearly expect psychologists to adhere to the highest standards for understanding psychology principles and theory, tests and measurement, and other aspects affecting the evaluation of individuals.

Research suggests that foster and adoptive parent applicants sometimes respond more truthfully to structured questionnaires than face-to-face interviews when the questions apply to objective data (an explanation for why the questions asked on applications are important) (Crea, Barth, & Chintapalli, 2007).

Adding the structured tests psychologists rely on to gather data will enhance the screener's confidence that subjectivity and personal biases will be minimized, thus providing back-up data to the application.

The consulting psychologist's evaluation is an excellent way to add objective, quantifiable, uniform information to a case that may have many loose ends. Screeners do not refer the clear-cut cases for further evaluation. It is the hard-to-determine cases that are referred for a psychological consult; therefore, the more empirically based data that can be generated the better. Psychologists must take their role very seriously and strive to add the most salient data to assist in building a strong case. The evaluation should not stray far from the quantifiable measurements and tools available to psychologists, yielding to the scientific side of the practice. The evaluation should thoroughly cover all aspects of the referral question, but it may go beyond the initial referral question when other relevant data emerges during the process (American Psychological Association, 2002).

The Report

A psychologist must approach report writing with a good understanding of how the report will be used, by whom it will be used, and how it will be integrated with other data. The decision process should consider all data. The psychological report is a narrative of everything the evaluation has produced. It is an official document that becomes part of the cumulative file on the applicant and may prove to be an important factor in the outcome of the application.

The report should provide needed data for the screener to be able to know how this applicant compares with other individuals who have taken the same assessment and what the comparison actually implies. Being able to make those normative comparisons is an advantage of formal psychological testing.

Depending on the reader of the report, psychologists may need to explain briefly some principles of psychological testing such as reliability, validity, or standard of measure, particularly if the applicant will read the report. The standard of practice regarding the distribution of such a report varies between jurisdictions and agencies. It is a more prudent approach to assume the applicant may read the report at some point. It should be written in a manner that is designed primarily to meet the needs of the referring agency, yet can be read by the applicant either before or after placement decisions are made.

Psychological reports should be written in clear and understandable language, avoiding as much professional jargon as possible. The length will vary because of the referral question; however, it should only be as long as necessary to comprehensively address the issues. Either the report or accompanying cover letter should clearly state the questions that were to be addressed. The psychologist will need to list anyone interviewed in person or by phone and how much time was spent with each. A list should be provided of all documents reviewed in relationship to the evaluation, such as the home study, interview notes, medical or psychiatric records, educational data, and legal documents.

The report should contain summaries of tests and interviews. Sometimes direct quotes can be more helpful than interpretations of what was said. Each report should end with a conclusion and recommendation section. Any diagnostic impressions should be reported along with summative data and recommendations that are responsive to the referral questions. The written report should avoid inflammatory language, examiner bias, and value judgments (Ackerman, 1999).

Words of Warning: Ways to Avoid the Pitfalls

First and foremost, the consulting psychologist should have an excellent reputation in the professional community. He or she should be known for expertise in the practice areas relevant to the assessment of prospective foster and adoptive parents. The psychologist's ability to conduct comprehensive evaluations and clearly articulate the results should be well documented.

To Avoid Reports Being Too Vague and General and Not Contributing to the Body of Data, the Screener Should:

- be very specific in the questions addressed by the psychologist.
- point out discrepancies between self-report and observational reports by others.
- make all information available to the psychologist.
- help the applicants understand that it is in their best interest to be open and honest with the psychologist.
- inform the applicant that the agency makes placement decisions, not the psychologist.
- inform the psychologist what information may and may not be specifically stated in the report because of the confidential nature of some of the data.
- make sure the psychologist has expertise in adult assessment of psychopathology, marriage and family, personality and parenting.
- make sure the psychologist understands the responsibility of the consultation and is willing to assume the responsibility.

To Avoid Having All Reports Biased toward Pathology:

- make sure the referral questions are not replete with subjective data that may bias the psychologist.
- eliminate any possible vested interest in finding problems for which the psychologist may provide services by having the consulting psychologist sign a written agreement that he or she may not accept the applicant as a patient after the evaluation.
- make sure the consulting psychologist does not have a reputation of letting personal and moral values color his or her interpretation of the data.
- present the issues in behavioral terms, avoiding terms that have multiple meanings.

CHAPTER TWELVE

Psychological Consultations: When Parents Have Mental Health Problems

There is little empirical data available specific to adoptive and foster families and the prevalence of mental illness, but with one in four adults in the United States suffering from a diagnosable mental illness, it is fair to assume those numbers as a reasonable baseline percentage for adoptive and foster parent applicants (Kessler, Berglund, Demler, Jin, & Walters, 2005). In other words, statistically you can expect one in four applicants to suffer from some form of mental illness. The question for researchers to answer in future studies is whether the prevalence of mental illness among adoptive and foster care applicants is higher or lower than the average seen in the general population. The experience of some social workers is that the percentage may be higher because there is anecdotal evidence that some applicants apply for adoptive or foster children as a subterfuge for seeking counseling for personal or relationship issues.[1] Others may feel that having a child in the home will be a solution to their underlying mental health problems.

Often, the lack of understanding, associated stigma of the labeling, and personal fears hinder the sufferers from acknowledging the illness and seeking treatment. In the adoptive and foster parenting screening process, it is reasonable to expect that those applicants who did not approach a social services agency for help with mental health disorders will be reluctant to volunteer the severity or details of any mental health challenges. Sometimes applicants fear that they will be turned down if they tell too much or anything at all. However, if telling is imperative, they may try to minimize symptoms or recent history.

Parenting skills are always of concern to mental health providers. The influence that parents have on their children is considered crucial in the child's development,

---

1. Experienced social workers know that adoptive and foster home applicants sometimes have ulterior motives for applying for children. For example, one partner may use the interview process to indirectly seek marriage counseling or use the process to get validation from a social worker that the partner's unusual behaviors are within normal limits.

emotional health, and long-term achievement. Commonly exhibited parenting skills are often grouped together into specific styles. These styles or clusters have been found to be associated with long-term outcomes. As indicated in a 2006 British study, when things go wrong, adults usually become either self-critical or self-reassuring (Irons, Gilbert, Baldwin, Baccus, & Palmer, 2006). Findings suggest that parenting styles and attachment experiences in childhood are major contributors to adult problem-solving skills and vulnerabilities to mental health disorders. When children are subjected to parental rejection instead of warmth, they internalize that negativity and it becomes the foundation for negative self-evaluation (Irons et al., 2006).

Poor parenting has been linked to mental health problems for a very long time (Chambers, Power, & Durham, 2004).

This supports delving into psychological problems within the screening process. Screeners should not hesitate to seek the expertise of a psychologist to evaluate underlying factors associated with identified diagnoses, symptom identification, and parenting styles and their potential effect on placement decisions and follow-up.

Many parents who are diagnosed with a mental disorder successfully parent their children. Having the diagnosis alone seldom dictates outcomes. This chapter offers screeners a review of the impact a mental illness can have on parenting skills, briefly describes assessment instruments, and offers recommendations for parents who face mental health challenges.

A psychological evaluation can confirm a suspected diagnosis of a mental illness or provide insight into the possible parenting challenges associated with mental disorders. Multiple methods of assessment have long been the most effective way of providing the best information for professionals to get a reliable snapshot of a situation. The standard home study screening interview offers a single method of data gathering. Biases, along with inaccuracies in informant data, can complicate the screening process when applicants try to hide issues in an effort to present themselves in the best possible way. Applicants may minimize or exaggerate aspects of their life that they feel are important in influencing the placement decision. As with many important decisions where questions linger, having added professional input from a slightly different perspective may provide a useful basis for decision making.

Consulting psychologists will likely use multiple evaluation methods, including both objective and subjective assessments. Although the unstructured nature of a clinical interview may evoke significant reactions that the psychologist will interpret, standardized tests conducted under strict protocol may evoke different reactions. Data collected may lead to a diagnosis, confirm a diagnosis or provide conclusions and recommendations to be considered in placement decisions or assist in post-placement follow-up.

Psychologists and the referring screener must be cautious not to overinterpret tests that lack normative data for the adoptive and foster parenting applicants. In a 1994 article, John E. Dalton warned practitioners against using typical interpretations of the data without having an appropriate representation in the normative sample. He used the Minnesota Multiphasic Personality Inventory (MMPI) and

Marlowe-Crowne Social Desirability Scale to determine typical adoptive applicant profiles. In the study, the adoptive applicants showed a higher level of defensiveness, particularly female applicants. On the Marlowe-Crowne, their scores reflected a stronger need to present an image of strong moral character and virtuousness than nonapplicants. When analyzed using the standard procedure, one might conclude that more defensive people apply for adoption; however, these results may reflect on the adoption application process and the assumption that it creates defensiveness and a need to meet certain moral and virtuous criterion rather than focus on the individual's enduring personality. Furthermore, the male applicants scored high on the Mf scale of the MMPI, which is associated with higher educational levels and suggests a desire to be perceived as nurturing and family oriented. Female applicants scored low on the same scale in spite of a high educational level. If one uses normative data for interpretation only, the female applicants are described as likely to be passive, submissive, and yielding. Profiles of both male and female applicants in the study suggested they were rather superficial and flighty in social situations. This study points out that although consultation can be extremely valuable, psychologists must be very cautious in using normative data and particularly computer-generated interpretations, which are not applicable to the uniqueness of the adoptive or foster care application situation (Dalton, 1994).

Depression

In a recent study funded through a collaboration of government entities and private, nonprofit organizations, it was found that of the millions of adults affected by major depression each year, about 7.5 million are parents whose disorder affects 16 million children under the age of 18 and thus puts them at risk for a wide range of problems. The problem increases when data include another 4 percent who suffer from a milder, yet chronic form of depression. Parents with depression were found to have deficits in their caregiving ability, nurturance, and their ability to take care of the material needs of their children.[2] Of great concern is the fact that depression is usually accompanied by a substance abuse diagnosis and at least one psychiatric disorder, with anxiety and personality disorders the most frequently co-occurring mental health challenges.[3]

Because adoptive and foster parents come from the general population, it is a given that some applicants suffer from depression. Most men, and many women, who suffer from depression do so in silence. Those who ignore the symptoms in hopes that the problem will go away seldom get their wish. Special occasions, vacations, or anticipation of events can help them feel fairly good from time to time. The excitement and anticipation of adoption or fostering a child may help create a positive

---

2. See National Research Council and Institute of Medicine of the National Academies, 2009, *Depression in parents, parenting, and children: Opportunities to improve identification, treatment, and prevention.*

3. Ibid.

environment, and symptoms from depression may subside for a while, but invariably the symptoms will return. Even when the severity of symptoms seems to be related to specific situations, no life is immune to life disappointments and challenges, so without treatment, symptoms usually reoccur. Often, sufferers deal with episodic bouts of major depression lasting months along with enduring milder depression or dysthymia. Most individuals who have had at least one episode of major depression can expect five or six more major episodes in their lifetime. The good news for depression sufferers is that it is one of the most treatable psychiatric disorders.[4]

How Does Depression Affect Parenting?

In the 1970s and early 1980s research on children of parents who suffer from depression found that they had as many adjustment, behavioral, and mental health problems as children of parents who have a diagnosis of schizophrenia. Some hypotheses focused solely on the genetic link; however, twin and adoption studies indicated that genetics can only partially account for problems encountered by children of parents who have psychiatric disorders.[5]

Research findings indicate that depressed mothers tend to evidence constricted affect, are more negative, and describe their children as having more problems than would be the case with nondepressed mothers. Their children are more often referred by both parents and teachers for treatment because of behavioral and emotional problems. Depressed mothers reportedly have more difficulty applying consistent discipline, pay less positive attention to their children, and are at a higher risk for verbal aggression toward their children. Depressed mothers of young children are more hostile and withdrawn than nondepressed mothers. They show less warmth to their children (Kase, n.d).

In families where both parents are depressed, there is more alcohol and substance abuse, poverty, violence, cultural isolation, and marital conflict that results in poor parenting. Their children are at high risk for temperament problems and insecurity and are generally less happy. They exhibit poorer social skills and more vulnerability to depression, tend to self-blame, and report less self-worth. They have more difficulty handling personal stress. There is a higher risk of childhood depression in children, even as young as preschool, when they are cared for by a depressed parent (Luby, 2010).

Depression, which is often accompanied by anxiety, is among the risk factors that compromise parental effectiveness. Dr. William Beardslee of Children's Hospital in Boston warns that the risk to children living in homes with a parent who is depressed differs depending on the child's age. The vulnerability of infants and adolescents, more than middle-age children, has been identified. Depressed moms may be less

---

4. Ibid.

5. Ibid.

attentive or less able to respond in a healthy way to their babies' needs. Adolescents tend to experience stress from their depressed parent (Beardslee, Wright, Gladstone, & Forbes, 2008; Carlson & Waller, 2001).

Assessments Used for Depression

Agencies may find formal psychological assessments helpful in clarifying subtle hints of problems detected during the screening process. A consulting psychologist will help determine whether simple statements made during the screening—labeled as fleeting feelings—may actually be hints of significant problems that need to be considered in the placement process.

Since 1961, Aaron Beck and his associates have developed a series of tests to assess symptoms of depression, anxiety, and suicide ideation often diagnosed together. The inventories are typically quick and easy to administer and score. They are easy for the clients to understand, highly reliable, and valid. Administration usually takes less than 15 minutes. The Beck Depression Inventory (Carlson & Waller, 2001), the Beck Hopelessness Scale (Weinberg & Werner, 1998), the Beck Anxiety Inventory (Dowd & Waller, 1998), and the Beck Suicide Ideation (Hanes & Stewart, 1998) can be administered separately or together to combine information into a comprehensive profile. Although only considered screening instruments, the tests identify symptoms according to *DSM* criteria.

Pessimism/hopelessness and suicide ideation are often viewed as clinically relevant indicators. The Revised Hamilton Rating Scale for Depression has two forms: the Clinical Rating Form for the clinician and the Self-Report Problem Inventory Form for the patient. Both forms are designed to evaluate depressive symptoms as to severity, intensity, and frequency (Reynolds & Kobak, 1998).

The Reynolds Depression Screening Inventory is a revision of the classic Hamilton Depression Rating Scale. It is a screening for the severity of current depressive symptoms, including moods and cognitive, somatic, neuro-vegetative, psychomotor, and interpersonal areas. Administration takes about 10 minutes. Clinical data concerning depressive symptoms, recommendations, and treatment are discussed in the manual (Campbell & Flanagan, 2001).

The State Trait Depression Adjective Checklists (ST-DACL) is easy to administer and score. This self-administered test usually takes less than five minutes to complete. The ST-DACL is based on 171 adjectives used to describe feelings of individuals diagnosed as markedly or severely depressed. Any clinical applications should be made only in conjunction with other measures (Barona, Carlson, & Waterman, 1998).

Typical Recommendations and Concerns to Be Addressed

- Extra caution should be taken when placing an infant or adolescent in a home with a parent who has a history of depression. Children at these ages evidence a particularly high need for their parents to be "emotionally available" to help buffer the developmentally related stressors they experience. Demands of infancy, combined with the caregivers' own stressors related to depression, could be too overwhelming.

- Parental depression must be acknowledged, and ongoing treatment including therapy and medication is imperative. Early symptom identification of a depressive episode lessens the impact on the family.
- Parents who are depressed must discuss the illness with their children and help them understand that they are not to blame. They also should help them address their own fears and concerns.
- Involve friends and family in the care and support of the children of a depressed parent. Keep the foster or adoptive agency informed. Do not try to hide symptoms or the need for support.

Anxiety Disorders

Anxiety disorders are serious psychiatric illnesses that interfere with work, social activities, relationships, and other activities of daily living. Symptoms of anxiety can mimic life-threatening heath emergencies such as heart attack, psychiatric breakdown, or neurological disorders. Of the variety of anxiety disorders, specific phobias are the most common. Less common, but more disabling, panic disorder and obsessive–compulsive disorder are among the top 20 most disabling of all medical disorders in individuals 15 to 44 years of age (Kitchener, Jorm, & Kelly, 2009).

During the adoptive and foster parent application process, it can be expected that applicants may evidence some anxiety in fear of not being approved. Even this potentially happy event can create stress and anxiety. When stress, even good stress, creates a feeling of being overwhelmed and inhibits normal functioning, it exceeds the limits of normal stress response and should not be ignored. Applicants who report current symptoms of extreme anxiety, nervousness, or unrealistic fears warrant further evaluation. Concerns may increase if they report childhood anxiety or recall their childhood experience as having a parent who was very controlling or lacked warmth (Van der Bruggen, Stams, & Bogels, 2008).

Most often, anxiety disorders originate during childhood and adolescence. If not treated, distress, withdrawal, panic, or ritualistic behaviors often develop in an effort to relieve the associated stress. Young people with certain anxiety disorders learn to function fairly well by simply avoiding stress-provoking activities, but as they mature and assume adult responsibilities, such as jobs and family, anxiety can become unmanageable. As a parent, the challenges of an anxiety disorder affect the entire family, particularly in the area of parenting (Kessler et al., 2005).

How Do Anxiety Disorders Affect Parenting?

Children are adversely affected by the parenting styles of individuals who have anxiety disorders. Through their own self-reports, parents with anxiety problems are described as less nurturing and more restrictive. In one study, their children did not specifically report a lack of warmth, but reported significantly more overprotectiveness as compared with other parents. Children raised in a home with an over-anxious parent are significantly more likely to be diagnosed with an anxiety disorder. Although there are genetic contributions for familial transmission of anxiety, research has indicated that there are substantial environmental contributions as well. Much of the research suggests that adverse influence is largely related to parenting style (Lindhout et al., 2006).

Particular concerns are associated with parents who are diagnosed with panic disorder, mostly affecting female parents. These mothers of very young infants (four to eight months) showed less sensitivity than mother who were not diagnosed, and by the time the child was 14 months old, the mothers displayed more anger toward their children than mothers who were not diagnosed (Lindhout et al., 2006). In addition, findings suggest that children of a panic-disordered parent are at high risk for developing agoraphobia or obsessive–compulsive disorder, both anxiety disorders, whereas children who suffer from social phobia or separation disorder typically come from homes with parents who share the same diagnosis (Lindhout et al., 2006).

A recent meta-analytic review found more data to suggest a stronger relationship with *parental control*, defined as pressure put on the child to think, feel, or behave in desired ways, than parental anxiety itself. The affected children are more often school-age girls of high socioeconomic status. Findings also report a higher correlation between childhood anxiety disorders and parentally controlling environments than parental rejection. Several studies have suggested that anxious parents often use guilt, possessiveness, and low affection toward the child. The mothers are considered colder, more critical, and catastrophizing than others without similar diagnoses. They are observed to be intrusive and seek to impede independence in their children. The quality of mother–child attachment is often considered poor (Van der Bruggen et al., 2008).

In general, anxiety disorders are not all equal. The impact on family and parenting varies greatly. Anxiety disorders have an increased comorbidity rate with other psychiatric disorders, particularly with depression, personality disorders, and alcohol or substance abuse.

Assessments Used to Determine Anxiety Disorders

The Beck Anxiety Inventory (BAI), administered in about 10 minutes, is easy to score. Items represent an anxiety symptom that is rated for severity. The test is designed to measure symptoms of anxiety that are only minimally shared with depression (Dowd & Waller, 1998).

The Clark-Beck Obsessive–Compulsive Inventory (CPOCI) usually takes about 15 minutes to complete and is often used as a complimentary instrument to the Beck measures. The test screens for obsessive and compulsive symptoms. The 25 symptoms represented on the test evaluate 14 obsessive symptoms and 11 compulsive symptoms. The results are closely associated with the *DSM-IV* diagnostic criteria (Cellucci, 2005).

The Coping Resources Inventory for Stress (CRIS) measures coping resources such as personal behaviors, attitudes, beliefs, physical being, and financial resources. The inventory is rooted in the theory that considers stress to be a product of "inequality between perceived demands and perceived resources." It is thought that if an individual can identify his or her personal resources, he or she can apply those resources to reduce stress (Weinberg & Werner, 1998).

The Life Stressors and Social Resources Inventory—Adult Form (LISRES–A) is administered as a self-report questionnaire or semistructured interview. It was developed to evaluate an individual's life stressors, social resources, health, and well-being. It provides a comprehensive view of that individual's positive and negative life situation (Cooperstein & Stuart, 1998).

Typical Recommendations and Concerns to Be Addressed

- The client should acknowledge the anxiety disorder and seek a comprehensive evaluation, diagnosis, and treatment with a commitment to set goals of learning coping skills, anger management, and other goals relevant to parenting skills.
- The screener should help family members understand that anxiety disorders are more than just nervousness or worry. They should be encouraged to seek family support and assistance.
- You should advise the client not to self-medicate with alcohol or other non-prescribed drugs.
- You should be cautious not to solely rely on medication; learn and value skills in early identification and symptom reduction.
- Post-placement focus should include minimizing the effects of the parent's anxiety on the child.

Substance Use Disorders

Feeling lonely, anxious, bored, depressed, or wanting to just dull whatever the pain might be are typical reasons people give for their substance use. Often, simple failures, unfulfilled dreams, or difficult situations are temporarily silenced by socially accepted substances like alcohol or legal drugs. It is when these short-term episodes of substance abuse evolve beyond occasional use into abuse and dependency that devastating consequences usually occur. Families are torn apart when parents choose substances to mask or avoid problems rather than confronting them. When life issues are treated with substances, they can easily escalate into physical injury, aggression, antisocial behavior, sexual risk taking, health problems, depression, anxiety, suicide, and self-injury (Kitchener, Jorm, & Kelly, 2009).

Understanding the causes of substance use disorders is usually complex and replete with emotional enmeshment. Almost 4 percent of adults in the United States have a substance use disorder each year, primarily alcohol. Half of the individuals with a substance use disorder are no older than 20 years of age, with many having started their substance use in early adolescence. And the numbers rise to 75 percent of those with substance use disorders by age 27 (Grant et al., 2004).

Male individuals are represented twice as often as female individuals. Individuals with mood disorders, anxiety, or psychosis often use substances to self-medicate and, therefore, are about three times more likely to be diagnosed with substance abuse disorders. It is interesting to note that it is sometimes difficult to determine which disorder caused the other, the depression and anxiety or the substance use (Grant et al., 2004).

How Do Substance Use Disorders Affect Parenting?

One in four children in the United States under the age of 18 live in families that are affected by alcohol abuse or dependency. This does not include children in homes where parents are drug dependent (Grant et al., 2004). The problems associated with these children living with an addicted person are multilayered, mutigenerational, and pervasive. Too often these children suffer alone. Sometimes the damage is not apparent until years later, after the individuals fail academically, fail in their relationships, experience encounters with the law, and battle substance abuse. Hurt and angry, these individuals often feel they were denied a childhood and were forced to care for their addicted parent (Grant et al., 2004).

Mothers who have substance use disorders have been found to have a more intrusive and threatening style of parenting. Attachment disorders are common, as are later developmental issues including physical, educational, and emotional problems. Probably most well known as associated with substance use disorders is the risk of abuse and neglect. Social services agencies report a high rate of child maltreatment cases that involve parents who have a diagnosed substance use disorders (Edwards, 1999).

Children from the homes of heavy substance users have a high rate of behavioral and psychiatric problems and are more likely to misuse substances themselves. They often show aggression in situations with authority and are seen as cold and unresponsive. They are often seen as problem children with conduct disorders that interfere with school and social interactions. Some of these behaviors are considered learned from the example of their parent; others are considered to have developed in response to the substance-using parent's style and the environment, which is often chaotic, lacking in routine, and socially isolated ("Children of Addicted Parents: Important Facts," 2003).

Often accompanying substance use is marital conflict. Such conflict has been associated with childhood risk for the typical behavior problems mentioned above; however, there are some children who cope differently and internalize the conflicts as their fault. These children are at high risk for long-term psychopathological outcomes. Childhood trauma, including chaotic environments, is being looked at for its contribution to adult relationship problems, physical health problems, and stress-related mental health problems (Grant et al., 2004).

Assessments to Identify Substance Use Disorders

Drug Abuse Screen Test (DAST-20). The DAST-20 is a screening test that assesses possible drug usage. This 20-item, easy to administer, single-score inventory focuses on features of drug dependence, withdrawal symptoms, and several other typical behaviors of abuse of prescribed, over-the-counter, and illicit drugs (Ash & Rain, 1998).

Substance Abuse Subtle Screening Inventory–3 (SASSI-3). The SASSI-3 is an inventory designed to assess characteristics of substance dependence disorder. It is very short and easily to administer yielding results on five clinical scales, two ancillary scales, and one validity scale (Fernandez & Pittenger, 2003).

Rapid Alcohol Problem Screen (RAPS4). The RAPS4 is a four-question brief screening available in the public domain. The four questions pertain to remorse, amnesia, performance, and starter drinking behavior (Cherpitel, 2002).

Marital Satisfaction Inventory–Revised (MSI-R). Although not a test specifically designed to identify substance use disorders, the MSI-R is an excellent test that could be used early on in the consultation to open the door for exploring issues that are often present in substance use disorders. The MSI-R evaluates one's level of satisfaction or dissatisfaction in relationships. It also helps identify a couple's strengths and weaknesses and assess the home environment. Available in the public domain, the MSI-R seems especially well suited for clinical settings. The inventory is popular with clinicians, and the revised version provides stronger psychometrics (Bernt & Frank, 2001).

Typical Recommendations and Concerns to Be Addressed

- If placement is approved, the agency must follow up often and for an extended period of time.
- Be aware of stressors and triggers. Individuals with substance use disorders are at a higher risk for suicidal gesturing.
- Be aware of other mental health problems that often accompany substance use disorders.
- Insist on ongoing participation in some type of support group.

Personality Disorders

Personality disorders are typically grouped into three categories: cluster A, which includes paranoid, schizoid, and schizotypal personality disorders; cluster B, which includes antisocial, borderline, histrionic, and narcissistic personality disorders; and cluster C, which involves behaviors of extreme anxiety or fearfulness and includes avoidant, dependent, and obsessive–compulsive personality disorders. These 10 separate personality disorders differ greatly in severity and impact on the individual's life. As with most psychiatric disorders, there is a large overlap in behaviors, and many individuals are diagnosed with more than one personality disorder from different clusters.

The diagnosis of a personality disorder involves the evaluation of long-term behavioral patterns across multiple settings. Often symptoms are further exacerbated by stress. Personality disorders must not be diagnosed if they appear only during Axis I disorders (American Psychiatric Association, 2000).

Cluster B (antisocial, borderline, histrionic, and narcissistic) personality disorders sometimes can be difficult to detect. Screeners and psychologists must be very thorough in examining the applicant's childhood history and their parents' style of parenting, looking for clues of early childhood environments that are known to have an adverse effect on the individual in adulthood. For example, adult antisocial personality characteristics are associated with having been exposed to an uncaring, yet overly protective and intrusive parenting style. As children, these adults often had very strict, authoritarian parents (Rhule, McMahon, & Spieker, 2004). According to biosocial theory, borderline personality disorder develops as a result of an emotionally vulnerable child who is exposed to an "invalidating environment" from an early age (Kiehn & Swales, 2002).

It is possible for individuals with personality disorders to proceed through the screening process with only subtle hints of symptoms. Screeners may overlook or rationalize idiosyncratic characteristics during the interviews. Although many individuals with personality disorders may be able to maintain effective interpersonal skills during screening, screeners should identify subtle features and probe further into those features. Depending on those results, a psychological consult may be dictated to delve deeper into the psychological characteristics of the individual to possibly identify enduring patterns of problematic behaviors.

How Do Personality Disorders Affect Parenting?

Personality disorders can have devastating effects on families and parenting acumen. The parenting practices of individuals with personality disorders are often responsible for creating a destructive emotional environment. Children raised in these dysfunctional family units often develop significant psychiatric illnesses.

A 2006 review of research reported that parental possessiveness, inconsistent discipline, low communication, and low praise of the child were found in individuals with personality disorders (Johnsoti, Cohen, Kasen, Ehrensaft, & Crawford, 2006). Furthermore, those with comorbid substance abuse, depression, or anxiety disorders show even more destructive parenting behaviors (Johnsoti et al., 2006).

Abusive parents are commonly diagnosed with antisocial, narcissistic, or borderline personality disorders. From 66 percent to 70 percent of mother's involved in legal proceeding concerning child care were diagnosed with borderline personality disorder (Mason & Kreger, 1998).

Individuals with borderline personality disorders have few internal controls to guide their response to their own child's emotional needs. Their own damaged self-image remains the main focus of their emotional energy, usually at the expense of relationships. Volatile and erratic behavior along with stress-related paranoia and dissociation can be confusing for children who are often made to feel guilty and responsible for the family unrest. Female parents are diagnosed with borderline personality more than male parents, and the adverse impact is found to be more pronounced in their female children (Newman, Stevenson, Bergman, & Boyce, 2007).

Poor parenting is often associated with personality disorders, in part, because of the parent's deficits in affective regulation. These parents are overly sensitive to stressors while being unable to manage their psychological experiences of anxiety, anger, hostility, or arousal. There is strong evidence for contributions of both nature and nurture in the multigenerational diagnoses of personality disorders. Also of great concern to mental health professionals is the lack of improvement that treatment has on the parenting styles of individuals with personality disorders (Choca & Widiger, 2001).

Assessments Typically Used in Diagnosing Personality Disorders

Million Clinical Multiaxial Inventory–III (MCMI-III). The MCMI-III is a 175-item true–false, self-report test inventory designed to measure personality disorders. It is popular because it is shorter than the MMPI-2 but is considered as reliable and valid in identifying psychopathology (Archer, 1992).

Minnesota Multiphasic Personality Inventory–2 (MMPI-2). The MMPI-2 requires an eighth-grade reading level, is recommended for clients at least 18 years old, and usually takes about 90 minutes to complete. This new version of the MMPI offers changes in items for clarity, updating, and deleting repeated items. Although black–white differences on the MMPI may be statistically significant, there are small mean differences. Knowledge of psychopathology is necessary to interpret the MMPI-2. This test continues to be a valuable tool for the skilled clinician who is familiar with the criticisms and its uniqueness (Boyle & Kavan, 1995).

Personality Assessment Inventory (PAI). The PAI is considered an alternative to the MMPI for assessing abnormal personality traits. This self-report questionnaire has 344 items, but there is a short version of 160 items. Designed for adults with at least a fourth-grade reading level, the PAI uses a four-point response format (Newmark, 1985).

Rorschach. The Rorschach has mesmerized the public for many years and is probably the most widely recognized psychological test. Its mysterious nature contributes to it sometimes being considered the ultimate psychological test. The test has 10 cards with inkblots on them, five of which are black and gray and five with colors on a white background. Only well-trained clinicians should administer, score, or interpret the Rorschach. Although subjective and frequently criticized, it is considered an excellent test to use when problem-solving capabilities, emotional operations, interpersonal functioning, and self-concept are of concern (Conoley & Impara, 1995).

Rotter Incomplete Sentences Blank (RISB). The RISB is a projective measure that presents short sentences stems to the individual for him or her to complete the thought. Scoring considers omissions and incomplete responses, conflict responses, positive responses, and neutral responses. Only skilled clinicians with a good knowledge of personality dynamics should administer and interpret the RISB. With high face validity, caution is advised because of responses that are amenable to distortion, depending on the lack of self-insight, or conscious and unconscious motives of the respondent (Conoley & Impara, 1995).

Six Factor Personality Questionnaire (SFPQ). The SFPQ usually takes about 20 minutes to complete. It measures six broad domains of personality derived from the 108 items, using a five-point response scale. The SFPQ requires a fifth-grade reading level and is appropriate for use across a wide range of ages and backgrounds and in a variety of settings (Jenkins, Plake, Impara, & Spies, 2003).

Sixteenth Personality Factor Questionnaire, Fifth Edition (16PF). The 16PF is a test of personality that is intended for use with normal adults with no psychiatric diagnoses. The test is written on a fifth-grade reading level. The 16 factors assessed are evaluated as a dichotomy, yet with neither being a negative factor. In addition there are five global scores and three response style indices. The interpretations of the results is considered complex (McLellan, 1995).

Structured Interview for the Five-Factor Model of Personality (SIFFM). The SIFFM is a structured interview with 120 items designed to measure five factors of personality in a dichotomous format. The SIFFM is consistent with the criteria for Axis II (personality) *DSM* disorders and, in part, is based on the Revised NEO Personality Inventory. The interview format is popular among clinicians. An understanding of psychopathology, personality, and structure interviewing is necessary to interpret the data (Mastrangtlo, 2003).

Tennessee Self-Concept Scale (TSCS-2). The TSCS-2 is a simple 82-item, paper–pencil assessment that takes about 20 minutes to complete. The TSCS-2 is based on six scales designed to assess conflicts in one's self-view. Clinicians find the TSCS-2 beneficial when combined with other clinical data (Brown, 1998).

Thematic Apperception Test (TAT). The TAT contains 31 pictures, some specific to adult females and adult males, some specific to boys and girls from seven to 14 years of age, and some applicable to all clients. The TAT assesses personality by eliciting fantasy as a result of projecting past experience and present needs in response to ambiguous picture stimuli. Verbatim recording of responses is used as much as possible. The TAT is considered very hard to interpret and reports insufficient validity. There is an absence of consensual scoring. The TAT is not recommended to be used alone. Even formal training for use of the TAT is generally inadequate. TAT is now considered obsolete by many (Dana, 1985).

Typical Recommendations and Cautions

- Postplacement follow-up must include long-term commitment to therapy by a therapist with expertise in treating personality disorders. Personality disorders can be difficult to treat.
- Some individuals with high and unrealistic expectations of parenting may find that joy quickly diminishing as challenges come. Agencies must be vigilant in providing long-term follow-up and support for parents who have personality disorders.

Appendix

Chapter 2 (First Contact)

Question 1: How long have you been considering adoption/foster parenting? _____

_____

Question 2: Why do you think the time is right for adoption/foster parenting? _____

_____

Question 3: Are you able to have birth children? _____

_____

Question 4: How does it make you feel that you can't have birth children?_____

_____

Question 5: Have you ever applied elsewhere to adopt children?_____

_____

Question 6: What age child would you like to adopt? _____

_____

Question 7: Describe the child that you think would fit best into your home? _____

_____

Question 8: Would you be able to accept a child who has special needs? _____

_____

Question 9: How do you think that adoption will change your life? _____

_____

Question 10: What do you think is the most difficult thing about raising an adopted or foster child?_____

_____

Question 11: How does your extended family feel about you adopting/ fostering a child? _____

_____

Question 12: How would you feel about adopting/fostering a child with developmental disabilities? _____

_____

Question 13: How would you feel about adopting/fostering a physically challenged child?_____

_____

Question 14: How do you feel about adopting/fostering a child with emotional problems? _____

_____

Question 15: How would you feel about adopting/fostering a child who had been sexually, emotionally or physically abused by his or her parents or caregivers?_____

_____

Question 16: How would you feel about adopting/fostering a child of a different race? _____

_____

Question 17: How would you feel about adopting/fostering a child of a different religion?_____

_____

Question 18: How would you feel about adopting/fostering a child whose birth parents are under court order not to try to contact the child? _____

_____

Question 19: How would you feel about adopting/fostering a child whose parent is in prison? _____

_____

Question 20: How would you feel about adopting/fostering a juvenile offender? _____

_____

Question 21: How would you feel about adopting/fostering siblings?_____

_____

Chapter 4 (Individual Interview)

Question 1: Could I please have the names and ages of your parents?
(Note: This information may already be provided on the application form) _____

_____

Question 2: Could I please have the names, ages, and addresses of your siblings?
(Note: This information may already be requested and provided on the application)

_____

_____

Question 3: Have your parents or siblings ever been arrested or convicted of a crime?

_____

_____

Question 4: How would you describe your childhood? Was it different in any important ways from your friends' childhoods? _____

_____

Question 5: How would you describe your partner's childhood? _____

_____

Question 6: How would you describe your relationship with your parents? _____

_____

Question 7: In what ways are your mother and father different? _____

_____

Question 8: Who is dominant in your family, your father or your mother?_____

_____

Question 9: Were you ever emotionally, sexually, or physically abused as a child?____

_____

Question 10: Which of your parents was the most loving? _____

_____

Question 11: Did your parents ever have arguments about your behavior?
If so, describe the behavior that provoked the arguments. _____

_____

Question 12: Did you ever feel you had to "walk on eggshells" around your parents or siblings?_____

_____

Question 13: What are the highlights of your childhood?_____

_____

Question 14: Did you undergo any traumatic events as a child? _____

_____

Question 15: Did either of your parents have previous marriages? If so, please tell me about them and explain why and how the marriages ended. _____

_____

Question 16: Have your parents ever had a marital separation?_____

_____

Question 17: How were you disciplined as a child? _____

_____

Question 18: Were your parents fair when disciplining you? _____

_____

Question 19: Tell me about your relationships with your siblings._____

_____

Question 20: What quality of yours do you think your partner most appreciates?

_____

_____

Question 21: What do you find most attractive about your partner?_____

_____

Question 22: Who are your partner's best friends?_____

_____

Question 23: What are your partner's life dreams?_____

_____

Question 24: Does your partner listen to you when you talk? _____

_____

Question 25: Who is your best friend? _____

_____

Question 26: When you have disagreements with your partner, how do you solve them? _____

_____

Question 27: What is the worst argument you ever had with your partner and how was it resolved? _____

_____

Question 28: Has your partner ever struck you during an argument? _____

_____

Question 29: At what age did you become sexually active? _____

_____

Question 30: How often do you and your partner have sex? _____

_____

Question 31: Does your partner bear any grudges because of previous sexual relationships you had? _____

_____

Question 32: (for males) Have you ever dressed as a woman? _____

_____

Question: 33: Does your partner find it difficult to forgive you when you make mistakes, and do you find it difficult to forgive yourself when you make mistakes?

_____

_____

Question 34: Does your spouse get upset if you don't keep him advised of where you are at all times, and do you ever have arguments about you spending time with people your spouse does not approve of? _____

_____

Question 35: Does your partner know what pleases you sexually? _____

_____

Question 36: Have you and your partner ever had a marital separation? _____

_____

Question 37: Have you ever filed charges against your partner for assault or have you ever had reason to file charges but didn't?_____

_____

Question 38: Who makes most of the decisions in your relationship, you or your partner? _____

_____

Question 39: Do you ever feel you have to "walk on eggshells" around your partner?

_____

_____

Question 40: Do you and your partner ever have disagreements about the role of religion in your relationship? _____

_____

Question 41: Do you ever see yourself in your partner? _____

_____

Question 42: How would you describe your first years in school? Did you have any bad experiences? Were you able to make friends with the other students?

_____

_____

Question 43: Tell me about the best teacher you ever had. What made her or him special?_____

_____

Question 44: Tell me about the worst teacher you had. What made her a bad teacher?

_____

_____

Question 45: How would you describe your high school experiences?

_____

_____

Question 46: Did you participate in any extracurricular activities in high school?

_____

_____

Question 47: How many books do you have in your home? _____

_____

Question 48: Were you ever bullied by other students? _____

_____

Question 49: Are you happy with your current job (or position)? _____

_____

Question 50: Do you see yourself staying there until retirement? _____

_____

Question 51: How would you describe your relationship with your boss?_____

_____

Question 52: How often do you go to work early? How often do you work late?

_____

_____

Question 53: Have you ever resigned from a job without having a replacement job?

_____

_____

Question 54: Have you ever been fired? _____

_____

Question 55: Have you ever been the target of a conspiracy by jealous co-workers?

_____

_____

Question 56: Have you ever been reprimanded at work for losing your temper with customers or co-workers? _____

_____

Chapter 7 (Parenting Attitudes)

Question 1: Under what circumstances were children in your home? _____

_____

Question 2: What would you want to do differently with foster or adoptive children that you didn't do with your birth children or children who you cared for on a regular basis? _____

_____

Question 3: (For applicants with children in the home). Have your children ever been referred to undergo counseling at school for behavioral problems? _____

_____

Question 4: Have your children ever run away from home? _____

_____

Question 5: Have your children ever had encounters with the police?_____

_____

Question 6: How do you disciple your children? _____

_____

Question 7: Did your parents spank you on a regular basis? If so, do you feel that it had the desired results? _____

_____

Question 8: Do you consider scolding and statements of disapproval to be appropriate parenting techniques? _____

_____

Question 9: Have you ever kept other people's children in your home overnight or for an extended period of time? If yes, how did you feel when they returned to their parents?_____

_____

Question 10: As an adult, have you ever had a dog or a cat? If so, how did you correct your pet when it displayed bad behavior? _____

_____

Question 11: Have you ever had to leave work to take care of your pet? If so, did you get in trouble with your boss? _____

_____

Question 12: Have you ever given away a pet that you no longer had time for?

_____

_____

Question 13: (If the applicants have siblings with children) If something happened to your siblings, would you want to raise their children? _____

_____

Question 14: Do you and your spouse agree on how children should be disciplined? If not, how do you differ? _____

_____

Question 15: Do you think that children have a good understanding of a parent's need for love? _____

_____

Question 16: Have you ever been shown disrespect by a child and not understood why? _____

_____

Question 17: From your experience, what is the best way to get a child to stop doing something you don't want them to do? _____

_____

Question 18: (For open adoptions) If you told your 14-year-old adopted daughter that she could not smoke, and the birth mother told her that she could smoke, how would you handle the situation? _____

_____

Question 19: If you had negative information about your child's birth parents, at what point would you share it with your child? _____

_____

Question 20: Do you think it is possible for a child to love two parents equally?

_____

_____

Question 21: What do you think is the biggest disappointment that a parent can have with a child? _____

_____

Question 22: Do you think that you are responsible for whether your child loves you?

_____

_____

Question 23: If you are ill, who takes care of you? _____

_____

Question 24: If your pets are ill, who takes care of them? _____

_____

Question 25: Tell me about the last time you nursed your partner when he or she was ill? _____

_____

Question 26: When was the last time you made dinner for your partner?_____

_____

Question 27: If you hurt your partner's feeling, whether intentionally or unintentionally, how do you handle the fallout? _____

_____

Question 28: When your partner is not feeling well do you inquire about them during the day? _____

_____

Question 29: (for single applicants who want opposite-sex children) Do you have friends or family members of the opposite sex who can serve as same-sex role models for an opposite-sex child placed with you? _____

_____

Legal Glossary

–A–

Acquittal—A release or discharge of a liability or obligation.

Adoption assistance—Financial support for adoptive parents of children identified with special needs who are adopted from the public foster care system.

Adoption decree—Legal document awarding the adoptive parents full parental rights to the child adopted.

Adjudication—Pronounce a judgment or decree.

Admissible evidence—Evidence that is permitted to be introduced in a civil or criminal proceeding or trial.

Affiant—The person who makes and subscribes an affidavit.

Affidavit—A sworn written statement, signed and witnessed by an authorized official, such as a notary public.

Affirmation—The formal declaration that an affidavit is true.

Affirmative defense—A defense that is raised that excuses or justifies the behavior on which the lawsuit is based.

Answer—A written statement by the defendant in a lawsuit that answers each allegation contained in the plaintiff's complaint.

Answers to interrogatories—A written statement by a party that addresses each question or interrogatory asked by the other party.

Appeal—A proceeding brought to a higher court to review a lower court decision.

Appellate court—A court that has jurisdiction to hear appeals and review a lower court's holding or procedures.

Appellee—The party against whom an appeal is taken.

Arbitrator—A neutral, disinterested person chosen by the parties to hear evidence concerning the dispute.

Arrest—To take into custody by legal authority.

Assumption of risk—A legal doctrine under which a party may not recover for an injury received when that person had voluntarily exposed himself or herself to a known danger.

–B–

Bench trial—A trial without a jury in which a judge decides the facts and verdict.

Beneficiary—In a trust, a person who is named to receive benefits. In a will, someone who is named to receive property or benefits.

Best evidence—Primary evidence, or, the best evidence available. For instance, an original signature on a document is "best evidence," a photocopy of that document is "secondary evidence."

Beyond a reasonable doubt—The standard in a criminal case requiring that the jury find the evidence be so conclusive that all reasonable doubts are removed from the mind of the ordinary person.

Breach—The violation of a law, right, or duty, either by commission or omission.

Breach of contract—An unjustified failure to carry out the terms of a contract.

Brief—A written argument by an attorney arguing a case. This document contains a summary of the facts of the case, relevant laws, and an argument of how the law applies to the fact situation.

Burden of proof—The necessity or duty of affirmatively proving facts in dispute on an issue raised between the parties in a lawsuit.

Bylaws—Rules or laws adopted by a corporation that govern its actions.

–C–

Calendar—List of cases scheduled to be heard in court.

Capacity—Have mental ability or legal authority.

Case law—Law established by previous judicial opinions and decisions of appellate courts.

Cause—A lawsuit or action litigated in court.

Cause of action—A specific legal claim based on facts upon which a person seeks compensation in court.

Certiorari—A writ of review issued by a higher court to a lower court.

Challenge—An objection.

Change of venue—Moving a lawsuit to another jurisdiction.

Circumstantial evidence—All inferential evidence except eyewitness testimony.

Civil procedure—The rules and process by which a civil case in either federal or state court is tried and appealed.

Class action—A lawsuit brought by one or more persons on behalf of a larger group.

Closing argument—The summary closing statement to the trier of facts.

Code of Federal Regulations—An annual publication that states the federal agency's regulations.

Common law—Law established in colonial and precolonial times based on earlier cases.

Comparative negligence—The simplest way of thinking about comparative negligence is that the damages awarded to the victim are decreased in direct proportion to his or her own negligence. For example, if a jury determines a plaintiff's damages to be $100,000, and finds that the plaintiff is 30 percent at fault, the plaintiff would be awarded $70,000 against the defendant.

Contributory negligence—The term contributory negligence is often used to describe the actions of an injured person that may have also caused or contributed to that person's injury. Where contributory negligence law is in force, if the plaintiff in any way contributed to his or her own injury, the plaintiff is barred from recovering damages. The extreme consequence of this approach has led to its being severely limited or abandoned in many jurisdictions.

Complainant—The party who complains or sues.

Confidential communication—Information exchanged between two people who have a relationship in which private communications are protected by law, and who intend that the information be kept confidential.

Consent—Agreement.

Contempt of court—Willful disobedience of a court's official court order.

Continuance—Postpone a legal proceeding to a later date.

Counterclaim—A claim made by a defendant in a civil lawsuit against the plaintiff.

Cross-claim—A pleading that asserts a claim arising out of the same subject action as the original complaint against another party.

Cross-examination—The questioning of a witness produced by the other side.

–D–

Damages—Money awarded by a court to a person injured by the unlawful conduct of another party.

Decree—An order of the court.

Deposition—Testimony of a witness or a party taken under oath outside the courtroom. The transcript of that testimony becomes a part of the case record.

Direct evidence—Proof of facts or evidence.

Direct examination—Initial questioning of witnesses by the party on whose behalf they are called.

Discovery—Pretrial procedures for obtaining facts and information about the case.

–E–

Entity—A legally recognized organization.

Entry—A statement of conclusion reached by the court and recorded by the court.

Estoppel—An impediment that prevents a person from asserting or doing something because that impediment contradicts the person's previous assertions or acts.

Evidence—Information presented in testimony or in documents that is used to persuade the fact finder.

Exceptions—A declaration by a party reserving the right to appeal a court's ruling upon a motion.

Exhibit—A document or other item introduced as evidence during a trial or hearing.

–F–

Felony—A serious criminal offense. An offense punishable by imprisonment for a term exceeding one year.

Fiduciary—A person or institution who manages money or property for another.

Finding—Formal conclusion by a judge on issues of fact.

Foster care—Temporary placement of a child with a family or individual other than the child's birth parents, resulting from reasons related to neglect, abuse, or abandonment.

Fraud—An intentional false representation of a matter that is meant to deceive.

–G–

Gross negligence—Failure to use even the slightest amount of care in a way that demonstrates willful disregard for the safety of another person.

Guardian—Court-appointed individual responsible for the control and management of a child's care and property.

Guardian ad litem (GAL)—Court-appointed individual, not necessarily a lawyer, whose duty it is to represent the best interests of a child, born or unborn.

Guardianship—The legal right given to a person to be responsible for the care of a person deemed incapable of providing life's necessities for himself or herself.

–H–

Harmless error—An error committed during trial that was either corrected or was not serious enough to affect the outcome of the trial.

Hearsay—Statements by a witness who did not see or hear the incident in question but heard about it from someone else; such secondhand assertions are usually not admissible as evidence in court.

Home study—Collection of information, home observation, and interviews with applicants to determine and approve their fitness as foster or adoptive parents.

Hostile witness—A witness whose testimony is not favorable to the party who calls him or her as a witness.

Hung jury—A jury whose members cannot agree upon a final verdict.

–I–

Impeach a witness—An attack on the credibility or believability of a witness.

Implied contract—A contract not created or evidenced by the explicit agreement of the parties but one inferred by law.

Incapacity—Lack of legal ability to act; disability, incompetence; lack of adequate power.

Incompetent—One who lacks ability, legal qualification, or fitness to manage his or her own affairs.

Independent adoption—Adoption that takes place without the involvement of a public or private adoption agency.

Indian Child Welfare Act of 1978—Act that regulates the placement and adoption of Native American children.

Individualized education plan (IEP)—A formal plan designed to delineate educational objectives for children with diagnosed learning disabilities.

Injunction—A court decision commanding or preventing a specific act.

Intentional tort—Wrong perpetrated by one who intends to break the law.

Interlocutory—Temporary; provisional; interim; not final.

Interrogatories—A set or series of written questions propounded to a party, witness, or other person having information or interest in a case; a discovery device.

Interstate Compact on Adoption and Medical Assistance (ICAMA)—Legal contract between member states that children with special needs who are adopted within a state will continue to receive medical benefits upon moving to another state.

Interstate Compact on the Placement of Children (ICPC)—Interstate contract that regulates adoptions across states.

Irrevocable consent—Consent to make an adoption plan that has been signed by a birth parent and can no longer be withdrawn.

–J–

Joint and several liability—A legal doctrine that makes each of the parties who are responsible for an injury liable for the entire amount of damages awarded.

Judicial review—The authority given to a court to review the official actions of another branch of government.

Jurisdiction—Authority to act within a defined legal area.

Justiciable—Issues and claims that are capable of being properly examined in court.

–K–

Kinship placement—Legal adoption by a biological relative.

–L–

Leading question—A question that suggests the answer desired of the witness.

Legal guardian—Individual who is able to make decisions for a child in the absence of an adoption, which cannot take place without consent from the birth parent, state, or individual with custody.

Legal risk placement—Situation in which a child is placed with a family prior to becoming legally free for adoption, with the understanding that the family will adopt the child upon termination of parental rights.

Legally free—Youth who is available for adoption due to termination of parental rights.

Liable—Legally responsible.

Licensing boards—State agencies created to regulate the issuance of licenses.

Litigant—A party to a lawsuit.

Litigation—A lawsuit; a legal action, including all proceedings therein.

–M–

Malfeasance—The commission of an unlawful act.

Minor—A person under the age of legal competence.

Misfeasance—Improper performance of a lawful action.

Mistrial—An invalid trial, caused by a fundamental error.

Mitigating circumstances—Circumstances that do not constitute a justification for an offense but that may be considered as reasons for reducing the degree of blame.

Moot—A case or point that is not subject to a judicial determination because it involves an abstract question.

Motion—An application made to a court or judge that requests a ruling or order in favor of the applicant.

Motion in limine—A motion made by counsel requesting that information which might be prejudicial not be allowed to be heard in a case.

Multiethnic Placement Act of 1994 (MEPA)—Statute barring color, race, or national origin of a child of prospective parent to be used to impede the child's placement.

Mutual assent—A meeting of the minds; agreement.

–N–

Negligence—Failure to use care which a reasonable and prudent person would use under similar circumstances.

Nonfeasance—Nonperformance of an act which should be performed.

Nonidentifying information—Information such as health and history, which does not include names, birth dates, addresses, telephone numbers, or other distinguishing information.

Nonrelative adoption—Adoption by an individual unrelated to the youth.

Notary public—Individual with the appointed authority to act as an unbiased witness to endorse official documents.

Notice—Formal notification to the party that has been sued in a civil case of the fact that the lawsuit has been filed.

–O–

Oath—A solemn pledge made under a sense of responsibility in attestation of the truth of a statement or in verification of a statement made.

Objection—The process by which one party takes exception to some statement or procedure. An objection is either sustained or overruled by the court.

Open adoption—Adoption in which some extent of contact and communication is maintained between adoption parties after finalization.

Opening statement—The initial statement made by attorneys for each side, outlining the facts each intends to establish during the trial.

Order—A court's mandate, command, or direction.

Original birth certificate—Birth certificate issued at birth, prior to making an adoption plan.

Overrule—A judge's decision not to allow an objection.

–P–

Parens patriae—State's legal ability to terminate parental rights and assume responsibility for the children in question.

Parental rights—Legal responsibilities and benefits which are associated with raising a child.

Passive adoption registry—Adoption registry which requires that both parties consent to the release of information. A registry administrator then attempts to match individuals and notifies parties if a match has been made.

Paternity—Identification of father of a child.

Paternity testing—Determination through testing of DNA whether an individual has a paternal biological relationship to an individual.

Permanency planning—Planning for family reunification or for termination of parental rights so that a child may be adopted.

Petitioner—The person filing an action in a court of original jurisdiction.

Plaintiff—A person who brings an action; the party who complains or sues in a civil action.

Posttraumatic stress disorder (PTSD)—Psychological condition resulting from anxiety produced from highly traumatic experiences.

Precedent—Laws established by previous cases which must be followed in cases involving identical circumstances.

Presumed father—Legal father of a child, unless proven otherwise through paternity testing.

Prima facie case—A case that is sufficient and has the minimum amount of evidence necessary to allow it to continue in the judicial process.

Punitive damages—Money award given to punish the defendant or wrongdoer.

Putative father—Unmarried male who claims to be the father of a child for whom paternity is in question.

Putative father registry—Registry for unmarried males who claim paternity for a child in question, and which has not been proven. Individuals registered are consulted in cases of adoptions.

−R−

Rebuttable presumption—Statement assumed to be true unless proven otherwise.

Remand—To send a dispute back to the court where it was originally heard.

Reply—The response by a party to charges raised in a pleading by the other party.

Residential care facility—Facility that houses children with severe emotional, mental, and behavioral challenges, and whose goal is to help its residents overcome such issues in order to better function in their everyday lives.

Reversible error—A procedural error during a trial or hearing sufficiently harmful to justify reversing the judgment of a lower court.

–S–

Special needs—Broad term that may refer to a child with mental, physical, or emotional disabilities, or to a child who is difficult to place, such as in cases of sibling groups.

Sovereign immunity—The doctrine that the government, state or federal, is immune to lawsuit unless it give its consent.

Standing—The legal right to bring a lawsuit. Only a person with something at stake has standing to bring a lawsuit.

Subpoena—A command to appear at a certain time and place to give testimony upon a certain matter.

Subpoena duces tecum—A court order commanding a witness to bring certain documents or records to court.

Summary judgment—A procedural device used during civil litigation to quickly dispose of a case without going to trial. It is invoked when there is no dispute as to the material facts of the case and one party is entitled to judgment as a matter of law. In legalese, summary judgment is appropriate if the party making a request of the court demonstrates that there is "no genuine issue as to any material fact" and that it is "entitled to a judgment as a matter of law."[1]

In applying this standard, courts view the evidence and all reasonable inferences derived from the evidence in the light most favorable to the party opposed to the request before the court.[2] An issue of fact is "genuine" if "the evidence allows a reasonable jury to resolve the issue either way."[3] A fact is "material" when it is essential to the proper disposition of the claim. The party initiating the court action bears the burden of demonstrating an absence of a genuine issue of material fact and entitlement to judgment as a matter of law.[4] In attempting to meet that standard, the party requesting the court action does not need to negate the other party's claim. Rather, that party needs simply to point out to the court a lack of evidence for the other party on an essential element of that party's claim. It should be noted that summary judgment is not what some critics call a "disfavored procedural shortcut." Indeed, it is an important procedure "designed to secure the just, speedy and inexpensive determination of every action."[5]

---

1. Fed. R. Civ. P. 56(c).

2. *Burke v. Utah Transit Auth. & Local 382*, 462 F.3d 1253, 1258 (10th Cir. 2006).

3. *Haynes v. Level 3 Communications, LLC*, 456 F.3d 1215, 1219 (10th Cir. 2006).

4. *Celotex Corp. v. Catrett*, 477 U.S. 317, 322–23 (1986).

5. *Celotex*, 477 U.S. at 327 (quoting Fed. R. Civ. P. 1).

Supplemental Security Income (SSI)—Federal income supplement for blind, disabled, or senior people with little income.

–T–

Termination of parental rights (TPR)—Decision by a court to end a parent's rights to a child, which may or may not be voluntary.

Therapeutic foster home—Foster homes in which parents have been specifically trained to care for children and adolescents with behavioral, physical, or mental health disorders.

Title IV-E—Federal assistance program under Social Security Act.

Trial brief—A written document prepared for and used by an attorney at trial. It contains the issues to be tried, synopsis of evidence to be presented and case and statutory authority to substantiate the attorney's position at trial.

–U–

Ultra vires—Latin for beyond powers. Conduct by a corporation or its officers that exceeds the powers granted to it by law.

–V–

Vacate—To set aside.

Venue—State laws or court rules that establish the proper court to hear a case.

Voir dire—The preliminary examination made in court of a witness or juror to determine their competency or interest in a matter.

–W–

Waiting child—Child who is legally free for adoption.

Writ—A judicial order directing a person to do something.

Wrongful adoption—Adoption in which known information regarding the youth is not released to the adoptive parents and if it had, the adoption would not have occurred.

References

Abel, G., Becker, J., Cummingham-Rathner, J., & Rouleau, J. (1988). Multiple para-philic diagnoses among sex offenders. *Bulletin of the American Academy of Psychiatry and the Law, 16,* 153–168.

Ackerman, M. J. (1999). *Essentials of forensic psychological assessment.* New York: John Wiley & Sons.

Alan Guttmacher Institute. (2002). *In their own right.* New York: Author.

American Psychiatric Association. (2000). *Diagnostic and statistical manual of mental disorders* (4th ed., text rev.). Washington, DC: Author.

American Psychological Association. (1994). Guidelines for child custody evaluation in divorce proceedings. *American Psychologist, 49,* 677–680.

American Psychological Association. (2002). *Ethical principles of psychologists and code of conduct.* Retrieved from http://www.apa.org/ethics/code/index.aspx

American Psychological Association. (2010). Parenting expert warns against physi-cal punishment. Retrieved from http://www.apa.org/news/press/releases/2010/05/corporal-punishment.aspx

Appleton, W. S. (1981). *Fathers and daughters.* New York: Doubleday.

Archer, R. P. (1992). Minnesota Multiphasic Personality Inventory–2. In J. J. Kramer & J. C. Conoley (Eds.), *The eleventh mental measurements yearbook* (pp. 546–561). Lincoln, NE: Buros Institute of Mental Measurements.

Arehart-Treichel, J. (2006, May 19). Pedophilia often in headlines, but not in research lab. *Psychiatric News, 37.*

Ascione, F. R. (1998). Battered women's reports of their partners' and their children's cruelty to animals. *Journal of Emotional Abuse, 1,* 119–133.

Ash, P., & Rain, J. S. (1998). Drug Abuse Screening Test. In J. C. Impara & B. S. Plake (Eds.), *The thirteenth mental measurements yearbook* (pp. 379–381). Lincoln, NE: Buros Institute of Mental Measurements.

Associated Press. (2010, April 9). *Adoption freeze urged after woman returns boy to Russia.* Retrieved from www.usatoday.com/news/world2010-04-09-adoption-freeze_N.htm

Associated Press. (2010, July 13). *Mom jailed over sex with 14-year-old son.* Retrieved from www.msnbc.msn.com

Bancroft, A., Wilson, S., Cunningham-Burley, S., Backett-Milburn, K., & Masters, H. (2004). *The effect of parental substance abuse on young people.* York, United Kingdom: Joseph Rowntree Foundation.

Barona, A., Carlson, J., & Waterman, B. (1998). State Trait-Depression Adjective Checklist. In J. C. Impara & B. S. Plake (Eds.), *The thirteenth mental measurements yearbook.* Lincoln, NE: Buros Institute of Mental Measurements.

Beardslee, W. R., Wright, E. J., Gladstone, T.R.G., & Forbes, P. (2008). Long-term effects from a randomized trial of two public health preventive interventions for parental depression. *Journal of Family Psychology, 21,* 703–713.

Beaty, L. A., & Alexeyev, E. B. (2008). The problem of school bullies: What the research tells us. *Adolescence, 43,* 1–11.

Bell, A., & Weinberg, M. (1978). *Homosexualities: A study of diversity among men and women.* New York: Simon & Schuster.

Bernt, F., & Frank, M.L.B. (2001). Marital Satisfaction Inventory—Revised. In B. S. Plake & J. C. Impara (Eds.), *The fourteenth mental measurements yearbook* (pp. 710–714). Lincoln, NE: Buros Institute of Mental Measurements.

Berry, M., Barth, R., & Needell, B. (1996). Preparation, support and satisfaction of adoptive families in agency and independent adoptions. *Child and Adolescent Social Work Journal, 13,* 157–183.

Biddulph, S. (2004). *Raising boys.* Berkeley, CA: Celestial Arts.

Biller, H. (1993). *Fathers and families: Paternal factors in child development.* Westport, CT: Auburn House.

Boyle, G. J., & Kavan, M. G. (1995). Personality Assessment Inventory. In J. C. Conoley & J. C. Impara (Eds.), *The twelfth mental measurements yearbook* (pp. 764–768). Lincoln, NE: Buros Institute of Mental Measurements.

Brooks, D. (2010, July 9). The medium is the medium. *New York Times.* Retrieved from www.nytimes.com/2010/07/09/opinion/09brooks.html

Brown, R., & Hattie, J. (1998). Tennessee Self-Concept Scale. In J. C. Impara & B. S. Plake (Eds.), *The thirteenth mental measurements yearbook* (2nd ed.). Lincoln, NE: Buros Institute of Mental Measurements.

Campbell, M. H., & Flanagan, R. (2001). Reynolds Depression Screening Inventory (RDSI). In J. C. Impara & B. S. Plake (Eds.), *The fourteenth mental measurements yearbook* (pp. 1022–1027). Lincoln, NE: Buros Institute of Mental Measurements.

Carlson, J. T., & Waller, N. G. (2001). Beck Depression Inventory II. In J. C. Impara, & B. S. Plake (Eds.), *The fourteenth mental measurements yearbook* (pp. 121–124). Lincoln, NE: Buros Institute of Mental Measurements.

Cellucci, T. (2005). Clark-Beck Obsessive-Compulsive Inventory. In R. A. Spies & B. S. Plake (Eds.), *The sixteenth mental measurements yearbook* (pp. 205–207). Lincoln, NE: Buros Institute of Mental Measurements.

Chambers, J., Power, K., & Durham, R. (2004). Parental styles and long-term outcome following treatment for anxiety disorders. *Clinical Psychology and Psychotherapy, 11,* 187–198.

Cherpitel, C. J. (2002). Screening for alcohol problems in the U.S. general population: Comparison of the CAGE, RAPS4, and RAPS4-QF by gender, ethnicity and service utilization. *Alcoholism: Clinical and Experimental Research, 2,* 1686–1691.

Child Trends Data Bank's analysis of General Social Survey of 2008. Retrieved from http://www.childtrendsdatabank.org/?q=node/187

Children and Family Research Center, School of social Work, University of Illinois at Urbana-Champaign. (2004, February). *Multiple placements in foster care: Literature review of correlates and predictors.* Retrieved from http://www.cfrc.illinois.edu/LR pdfs/PlacementStability.LR.pdf

Children of addicted parents: Important facts. (2003). Retrieved from http://www.hopenetworks.org/Children%20of%20Addicts.htm

Choca, J. P., & Widiger, T. A. (2001). Million Clinical Multiaxial Inventory-III. In B. S. Plake & J. C. Impara (Eds.), *The fourteenth mental measurements yearbook* (2nd ed.). Lincoln, NE: Buros Institute of Mental Measurements.

Clark, L. (1985). *SOS! Help for parents: A practical guide for handling common everyday behavior problems.* Bowling Green, KY: Parents Press.

CNN. (2009, March 10). *Their paths crossed on YouTube on an August night last year.*

Cohen, L. J., & Galynker, I. (2009, June 8). Psychopathology and personality traits of pedophiles. *Psychiatric Times, 26.* Retrieved from www.psychiatrictimes.com/display,article/10168/1420331

Conniff, R. (2004). Reading faces. *Smithsonian Magazine.* Retrieved from http://www.smithsonianmag.com/science-nature/ReadingFaces.html

Conoley, J. C., & Impara, J. C. (Eds.). (1995). *The twelfth mental measurements yearbook.* Lincoln, NE: Buros Institute of Mental Measurements.

Cooperstein, M. A., & Stuart, R. B. (1998). Life Stressors and Social Resources Inventory—Adult Form. In J. C. Impara & B. S. Plake (Eds.), *The thirteenth mental measurements yearbook* (pp. 618–621). Lincoln, NE: Buros Institute of Mental Measurements.

Crea, T., Barth, R., & Chintapalli, L. (2007). Home study methods for evaluating prospective resource families: History, current challenges, and promising approaches. *Child Welfare League of America, 82,* 141–159.

Dalton, J. (1994). MMPI-168 and Marlowe-Crowne profiles of adoption applicants. *Journal of Clinical Psychology, 50,* 863–866.

Dana, R. H. (1985). Thematic Apperception Test (TAT). In C. S. Newmark (Ed.), *Major psychological assessment instruments* (2nd ed., pp. 695–697). Needham Heights, MA: Simon & Schuster.

Dickerson, J. (1972). A casework approach to foster homes. *Ontario Association of Children's Aid Societies Journal, 16,* 17–19.

Dickerson, J., & Allen, M. (2006). *The basics of adoption: A guide for building families in the U.S. and Canada.* Westport, CT: Praeger.

Dickerson, J., & Allen, M. (2007). *Adoptive and foster parent screening: A professional guide for evaluations.* New York: Routledge.

Dowd, T. E., & Waller, N. G. (1998). Beck Anxiety Inventory. In J. C. Impara & B. S. Plake (Eds.), *The thirteenth mental measurements yearbook* (pp. 97–99). Lincoln, NE: Buros Institute of Mental Measurements.

Edwards, J. (1999). *How substance abuse affects parenting.* Retrieved from http://www.bensoc.org.au/uploads/documents/how-substance-abue-affects-parenting-1

Ekman, P. (2003). *Emotions revealed.* New York: Henry Holt.

Ekman, P., & Friesen, W. (1975). *Unmasking the face.* New York: Prentice-Hall.

Erdberg, P. (1985). The Rorschach. In C. S. Newmark (Ed.), *Major psychological assessment instruments* (2nd ed., pp. 1033–1038). Needham Heights, MA: Simon & Schuster.

Espelage, J., & Swearer, S. (2002). *Words can hurt forever.* New York: Free Press.

Evan B. Donaldson Adoption Institute. (2005). *Overcoming barriers to the adoption of children from foster care.* . Retrieved from http://www.adoptioninstitute.org/XXX

Fanshel, D. (1966). *Foster parenthood: A role analysis.* Minneapolis: University of Minnesota Press.

Felthous, A. R., & Kellert, S. R. (1980). Aggression against cats, dogs, and people. *Child Psychology and Human Development, 10,* 169–177.

Felthous, A. R., & Lockwood, R. (1998). *Cruelty to animals and interpersonal violence.* West Lafayette, IN: Purdue University Press.

Fernandez, E. (1998). Beck Hopelessness Scale. In J. C. Impara & B. S. Plake (Eds.), *The thirteenth mental measurements yearbook* (pp. 122–124). Lincoln, NE: Buros Institute of Mental Measurements.

Fernandez, E., & Pittenger, D. J. (2003). The Substance Abuse Subtle Screening Inventory-3. In B. S. Plake, J. C. Impara, & R. A. Spies (Eds.), *The fifteenth mental measurements yearbook* (pp. 122–124). Lincoln, NE: Buros Institute of Mental Measurements.

Foli, K. J., & Thompson, J. R. (2004). *The post-adoption blues: Overcoming the unforeseen challenges of adoption.* New York: Rodale.

Franz, C. E., McClelland, D. C., & Weinberger, J. (1991). Childhood antecedents of conventional social accomplishments in midlife adults: A 35-year prospective study. *Journal of Personality and Social Psychology, 60,* 586–595.

Fritz, G. S., Stoll, K., & Wagner, N. N. (1981). A comparison of males and females who were sexually molested as children. *Journal of Sex and Marital Therapy, 7,* 54–59.

Garbarino, J., Espelage, J., & deLara, E. (2003). Words can hurt forever. *Educational Leadership, 60*(6), 18–21.

Gillo, D. G. (1973). *Violence against children.* Cambridge, MA: Harvard University Press.

Goldstein, H. S. (1982). Fathers' absence and cognitive development of 12–17-year-olds. *Psychological Reports, 51,* 843–848.

Gonsiorek, J. (1982). Results of psychological testing on homosexual populations. *American Behavioral Scientist, 25,* 385–396.

Grant, B. F., Stinson, F. S., Dawson, D. A., Chou, P., Duford, M. C., Compton, W., et al. (2004). Prevalence and co-occurrence of substance use disorders and independent mood and anxiety disorders: Results from the National Epidemiologic Survey on Alcohol and Related Conditions. *Archives of General Psychiatry, 61,* 807–816.

Hanes, K. R., & Stewart, J. R. (1998). Beck Scale for Suicide Ideation. In J. C. Impara & B. S. Plake (Eds.), *The thirteenth mental measurements yearbook.* Lincoln, NE: Buros Institute of Mental Measurements.

Hart, H. M. (2001). Generativity and social involvement among African Americans and white adults. *Journal of Research in Personality, 35,* 208–230.

Hartnett, M. A., Leathers, S., Falconnier, L., & Testa, M. (1999). Placement stability study. Urbana, IL: Children and Family Research Center.

Hutchinson, D. (1943). *In quest of foster parents: A point of view on homefinding.* New York: Columbia University Press.

Irons, C., Gilbert, P., Baldwin, M. W., Baccus, J. R., & Palmer, M. (2006). Parental recall, attachment relating and self-attacking/self-reassurance: Their relationship with depression. *British Journal of Clinical Psychology, 45,* 287–308.

Jayson, S. (2008, July 15). Married couples who play together stay together. *USA Today.* Retrieved from *www.usatoday.com/news/nation/2008-07-15-fun-in-marriage_N.htm*

Jenkins, J. A., Plake, B. S., Impara, J. C., & Spies, R. A. (Eds.). (2003). Six Factor Personality Questionnaire. In B. S. Plake, J. C. Impara, & R. A. Spies (Eds.), *The fifteenth mental measurements yearbook* (pp. 819–821). Lincoln, NE: Buros Institute of Mental Measurements.

Jespersen, A. F., Lalumiere, M. L., & Seto, M. (2009). Sexual abuse history among adult sex offenders and non-sex offenders: A meta-analysis. *Child Abuse & Neglect, 33,* 179–192.

Johnsoti, J., Cohen, P., Kasen, S., Ehrensaft, M., & Crawford, T. (2006). Associations of parental personality disorders and Axis I disorders with childrearing behavior. *Psychiatry: Interpersonal and Biological Processes, 69,* 336–350.

Kadushin, A., & Kadushin, G. (1997). *The social work interview: A guide for human service professionals.* New York: Columbia University Press.

Kaplan, H. I., & Sadock, B. (Eds.). (1995). *Comprehensive textbook of psychiatry* (6th ed.). Philadelphia: Williams & Wilkins.

Kase, L. M. (n.d.). *How depression affects your family.* Retrieved from http://www.parents.com/baby/health/postpartum-depression/how-depression-affects-your-family/?page=3

Kendler, K. S., Bulik, C. M., Silberg, J., Hetteman, J. M., Myer, J., & Prescott, C. A. (2000). Childhood sexual abuse and adult psychiatric substance use disorders in women. *Archives of General Psychiatry, 57,* 953–959.

Kessler, R. C., Berglund, P. A., Demler, O., Jin, R., & Walters, E. E. (2005). Lifetime prevalence and age-of-onset distributions of DSM-IV disorders in the National Comorbidity Survey Replication (NCS-R). *Archives of General Psychiatry, 62,* 593–602.

Kiehn, B., & Swales, M. (2002). An overview of dialectical behavior therapy in the treatment of borderline personality disorder. *Advances in Psychiatric Treatment, 8,* 10–16.

Kitchener, B. A., Jorm, A. F., & Kelly, C. M. (2009). *Mental health first aid USA.* Catonsville: Maryland Department of Health and Mental Hygiene, Missouri Department of Mental Health, and National Council for Community Behavioral Healthcare.

Koestner, R., Franz, C., & Weinberger, J. (1990). The family origins of empathic concern: A twenty-six-year longitudinal study. *Journal of Personality and Social Psychology, 58,* 709–717.

Kramer, L., & Conger, K. J. (2009). What we learn from our sisters and brothers: For better or worse. *New Directions for Child Adolescent Development, 126,* 1–12.

Kubler-Ross, E. (1969). *On death and dying.* New York: Scribner.

Langstrom, N., & Zucker, K. J. (2005). Transvestic fetishism in the general population: Prevalence and correlates. *Journal of Sex and Marital Therapy, 31,* 887–895.

Lanning, K. V. (2001). *Child molesters: A behavioral analysis* (4th ed.). Alexandria, VA: National Center for Missising & Exploited Children.

Laskow, L. (1992). *Healing with love: A breakthrough mind/body medical program for healing yourself and others.* San Francisco: Harper's.

Laumann, E., Gagnon, J. H., Michael, R. T., & Michaels, S. (1994). *The social organization of sexuality: Sexual practices in the United States.* Chicago: University of Chicago Press.

Lindhout, I., Markus, M., Hoogendijk, T., Borst, S., Maingay, R., Spinhoven, P., Van Dyck, R., & Boer, F. (2006). Childrearing style of anxiety-disordered parents. *Child Psychiatry and Human Development, 37,* 89–102.

Lleras, C. (2008). Social science research. *Social Science Journal, 37,* 888–902.

Luby, J. (2010). Preschool depression: The importance of identification of depression early in development. *Current Directions in Psychological Science, 19,* 91–95.

Lying? The face betrays deceiver's true emotions. (2008, April 24). *Science Daily* [Press release]. Retrieved from http://www.sciencedaily.com/releases/2008/04/080422 200952.htm

Maccoby, E. E., & Jacklin, C. N. (1974). *The psychology of sex differences.* Palo Alto, CA: Stanford University Press.

Markman, H., & Stanley, G. R. Unpublished study begun in 1996. Denver: University of Denver, Center for Marital and Family Studies. (Study is based on long-term evaluation of 306 Denver-area couples.)

Martyna, B. (2007, April–June) "Braam v. State of Washington." *Youth Law News,* 81p. 3d851 (2002).

Mason, P., & Kreger, R. (1998). *Stop walking on eggshells: Taking your life back when someone you care about has borderline personality disorder.* Oakland, CA: New Harbenger.

Mastrangelo, P. M., & Urbina, S. (2003). Structured Interview for the Five-Factor Model of Personality. In B. S. Plake, J. C. Impara, & R. A. Spies (Eds.), *The fifteenth mental measurements yearbook.* Lincoln, NE: Buros Institute of Mental Measurements.

McLellan, M. J., & Rotto, P. C. (1995). Sixteen Personality Factor Questionnaire. In J. C. Conoley & J. C. Impara (Eds.), *The twelfth mental measurements yearbook* (5th ed., pp. 946–950). Lincoln, NE: Buros Institute of Mental Measurements.

Medalie, J. H., & Goldbourt, U. (1976). Angina pectoris among 10,000 men: Psychosocial and other risk factors as evidence by a multivariate analysis of a five year incidence study. *American Journal of Medicine, 60,* 910–921.

Mendel, M. P. (1995). *The male survivor: The impact of sexual abuse.* London: Sage Publications.

Michael, R. T., Gagnon, J. H., Laumann, E. O., & Kotate, G. (1994). *Sex in America: A definitive survey.* Boston: Little Brown.

Mouttapa, M., Valent, T., Gallaher, P., Rohrbach, L. A., & Unger, J. B. (2001). Social network predictors of bullying and victimization. *Adolescence, 39,* 315–335.

Murray, S. L., Holmes, J. G., Griffin, D. W., Bellavia, G., & Dolderman, D. (2002). Kindred spirits? The benefits of egocentrism in close relationships. *Journal of Personality and Social Psychology, 82,* 563–581.

Nansel, T. R., Overpeck, M., Pilla, R. S., Ruan, W. J., Simons-Morton, B., & Scheidt, P. (2001). Bullying behaviors among U.S. youth. *JAMA, 285,* 2094–2100.

National Association of Social Workers. (2008). *Code of ethics of the National Association of Social Workers.* Washington, DC: Author.

National Poll on Children's Health, April 16, 2010. *C.S. Mott Children's Hospital, 9*(4). Retrieved from http://www.med.umich.edu/mott/npch/pdf/041510report.pdf

National Research Council and Institute of Medicine of the National Academies. (2009). *Depression in parents, parenting, and children: Opportunities to improve identification, treatment, and prevention.* Washington, DC: National Academies Press.

Newman, L., Stevenson, C., Bergman, L., & Boyce, P. (2007). Borderline personality disorder, mother–infant interaction and parenting perceptions: Preliminary findings. *Australian and New Zealand Journal of Psychiatry, 41,* 598–605.

North American Council on Adoptable Children. (n.d.). Retrieved from http://www.nacac.org/adoptionsubsidy/stateprofiles

Nudo, L. (2004). Fighting the real bullies. *Prevention, 56,* 123–124.

Olweus, D. (1993). *Bullying at school: What we know and what we can do.* Oxford, England: Blackwell.

Petty, R., & Brinol, P. (2003). Overt head movements and persuasion: A self-validation analysis. *Journal of Personality and Social Psychology, 84,* 1123–1139.

Pollack, D. (2003), Minimizing agency and worker liability. *Policy & Practice, 61,* 26.

Pollack, D. (2007b). Youth in residential facilities: What is negligent supervision? *ABA Children's Rights Litigation Committee, 10,* 8–10.

Pollack, D., & Popham, G. (2009). Wrongful death of children in foster care. *University of La Verne Law Review, 31*(1), 25–44.

Popenoe, D. (1996). *Life without father.* New York: Martin Kessler–Free Press.

Reynolds, W. M., & Kobak, K. A. (1998). Hamilton Depression Inventory. In J. C. Impara & B. S. Plake (Eds.), *The thirteenth mental measurements yearbook* (pp. 475–480). Lincoln, NE: Buros Institute of Mental Measurements.

Rhule, D., McMahon, R., & Spieker, S. (2004). Relation of adolescent mothers' history of antisocial behavior to child conduct problems and social competence. *Journal of Clinical Child and Adolescent Psychology, 33,* 524–535.

Roberts, M. (2005). *Study finds foster care may foster lifelong ills.* Retrieved from the Carter Center Web site: http://www.cartercenter.org//news/documents/doc2065.html.

Rosenfeld, A., Pilowsky, D., Fine, P., Thorpe, M., Fein, E., Simms, M., et al. (1997). Foster care: An update. *Journal of the American Academy of Child and Adolescent Psychiatry, 36,* 448–457.

Rothschild, K., & Pollack, D. (2008). When qualified immunity protects social workers from 42 U.S.C § 1983 lawsuits. *American Professional Society on the Abuse of Children Advisor, 20,* 7–10.

Rubin, D., Alessandrini, E. A., Feudtner, C., & Mandell, D. S., Localio, A. R., & Hadley, T. (2004). Placement stability and mental health costs for children in foster care. *Pediatrics, 113,* 1336–1341.

Schwartz, P., & Young, L. (2009). Sexual satisfaction in committed relationships. *Sexuality Research & Social Policy, 6*(1), 1–17.

Schweitzer, H., & Pollack, D. (2006). Ethical and legal dilemmas in adoption social work. *Family Court Review, 44,* 258–269.

Seals, D. (2003). Bullying and victimization: Prevalence and relationship to gender, grade level, ethnicity, self-esteem, and depression. *Adolescence, 38,* 735–747.

Siegel, B. (1990). *Love, medicine and miracles: Lessons learned about self-healing from a surgeon.* New York: Harper's.

Smith, T. W. (1998). *American sexual behavior: Trends, socio-demographic differences, and risk behavior.* Chicago: National Opinion Research Center, University of Chicago.

South Carolina Forcible Sex Crimes [Summary]. (1999). Columbia: South Carolina Law Enforcement Division.

Sourander, A., Jensen, P., Ronning, J. A., Niemela, S., Helenius, H., Sillanmaki, L., et al. (2007). What is the early adulthood outcome of boys who bully or are bullied in childhood? The Finnish "From a Boy to a Man" study. *Pediatrics, 120,* 397–404.

South Carolina Handbook for Foster Parents. (2008). Retrieved from https://dss.sc.gov/content/library/manuals/foster_care_licensing.pdf

Stanley, N., & Penhale, B. (1999). The mental health problems of mothers experiencing the child protection system. *Child Abuse Review, 6,* 35–40.

Steele, B. (1966). *Proceedings.* Paper presented at the Conference on Patterns of Parental Behavior Leading to Physical Abuse of Children, University of Colorado, School of Medicine, Boulder, CO.

Taylor, C., Manganello, J. A., Lee, S. J., & Rice, J. C. (2010). Mothers' spanking of 3-year-old children and subsequent risk of children's aggressive behavior. *Pediatrics, 125,* e1057–1065.

Toppo, G. (2010, May 31). Free books block "summer slide" in low-income students. *USA Today.* Retrieved from http://www.usatoday.com/news/education.2010-06-01-sukmmerreading01_st_N.htm

U.S. Department of Health and Human Services. (2001, April). *Adoption and foster care analysis and reporting system* (Report 5). Washington, DC: Government Printing Office.

U.S. Department of Health and Human Services. Numbers of children in, entering and exiting foster care (Publications and fact sheets for FY 2000 and FY 2006). Retrieved from http://www.childwelfare.gov/factsheets/fosterexhibit1

Van der Bruggen, C., Stams, G., & Bogels, S. (2008). Research review: "The relation between child and parent anxiety and parental control: A meta-analytic review." *Journal of Child Psychology and Psychiatry, 49,* 1257–1269.

Vargas, T. (2006, March 2). Mother admits killing daughter. *Washington Post.* Retrieved from www.washingtonpost.com/wp-dyn/content/article/2006/03/01/AR2006030102380

Watkins, S. A. (1989). Confidentiality and privileged communications: Legal dilemma for family therapists. *Social Work, 34,* 133–136.

Webster, D., Barth, R. P., & Needell, B. (2000). Placement stability for children in out-of-home care: A longitudinal analysis. *Child Welfare, 79,* 614–632.

Weinberg, S. L., & Werner, P. (1998). Coping Resources Inventory for Stress. In J. C. Impara & B. S. Plake (Eds.), *The thirteenth mental measurements yearbook.* Lincoln, NE: Buros Institute of Mental Measurements.

White, M., & Epston, D. (1990). *Narrative means to therapeutic ends.* New York: W. W. Norton.

Widom, C. S. (1995). *Victims of childhood sexual abuse: Later criminal consequences.* Washington, DC: U.S. Department of Justice, National Institute of Justice.

Willison, B. G., & Masson, R. L. (1986). The role of touch in therapy: An adjunct to communication. *Journal of Counseling and Development, 64,* 497–500.

Wolins, M. (1963). *Selecting foster parents.* New York: Columbia University Press.

Zanarini, M. C., & Frankenburg, F. R. (2001). Treatment histories of borderline inpatients. *Comprehensive Psychiatry, 42,* 144–150. Also see http://www.nimh.nih.gov/health/publications/borderline-personality-disorder-fact-sheet/index.shtml

Additional Reading

Abrahamson, A. C., & Baker, L. A. (2002). Rebellious teens? Genetic and environmental influences on the social attitudes of adolescents. *Journal of Personality and Social Psychology, 83,* 1392–1408.

Ackerman, M. J., & Kane, A. (1993). Psychological experts in divorce, personal injury and other civil actions. New York: John Wiley & Sons.

Ainsworth, M. D. (1978). *Patterns of attachment.* Hillsdale, NJ: Lawrence Erlbaum.

Alessandri, S. M., & Wozniak, R. H. (1987). The child's awareness of parental beliefs concerning the child: A developmental study. *Child Development, 58.*

Amato, P. R. (1988). Parental divorce and attitudes toward marriage and family life. *Journal of Marriage and the Family, 50,* 453–461.

Amato, P. R., & Booth, A. (2001). The legacy of parents' marital discord: Consequences for children's marital quality. *Journal of Personality and Social Psychology, 81,* 627–638.

Apgar, V., & Beck, J. (1973). *Is my baby all right?* New York: Trident.

Aries, P. (1965). *Centuries of childhood: A social history of family life.* New York: Vintage.

Bachrach, A. J., & Murphy, G. (Eds.). (1954). *An outline of abnormal psychology.* New York: Modern Library.

Ban, P. L., & Lewis, M. (1971, April). *Mothers and fathers, girls and boys: Attachment behavior in the one-year-old.* Paper presented at a meeting of the Eastern Psychological Association, New York.

Barron-Cohen, S. (2003). T*he essential difference: The truth about the male and female brain.* New York: Perseus.

Bassani, D. G., Padoin, C., & Veldhuizen, S. (2008). Counting children at risk : Exploring a method to estimate the number of children exposed to parental mental illness using adult health survey data. *Social Psychiatry and Psychiatric Epidemiology, 43,* 927–935.

Belsky, J. (1996). Parent, infant, and social–contextual antecedents of father–son attachment security. *Developmental Psychology, 32,* 905–913.

Biederman, J., Monuteaux, M. C., Faraone, S. V., Hirsheld-Becker, D. R., Henin, A., & Rosenbaum, J. F. (2004). Does referral bias impact findings in high-risk offspring for anxiety disorders? A controlled study of high-risk children of non-referred parents with panic disorder/agoraphobia and major depression. *Journal of Affective Disorder, 82,* 209–216.

Biederman, J., Petty, C., Faraone, S. V., Hirshfeld-Becker, D., Pollack, M. H., de Figueiredo, S., et al. (2006). Effects of parental anxiety disorders in children at high risk for panic disorder: A controlled study. *Journal of Affective Disorder, 94,* 191–197.

Blau, T. H. (1988). *The psychologist as expert witness.* New York: John Wiley & Sons.

Bower, T. (1981). *Development in infancy.* San Francisco: Freeman.

Brazelton, T. B. (1984). *The Infant Neonatal Assessment Scale.* Philadelphia: Lippincott.

Brodzinsky, D. M. (1990). *The psychology of adoption.* New York: Oxford University Press.

Burns, A., &Scott, C. (1994). *Mother-headed families and why they have increased.* Hillsdale, NJ: Lawrence Erlbaum Associates.

Calvo, R., Lazaro, L., Castro, J., Morer, A., & Toro, J. (2007). Parental psychopathology in child and adolescent obsessive–compulsive disorder. *Social Psychiatry and Psychiatric Epidemiology, 42,* 647–655.

Cleaver, H., Unell, I., & Aldgate, J. (1999). *Children's needs—Parenting capacity. The impact of parental mental illness, problem alcohol and drug use, and domestic violence on children's development.* London: Department of Health, The Stationery Office.

Cowley, G. (2003, September 8). Girls, boys and autism. *Newsweek.* Retrieved from http://www.newsweek.com/2003/09/07/girls-boys-and-autism.html

Crea, T., Barth, R., & Chintapalli, L. (2007). Home study methods for evaluating prospective resource families: History, current challenges, and promising approaches. *Child Welfare League of America, 82,* 141–159.

Daly, M., & Wilson, M. (1987). Risk of maltreatment of children living with stepparents. In R. Gelles & J. Lancaster (Eds.), *Child abuse & neglect: Biosocial dimensions.* New York: Aldine de Gruyter.

Eliot, L. (1999). What's going on in there? How the brain and mind develop in the first five years of life. New York: Bantam.

Empfield, M., &Bakalar, N. (1980). *Identity and the life cycle.* New York: W. W. Norton.

Erickson, E. H. (1963). *Childhood and society.* New York: W.W. Norton.

Fahlberg, V. I. (1991). *A child's journey through placement.* Indianapolis, IN: Perspective Press.

Feigelman, W., & Finley, G. E. (2004). Youth problems among adoptees living in one-parent homes: A comparison with others from one-parent biological families. *American Journal of Orthopsychiatry, 74,* 305–315.

Frisino, J., & Pollack, D. (1997). HIV testing of adolescents in foster care. *Journal of HIV/AIDS Prevention and Education for Adolescents and Children, 1*(1), 53–70.

Furstenberg, F. F., & Cherlin, A. J. (1994). *Divided families: What happens to children when parents part.* Cambridge, MA: Harvard University Press.

Garfinkel, I., & McLanahan, S. S. (1986). *Single mothers and their children.* Washington, DC: Urban Institute Press.

Gelles, R., &Lancaster, J. (Eds.). (1987). *Child abuse and neglect: Biosocial dimensions.* New York: Aldine de Gruyter.

Gelman, S. R., Pollack, D., & Weiner, A. (1999). Confidentiality of social work records in the computer age. *Social Work, 44,* 243–252.

Gibelman, M., Gelman, S., & Pollack, D. (1997). The credibility of nonprofit boards: A view from the 1990s and beyond. *Administration in Social Work , 21*(2), 21–40.

Gilmore, U., Oppenheim, E., & Pollack, D. (2004). Delays in the adoption and foster home interstate study process. *University of California-Davis Law School Journal of Juvenile Law and Policy, 8*(1), 55–94.

Gopfert, M., Webster, J., & Seeman, M. V. (1996). *Parental psychiatric disorder: Distressed parents and their families.* Cambridge, England: Cambridge University Press.

Gray, D. D. (2002). *Attaching in adoption: Practical tools for today's parents.* Indianapolis, IN: Perspectives Press.

Hansen, M., & Pollack, D. (2005). Unintended consequences of bargaining for adoption assistance payments. *Family Court Review, 43,* 494–510.

Hansen, M., & Pollack, D. (2006a). The regulation of intercountry adoption. *Brandeis Law Journal,45*(1), 105–128.

Hansen, M., & Pollack, D. (2006b). The subtleties of race and recruitment in foster care and adoption. *California NASW News, 32*(8), 6.

Hansen, M., & Pollack, D. (2008). Tradeoffs in formulating a consistent national policy on adoption. *Family Court Review, 46,* 366–374.

Hansen, M., & Pollack, D. (2010). Transracial adoption of black children: An economic analysis. In M. Goodwin (Ed.), *Baby markets: Money and the new politics of creating families* (pp. 133–144). Cambridge, England: Cambridge University Press.

Harris, J. R. (2000). The outcome of parenting: What do we really know? *Journal of Personality, 68,* 625–637.

Henry, M., & Pollack, D. (2009). Adoption in the United States: A reference for families, professionals, and students. Chicago: Lyceum Books.

Henry, M., Pollack, D., & Lazare, A. (2006). Teaching medical students about adoption and foster care. *Adoption Quarterly, 10*(1), 45–61.

Hetherington, E. M. (2002). *For better or for worse.* New York: W.W. Norton.

Hofferth, S. L., & Anderson, K. G. (2003). Are all dads equal? Biology versus marriage as a basis for paternal investment. *Journal of Marriage and Family, 65,* 213–232.

Jaffee, S. R., Moffitt, T. E., Caspi, A., & Taylor, A. (2003). Life with (or without) father: The benefits of living with two biological parents depend on the father's antisocial behavior. *Child Development, 74,* 109–126.

Kempe, C. H., & Helfer, R. E. (1972). *Helping the battered child and his family.* Philadelphia and Toronto: J. B. Lippincott.

Kerig, P. K., Cowan, P. A., & Cowan, C. P. (1993). Marital quality and gender differences in parent–child interaction. *Developmental Psychology, 29,* 931–939.

Kindlon, D., & Thompson, M. (2000). *Raising Cain: Protecting the emotional life of boys.* New York: Ballantine Books.

Klaus, M. H., & Kennell, J. H. (1976). *Maternal–infant bonding.* St. Louis: Mosby.

Kroska, A. (2003). Investigating gender differences in the meaning of household chores and child care. *Journal of Marriage and Family, 65,* 456–473.

Levin, A. (2009). Little attention paid to effect of parents' depression on their children. *Psychiatric News, 44*(13), 1–29.

Levine, M. (2002). *A mind at a time.* New York: Simon & Schuster.

Locke, J. (1999). *Some thoughts concerning education.* New York: Oxford University Press.

Loehlin, J. C., Willerman, L., & Horn, J. M. (1987). Personality resemblance in adoptive families: A 10-year follow-up. *Journal of Personality and Social Psychology, 53,* 961– 969.

Lykken, D. (1997). The American crime factory. *Psychological Inquiry, 8,* 261–270.

Lykken, D. (2000). The causes and costs of crime and a controversial cure. *Journal of Personality, 68,* 559–605.

MacKinnon-Lewis, C., Rabiner, D., &Starnes, R. (1999). Predicting boys' social acceptance and aggression: The role of mother–child interactions and boys' beliefs about peers. *Developmental Psychology, 35,* 632–639.

Maccoby, E. (1980). Social development, psychological growth and parent–child relations. New York: Harcourt Brace Jovanovich.

Maddi, S. R. (1976). *Personality theories: A comparative analysis.* Homewood, IL: Dorsey Press.

Marsh, J., & Pollack, D. (2002). Constitutional rights of foster parents to adopt foster children. *Adoption & Fostering, 26*(1), 71–73.

Marsh, J., & Pollack, D. (2003a). The federal government's role in child welfare—In plain language. *Fostering Families Today, 3*(3), 38–43.

Marsh, J., & Pollack, D. (2003b). Recent developments in adoption law. *Adoption Quarterly, 6*(3), 63–72.

Martinez, C. R. (2001). Preventing problems with boys' noncompliance: Effect of a parent training intervention for divorcing mothers. *Journal of Consulting and Clinical Psychology, 69,* 416–428.

Mason, S., & Pollack, D. (2005). Legal aspects of hyperactivity medication in the schools: What social workers need to know. *School Social Work Journal, 30*(1), 61–74.

Mass, H. S., & Engler, R. E. (1954). *Children in need of parents.* New York: Columbia University Press.

McGuinness, T., & Pollack, D. (2008). Parental methamphetamine abuse and children. *Journal of Pediatric Health Care, 22,* 152–158.

McLanahan, S., & Sandefur, G. (2001). *Growing up with a single parent.* Cambridge, MA: Harvard University Press.

Melina, L. R. (1998). *Raising adopted children: Practical reassuring advice for every adoptive parent.* New York: HarperPerennial.

Montague, D.P.F., &Walker-Andrews, A. S. (2002). Mothers, fathers, and infants: The role of person familiarity and parental involvement in infants' perception of emotion expressions. *Child Development, 73,* 1339–1352.

Murphy, J. M. (1999). *Coping with teen suicide.* New York: Rosen Publishing Group.

National Institute of Child Development. (2003). Do children's attention processes mediate the link between family predictors and school readiness? *Developmental Psychology, 39,* 581–593.

Neal, J. H. (1983). Children's understand of their parents' divorces. In L. Kurdek (Ed.), *Children and divorce: New directions for child development.* San Francisco: Jossey-Bass.

Osofsky, J. (1987). *Handbook of infant development.* New York: John Wiley & Sons.

Pertman, A. (2000). *Adoption nation.* New York: Basic Books.

Pettit, G. S., & Dodge, K. A. (2003). Violent children: Bridging development, intervention, and public policy. *Developmental Psychology, 39,* 187–188.

Phares, V. (1992). Where's poppa? A relative lack of attention to the role of fathers in child and adolescent psychopathology. *American Psychologist, 47,* 656–664.

Piaget, J. (1932). *The moral judgment of the child.* New York: Macmillan.

Piaget, J. (1967). *Six psychological studies.* New York: Random House.

Plomin, R., Loehlin, J. C., & DeFries, J. C. (1985). Genetic and environmental components of "environmental" influences. *Developmental Psychology, 21,* 391–402.

Pollack, D. (1992). Record retention management: A key element in minimizing agency and worker liability. *Journal of Law and Social Work, 3*(2), 89–95.

Pollack, D. (1993). Liability insurance for foster parents and agencies: The role of commercial insurers. *Journal of Law and Social Work, 4*(1), 33–40.

Pollack, D. (2002). The capacity of a mentally retarded parent to consent to adoption. *Child Law Practice, 21*(1), 10–12.

Pollack, D. (2003a). Human services and law. *Policy & Practice, 61*(1), 30.

Pollack, D. (2003b). Minimizing agency and worker liability. *Policy & Practice, 61,* 26.

Pollack, D. (2003c). Negligence and foster children—Who is responsible? *Fostering Families Today,* 28–30.

Pollack, D. (2003d). *Social work and the courts* (2nd ed.). New York: Brunner-Routledge.

Pollack, D. (2004). Getting informed consent—More than just a signature. *Policy & Practice, 62*(2), 28.

Pollack, D. (2005a). The capacity of a mentally challenged person to consent to abortion and sterilization [Practice Forum]. *Health & Social Work, 30,* 253–257.

Pollack, D. (2005b). Does accreditation lead to best practice? Maybe. *Policy & Practice, 63*(1), 26.

Pollack, D. (2005c). Financial accountability of human services agencies. *Policy & Practice, 63*(2), 24.

Pollack, D. (2005d). Individual liability of supervisors. *Policy & Practice, 63*(3), 26.

Pollack, D. (2005e). Intercountry adoption: Who are the good guys? *Policy & Practice, 63*(1), 28.

Pollack, D. (2006a). Accountable human services in every 'cents.' *California NASW News, 32*(7), 7, 19.

Pollack, D. (2006b). Child trafficking and international adoption. *Adoption Today, 8*(5), 39.

Pollack, D. (2006c). A law and technology challenge for human services. *Policy & Practice, 64*(4), 21.

Pollack, D. (2006d). The many faces of human services lawyers. *Policy & Practice, 64*(3), 26.

Pollack, D. (2006e). Risk assessment instruments in child protective services: Are they "evidence?" *American Professional Society on the Abuse of Children Advisor, 18*(2), 2–3.

Pollack, D. (2006f). Suicidal clients: Law, ethics, and documentation. *Policy & Practice, 64*(2), 24, 42.

Pollack, D. (2006g). Supervisors are personally liable. *California NASW News, 33*(3), 9, 16.

Pollack, D. (2007). Should social workers be mandated reporters of child maltreatment? An international legal perspective. *International Social Work Journal, 50,* 699– 705.

Pollack, D. (2009a). Child abuse investigations: Fibbing and fudging are wrong. *Policy & Practice, 67*(6), 20.

Pollack, D. (2009b). Do child protection workers deserve immunity when they misrepresent or fabricate evidence? *American Professional Society on the Abuse of Children Advisor, 21*(2), 18–19.

Pollack, D. (2009c). Legal risk, accountability, and transparency in social work. *International Social Work Journal, 52,* 837–942.

Pollack, D., & Cavanaugh, K. (2001). When foster children get hurt, who is responsible? *Family Support, 20*(3), 57–61.

Pollack, D., & Frisino, J. (2005). Federal confidentiality laws as barriers to communication between the juvenile justice system and the child welfare system. *Social Policy Journal, 4*(2), 39–50.

Pollack, D., & Marsh, J. (2004). Social work misconduct may lead to liability [Practice Update]. *Social Work, 49,* 609–612.

Pollack, D., & Marsh, J. (2005). Social work, ethics and the law. *NASW—NY Update, 29*(4), 9.

Prokop, M. S. (1986). *Kids' divorce workbook.* Warren, OH: Alegra House.

Reti, I. M., Samuels, J. F., Bienvenu, O. J., Costa, P. T., & Nestadt, G. (2002). Adult antisocial personality traits are associated with experiences of low parental care and maternal overprotection. *Acta Psychiatrica Scandinavica, 106,* 126–133.

Ross, E. (2003, January 24). *Study says broken homes harm kids more.* Associated Press, London.

Stolk, M. V. (1972). *The battered child in Canada.* Toronto: McClelland and Stewart.

Tanner, J. (1978). *Education and physical growth.* London: Hodder and Stoughton.

Teyber, E. (1992). *Helping children cope with divorce.* San Francisco: Jossey-Bass.

Theis, S.V.S. (1924). *How foster children turn out.* New York: State Charities Aid Association.

Thomas, M. (1996). *Comparing theories of child development.* New York: W.W. Norton.

Thompson, C., Mazer, M., & Witenberg, E. (1955). *An outline of psychoanalysis.* New York: Modern Library.

Wachtel, E. F. (1994). *Treating troubled children and their families.* New York: Guilford Press.

Wallerstein, J., & Blakeslee, S. (1996). *Second chances: Men, women, and children a decade after divorce.* Boston: Houghton Mifflin.

Wallerstein, J., Lewis, J. M., & Blakeslee, S. (2000). *The unexpected legacy of divorce.* New York: Hyperion.

Walton, G. E., Bower, N. J., & Bower, T. G. (1992). Recognition of familiar faces by newborns. *Infant Behavior and Development, 15,* 265–269.

Watnik, W. (1997). *Child custody made simple.* Claremont, CA: Single Parent Press, 1997.

Weiner, A., & Pollack, D. (1997). Urban runaway children: Sex, drugs, and HIV. In N. K. Phillips & S. L. A. Straussner (Eds.), *Children in the urban environment: Linking social policy and clinical practice.* Springfield, IL : Charles C Thomas.

Weiner, A., & Pollack, D. (2006). Urban street youth: Sex, drugs, and HIV. In N. K. Phillips & S.L.A. Straussner (Eds.), *Children in the urban environment: Linking social policy and clinical practice* (2nd ed., pp. 209–226). Springfield, IL : Charles C Thomas.

Wodrich, D. L. (1984). *Children's psychological testing: A guide for nonpsychologists.* Baltimore: Paul H. Brookes.

Index